Community Consultation

~~~~~~

*Strategies for Facilitating Change
in Schools, Hospitals, Prisons,
Social Service Programs,
and Other Community Settings*

Patrick O'Neill
Edison J. Trickett

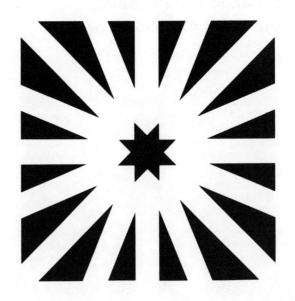

Community
Consultation

Jossey-Bass Publishers
San Francisco • Washington • London • 1982

COMMUNITY CONSULTATION
Strategies for Facilitating Change in Schools, Hospitals, Prisons,
Social Service Programs, and Other Community Settings
by Patrick O'Neill and Edison J. Trickett

Copyright © 1982 by: Jossey-Bass Inc., Publishers
433 California Street
San Francisco, California 94104
&
Jossey-Bass Limited
28 Banner Street
London EC1Y 8QE

Library of Congress Cataloging in Publication Data

O'Neill, Patrick.
Community consultation.

1. Social service consultants. 2. Community
organization. I. Trickett, Edison J. II. Title.
HV40.0'66 1982 361.8 82-48062
ISBN 0-87589-541-7

Manufactured in the United States of America

The paper in this book meets the guidelines for
permanence and durability of the Committee on
Production Guidelines for Book Longevity of the
Council on Library Resources.

JACKET DESIGN BY WILLI BAUM

FIRST EDITION

Code 8234

The Jossey-Bass
Social and Behavioral Science Series

Preface

〰〰〰〰〰〰〰〰〰〰〰〰〰〰〰〰〰〰〰〰〰〰〰〰〰〰〰〰〰〰〰〰〰

From the turn of the century, when the staff of Witmer's clinic in Philadelphia began going into the local public schools to help teachers with their students, the concept of consultation has had a long and increasingly complex history. It was incorporated into the child guidance movement of the 1920s, thrust into prominence during World War II when the military sought advice about many problems with psychological overtones, and accepted as a central component of the mental health professional's role in the 1950s. Now the idea of consultation as an intellectual activity and a professional role has taken firm hold.

The evolution of consultation in scope, sophistication, and complexity has been accompanied by an outpouring of literature. The sheer volume of published works is indicated by the fact that Mannino, MacLennan, and Shore (1975) included 1,136 references on mental health consultation published prior to 1973; Grady, Gibson, and Trickett (1981) surveyed the field from 1973 to 1978 and included 884 citations.

The diverse set of activities classified as consultation can be approached by examining three dimensions: the different professionals that have adopted consultation as a legitimate aspect of their professional role, the large number of settings in which consultants work, and the distinct models of consultation that are emerging. Consultation is now a clear professional activity of psychology, psychiatry, social work, business, counseling, education, nursing, and religion. Bruce Tefft, one of the pioneers of community psychology in Canada, found in a national survey that consultation occupied a major position in the professional life of community psychologists (Tefft, Hamilton, and Theroux, 1979). With respect to the variety of settings where consultation occurs, Grady, Gibson, and Trickett's (1981) annotated bibliography includes references to corrections, cross-cultural and international settings, schools, geriatric settings, government, hospitals and health agencies, industrial and business settings, the military, minority settings, religious settings, and social agencies. Very few organizational structures in our society are free from consultative intervention.

The increasing numbers of disciplines represented, and the extension of the practice of consultation to a wide variety of settings, signify a major evolution in an area that less than thirty years ago had hardly any published accounts of consultation activity. Yet these are not the only important developments for the field. Increasingly, consultation theories are being proposed. Models of consultation with such labels as behavioral, organizational, psychoeducational, systems, and traditional mental health consultation have been articulated. Such models are useful because they organize the experience of consultants, guide intervention, define the sociopolitical values inherent in the activity, and specify the criteria for successful outcomes.

As the field of consultation has become diversified, it has also become fragmented. Different varieties of consultation tend to become profession-specific, insulating one approach from another. To take just one example, entry issues occur in various settings and across disciplines, and articles discussing entry can be found in journals of all the various disciplines that train consultants. Nevertheless, the references that form the intellectual backdrop for those articles are usually restricted to only one discipline. Discrete—though conceptually similar—bodies of literature are springing up in different fields, raising the danger that generic issues will be overlooked. These generic issues, common across disciplines and settings, are the focus of this book.

We plan to step back from specific locales, models, and professions in order to take a broad look at the nature of the consultation experience. Our goal is to learn what is similar and important about consultation across varied settings, problems, viewpoints, and consultants. It is not our intention to develop or elaborate a new model of consultation. Nor do we aim to articulate a preferred *modus operandi* or to specify how consultation should be evaluated. Rather, we want to develop an appreciation for the way in which settings, clients, and the consultant's personal qualities all play a part in fashioning the issues of consultation.

We see consultation as a series of linkages. First the consultant is linked to the client, whether that client be a single person, a group, a complex organization, or the community at large. In Part One of the book, issues surrounding this linkage are examined, including consultant-setting fit and the contract (explicit or implicit) that defines the formal relationship between consultant and client.

Our next focus—the crux of Part Two—is on the links among members of a particular group or among subgroups within a client organization. Much of the work of consultants, especially that described in the group process and organizational development literatures, deals with these interconnections. In Part Two we present ideas and case material highlighting the consultant's intervention to change the structure of a client group, to improve its internal processes, or both.

The client group is also linked to its own environment. It must gather resources to survive; it must receive and process information to guide its action; it must compete or cooperate with other groups in the community. In Part Three the linkages among community groups are brought into focus. We discuss the consultant's relationship to such concerns as prejudice, discrimination, and the problems of distribution of power.

These linkages are not limited to a particular professional

affiliation, nor to a particular type of setting, nor to a particular model of consultation. The social worker as much as the community psychologist must forge links with the client; relationships within an organization are as much an issue in prisons as in schools; the struggle for resources among groups in a common environment impinges on the work of a behavioral consultant as well as on a systems theorist.

These three linkages, then, provide the structure for the book. Within this structure, three themes recur in each area of focus. First, the consultant is defined as a resource; second, consultation is shaped by context; third, the ideas and assumptions of those involved in the consultation process, including consultant and client, determine whether the consultant will succeed or fail.

Defining the consultant as a *resource* to the client turns our attention to the consultant's personal qualities and the fit between these qualities and the features of the setting, an issue we take up in Part One. The consultant's status, training, and competencies will influence whether he or she can assist a client group with its internal linkages, our topic in Part Two. Finally, in the competition for resources among groups discussed in Part Three, consultants themselves constitute a scarce resource; and their efforts may improve their clients' long-term viability.

By the *context* of consultation we mean the interweaving of people, roles, and issues to create the fabric of a particular community setting. This concept is useful in understanding the importance of many aspects of consultation that are often overlooked. Some examples: In Part One we shall see that consultation is affected by the client's implicit assumptions about the omniscience of professionals—assumptions that may differ from those made explicit in the consultant-client contract. Case narratives in Part Two demonstrate the effect of context on the tensions among subgroups and problems in the smooth flow of communication in client organizations. In Part Three the resources available within the community—and the traditional patterns of animosity or affiliation—are contextual issues that link or divide community groups.

Another recurring theme is the importance of *ideas* in determining the outcome of consultation. In Part One, the consultant's relationship to a setting is governed by the ideas each party has about the other. In Part Two, shared assumptions are seen to hold community groups together and give them a sense of cohesion and mission. In Part Three, cognitive biases in selecting information and giving it meaning are implicated in the stereotypes that divide segments of the community.

These are generic themes that cut across professional affiliation and the formal structure of particular settings. The discipline in which a consultant was trained may determine what sort of resource the consultant will be, but the resource issue itself is a general one. The specific setting (school, prison, tenants' organization) may be an important contextual variable, but the significance of context is not limited to one class of settings. Profession and setting may shape the ideas that guide an intervention, but the power of ideas to prompt or restrain different sorts of action will be implicated in all interventions.

Rather than developing a single theory of consultation, we shall use our focus on linkages and the recurring themes of resource, context, and idea to help us understand consultants, their settings, and their tasks. Nevertheless, we are not atheoretical. In Chapter One we present two approaches that we believe are useful for thinking about issues raised in particular cases. These approaches are the ecological analogy and cognitive community psychology. The ecological analogy (Trickett, Kelly, and Todd, 1972) puts an emphasis on linkage, resources, and the context of intervention. The cognitive approach in the field of community consultation (O'Neill, 1981) emphasizes ideas—above all, the systematic cognitive biases that shape assumptions and impose meaning on experience. The guiding concepts drawn from ecological and cognitive frames of reference are detailed in Chapter One.

Any book which relies heavily on case studies must avoid the pitfall of selecting only cases, or aspects of cases, that conform to the authors' biases. We include many cases with implications that might be illuminated by reference to other work in the field: James Kelly's (1979) contrast of receptive versus resistant settings (Chapter Two); John Glidewell's (1959) discussion of the beginning contract (Chapter Three); William Gamson's (1968) distinction between the social control and social influence perspectives (Chapter Six); Saul Alinsky's (1946, 1971) insights into community organizing (Chapter Seven). When the work of other theorists seems helpful, we introduce their concepts into the analysis. By taking a heuristic approach, we permit cases to raise questions rather than merely trying to demonstrate the aptness of our own notions.

We shall not try to teach specific skills. In cases throughout the book, consultants will be seen employing a wide range of skills from persuasion to action research, from program development to conflict resolution. More important than prescribing particular skills, we believe, is the need to assess the environment to decide what skills are useful in a given situation. Some authors separate process and structural consultation and advocate one or the other. Our cases involve both sorts of activity and various mixtures. Rather than advocating that consultants adopt one mode over the other, we focus on the consultant's mandate and argue that it is essential to understand that mandate and determine the form of consultation it permits or dictates. Some authors make a sharp distinction between interventions aimed at preserving a system and those aimed at changing it. We shall see consultants working usefully in both modes. Rather than championing one over the other, our emphasis will be on the need for consultants to know the mode in which they are working and, moreover, to ask the crucial value questions that arise from social control and social influence. As we present a variety of settings, skills, and goals, our themes will be the importance of context and a view of the consultant as a resource within particular contexts.

Acknowledgments

Seymour Sarason and the students who passed through his Psychoeducational Clinic at Yale inspired our interest in community consultation. We also drew on the ideas and support of J. Auerbach, James Kelly, T. Vincent, G. A. Milton, Riley Hern, Susan Plath, and Macha MacKay.

In our reconnaissance of the case literature we depended on the skills of Margaret Grady, Wendy Chappell-Ivey, and Anne Toland. Our other research assistants were Sandra Gould, C. M. O'Neill, and Lynn Cheek. Various drafts benefited from comments by Catherine Landry, Paula Halpin, and Joan and Alice Toland. We owe a debt to those who suffered through the stages of manuscript preparation, including Elaine Curran, B. Donovan, Denise Aspinall, Marie Davidson, and Sherry Crowell.

Much of this book was written while Patrick O'Neill was receiving a Leave Fellowship from the Social Sciences and Humanities Research Council of Canada. We would like to thank the council, Acadia University, and the University of Maryland for the support that made this project possible.

September 1982   Patrick O'Neill
                                                            Wolfville, Nova Scotia

                                                            Edison J. Trickett
                                                            College Park, Maryland

Contents

The Authors

~~~~~~

Patrick O'Neill is director of graduate training, Department of Psychology, at Acadia University in the Annapolis Valley of Nova Scotia. He attended the University of Victoria as an undergraduate and then studied at Yale University where he received the Ph.D. degree in community clinical psychology. After joining the faculty at Acadia in 1974, he developed a community component for the graduate program. He has published theoretical and empirical papers on the application of cognitive concepts to community psychology and particularly to consultation.

Edison J. Trickett is professor of psychology and director of the Clinical Community Psychology Program at the University of Maryland. He is also president of the Community Psychology Division of the American Psychological Association. He studied at Trinity College and then did graduate work at Ohio State University where he received the Ph.D. degree in clinical psychology. He has held positions as postdoctoral fellow at Stanford University and faculty member at Yale University. In 1977 he joined the faculty of the University of Maryland. In a research program that expressed his strong interest in the assessment of environments, he developed the Classroom Environment Scale in collaboration with R. H. Moos. He has written extensively about the application of ecological principles in psychology.

For my mother, Catherine

—Patrick O'Neill

Community Consultation

*Strategies for Facilitating Change
in Schools, Hospitals, Prisons,
Social Service Programs,
and Other Community Settings*

1

Introduction: Basic Concepts and Processes

Community organizer Saul Alinsky once said, "I always think about the guy who had a castrated dog. Every time a bitch in heat would pass by, this dog would try to break the window to get out. One day this fellow had a friend over who saw this performance. The friend says, 'I don't get it. Why does your dog act this way, because if he did get out he couldn't do anything.' The dog's owner answered with great indignation, 'You don't understand. My dog is a consultant' " (Saunders and Alinsky, 1970, p. 74).

Our first task is to define the term *consultant* and then test our definition against Alinsky's acerbic castrated-dog metaphor. A consultant is someone who intervenes—a person whose intervention is temporary, who works with a system focus rather than an individual focus, and whose advice may be accepted or rejected as the client chooses. This definition separates consultants from those who occupy permanent roles in a system, from psychotherapists who deal primarily with individual problems, and from leaders whose opinions constitute directives rather than advice.

What features of this definition might justify Alinsky's disparaging view? There are two possibilities, one concerning

1

values, the other concerning power. On the matter of values, it might appear that a consultant, offering services to clients on a take-it-or-leave-it basis, lacks real commitment to the struggles in which a client group is involved. When the going gets tough, the consultant can always pack up and move on.

But this lack of commitment has no place in our view of consultation. The *sine qua non* of our definition is that consultants *intervene*. Their actions have consequences, and they are responsible for those consequences. The assertion that they give advice rather than directives is not meant to absolve consultants of responsibility but to restrain them from infringing on the rights of clients to make their own decisions. The fact that consultants do not impose their own values on the groups they help does not mean they lack values or adopt without question the values of any group that happens to hire them. Rather, the key concern is to match the values of the consultant with those of the client group. In our view, this is a central issue in the linkage between consultant and client. We found value congruence to be a matter of importance in many of the cases we reviewed while selecting material for this book. Apparently consultants do not use the adviser role to exempt themselves from commitment to values. Nor does it free them from value dilemmas.

The second issue that might have prompted Alinsky's harsh analogy is that of power. The castration image suggests a loss of potency, and again it might be based on the consultant's role as adviser rather than leader in a community group. Bertrand Russell (1938) defined power as the production of intended effects. The more power a group has, the more it can do what its members want and get what it needs. In that framework, the aim of consultation is the *facilitation* of intended effects. The consultant is one of the resources group members can draw on as they strive to meet objectives. The fact that consultants do not seek personal power—they do not, for example, contend for leadership roles in a group—does not make them impotent. Instead, like Alinsky himself, consultants can make important contributions to the efforts of community groups to do what they want and get what they need. In fact, our definition of consultation is broad enough to include the activity of organizers like Alinsky, whose work is discussed in a later chapter.

Viewing the consultant as a resource has practical implications. Rather than specifying the characteristics that make a Good Consultant, we assume that different characteristics, ranging from personal style to background training, constitute different sorts of resources. This approach differs from that of theorists who offer specific models and techniques as blueprints for consultation (among them Argyris, 1970; Caplan, 1970; Goodstein, 1978; Schmuck and Miles, 1971). Although we recognize that models and methods are valuable, our resource-based approach has a somewhat different frame of reference: The models that consultants espouse, and the techniques they use, are among the resources they bring to groups.

Whether the consultant's characteristics, techniques, and theories are useful, and the way in which they are useful, will depend on the context of consultation. This notion of context includes time and place, community traditions, the nature of the problem facing a community group, and the obstacles or opportunities in the environment. While researching cases for this book, we discovered that contextual issues are broader than any one class of settings. Thus our approach differs from those who classify consultation in terms of setting (see Platt and Wicks, 1979) or those who write about consultation to a certain setting such as schools (Alpert and Associates, 1982) or the criminal justice system (Monahan, 1976). Again, a setting-specific approach is obviously useful to consultants working in that setting. But it is limited in its power to illuminate contextual issues across settings. The impact of a particular context is less apparent when there are no other contexts for comparison. There may be important aspects of schools that make school consultation different from prison consultation. Or problems that arise in schools may be generic and emerge also in prisons and other organizations. These issues can be defined clearly only by looking at a variety of settings.

The Ecological Analogy

Linkage, resource, and context are three concepts that owe much to the ecological approach developed by James Kelly and his colleagues (Kelly, 1970; Trickett, Kelly, and Todd,

1972; Trickett, Kelly, and Vincent, in press). The analogy from biological ecology, translated into a framework for consultation, can be stated in the form of assertions. In the following paragraphs we examine some of these assertions.

Assertion One: *Consultation is an activity designed—most broadly—to intervene in the social context.* Understanding and intervention include the way people and settings are coupled: how, to use statistical terms, person, setting, and interaction variance account for the behavior of interest. This assertion also implies a criterion for distinguishing consultation from other forms of intervention such as psychotherapy: The orienting reflex of the consultant is toward improving aspects of the social environment. This objective does not imply any single model or any specific level of intervention. The community organizer may focus on changes in power relationships or the accruing of resources toward improving the community. The psychoeducational consultant may work on interpersonal problem-solving skills of teachers, and this may have an impact on the environment of a public school. The long-range implications of consultation are primarily systemic. This conclusion suggests our next assertion.

Assertion Two: *Because consultation aims for a systemic impact, an important source of knowledge is understanding of the social context where consultation occurs.* How one conceptualizes the world of settings often governs how consultation proceeds and succeeds. Early consultation literature was marked by a rash of "failure studies" that frequently hinged on the consultant's significant misreading of the environment. Whether the setting is a school classroom, the development of a new mental health facility, or the organizing of a neighborhood to obtain needed resources, gaining knowledge of those settings is a pivotal task of the consultant. The development of salient concepts and strategies for learning about the environment is a primary intellectual task for the field. Emphasis on the social context should yield an appreciation of the ways in which group processes, norms, policies, and social structures influence communities.

Assertion Three: *Cultural and institutional diversity is not only a fact of life, it is a positively valued fact of life for the consultant.* Similarly, consultants with different characteristics and backgrounds will be socialized in different ways by social settings. Several cases referred to in later chapters illustrate these points. With regard to differences in setting, McIntyre (1969) has offered his experience in two elementary schools in the same community. Although the schools had similar pupil populations and were formally alike, they varied remarkably in staff morale, receptivity to consultation, and implicit objectives. In terms of consultant differences, Gooden (1977) and Levy-Warren (1976), a black male and a white female, found themselves in very different roles while consulting to the same alternative high school. Our assertion states, however, that it is important not only to understand diversity of setting but to value it. The consultant works to promote tolerance for diversity in social systems and appreciates the various adaptations people make to their communities.

To summarize, then, consultation involves the interaction of consultants with various host settings and people of diverse backgrounds and cultures. Regardless of the focus of intervention—the classroom, the neighborhood, the prison—the long-range goal of consultation is to have an impact on the social setting. A primary intellectual activity is to develop ideas that document the impact of setting and cultural diversity on consultation itself.

Given these three assertions about the nature of consultation, we find that Kelly's ecological analogy offers a set of axioms that not only pose general questions for consultants across a wide variety of consultation efforts but also provide an orientation for viewing people, settings, the consultant's role, and the goals of consultation. The four ecological axioms outlined below concern the ways in which the consultant can gain knowledge about the settings of consultation.

Axiom One: *the principle of interdependence.* The principle of interdependence asserts that whenever a component of a natural ecosystem is changed there are alterations in the relationship among all other components in the ecosystem (Trickett, Kelly, and Todd, 1972). There are reciprocal relationships between persons and settings. It is the systemic linkage among the component parts of the setting that gives it a unique character, and it is the clarification of these linkages that helps the consultant understand aspects of the setting that might be improved. Since the attention to interdependence focuses on the setting as a nexus of persons, roles, policies, and practices, it mitigates against a personalistic approach to the understanding of behavior. It further suggests that interventions can be viewed not only in terms of the changes in the immediate environment but also in terms of how the changes radiate through other parts of the interdependent system.

Axiom Two: *the principle of adaptation.* While the principle of interdependence focuses the consultant's attention on the ways in which events, policies, and behavior are interconnected, the principle of adaptation focuses on the context of the setting. What are the environmental norms that shape the opportunities for people as well as constrain their behavior? "The adaptation principle is derived from experimentation in biological ecology concerning environmental factors affecting the survival of an organism. The premise of the ecosystem asserts that for an organism to survive over time it must be able to cope with environmental changes" (Trickett, Kelly, and Todd, 1972, p. 384). This axiom about the substantive nature of the environment directs attention to coping as a perspective for labeling and understanding behavior. Behavior is specifically tied to the norms, processes, and constraints of the context in which it occurs. The axiom also orients the consultant toward scanning the environment in an effort to understand how and why the setting defined the primary consultative issue as it did. Understanding the setting thus becomes a primary diagnostic task.

Axiom Three: *the principle of cycling of resources.* How resources in a setting are defined, constrained, and developed constitutes a central theme of consultation. The principle of cycling of resources focuses attention on those aspects of the setting that may be used to promote change. People, settings, and events may all serve as resources for understanding the setting, dealing with issues of crisis and development, carrying out the intervention program, and ensuring the long-range impact of the consultation effort. People are resources for both consultative interventions concerning individuals (such as the recruiting of a competent teacher to develop a relationship with a child) or institutional or community issues (such as the development of a governing board whose members have access to outside resources). A primary consultative task is thus to identify the resources within the environment.

The principle of cycling of resources advocates detailed observation of the setting in terms of the resources available for problem solving in areas relevant to the consultative task. It includes an assessment of persons, enduring structures of the environment, and events as resources for the improvement of the setting.

Axiom Four: *the principle of succession.* The succession principle in field biology focuses on the evolution and diversification of plant communities. At any point in time a community, like an individual, is partly a product of its history. The consultant should be concerned with the evolution of the policies, practices, ways of labeling problems, and norms that have resulted in a need for consultation. This principle also alerts the consultant to the value of determining how things come to be the way they are and the importance of respecting traditions and practices, even when they seem to serve no useful function. In addition to the historical perspective embodied in this principle, the succession principle orients the consultant to the potential consequences and goals of intervention. The consultant acquires knowledge of the past to understand the present, designs interventions based on that knowledge, and builds on the positive traditions of the setting to ensure the consultative impact.

The following three propositions concerning the design of consultative interventions flow from the four principles of ecology.

Proposition One: *Interventions are designed to be matched with the host environment.* Implicit in the preceding ecological axioms is the notion that interventions, if they are to take hold, are designed to respond specifically to the unique aspects of the setting. Here the focus for consultation is the fit between the proposed intervention and the context where the intervention is to be implemented. The consultant should draw support for the change process from people in the setting. Moreover, the consultant should avoid an overly technological approach to consultation that ignores differences in settings and focuses on a packaged approach to change. And, finally, the consultant should develop a reciprocal relationship with those in the setting who initiate the change. The setting determines the approach: Working with classroom teachers on behavior problems may require a different strategy in a school with a strict set of rules of behavior as contrasted with a school with fluid norms.

Proposition Two: *Priority is given to assessing the side effects of consultative intervention.* Because consultation occurs in an ongoing social context, and because social contexts are composed of numerous interdependent systems and subsystems, interventions often have side effects that are not intended by the consultant. Whether the intervention introduces a new service, mobilizes a segment of a community to agitate for resources, or forms a teacher's group to discuss classroom management, the very act of intervention alters past relationships. The phrase "unanticipated consequences" has often been a signal to think about the implications of intervention beyond the intended ones. The further connotation is that such outcomes may threaten the success of the intervention. The ecological analogy stresses two general points about side effects—that their predictability is related to the degree to which accurate reconnaissance of the environment precedes intervention and, further, that they may have positive as well as negative features.

Proposition Three: *Management and conservation of resources is an overriding goal.* Social ecology, like the biological model before it, implies a predominant concern with resources. We have said that impact on the social system is an overriding goal. We can add that this impact ought to be assessed primarily in terms of resource management, conservation, and development. These resources include local skills, community development, and the ability of social environments to enrich people's lives.

The ecological analogy offers us a framework in which to view consultation as a series of linkages, the consultant as a resource, and outcome as affected by context. Intervention takes place not only in a context of people, roles, and settings; it occurs also in a context of ideas. The recent development of cognitive community psychology (O'Neill, 1981) stresses the relevance of social cognition for understanding community phenomena.

A Cognitive Orientation

Information has been called the basic raw material on which organizations operate (Weick, 1969). The way in which a community group selects and interprets information affects its ability to gain and hold members, to compete for scarce resources, and to adapt to changing circumstances. Information relieves uncertainty. In Shannon's (1948) theory of communication a unit of information is the amount needed to remove doubt in the face of two equally likely alternatives. As information passes through a system—among group members, for instance, or among community groups—it can be altered by noise or distortion. Noise is random alteration; distortion is systematic alteration. According to Miller's (1978) theory of living systems, information is always distorted to some extent as it passes through a system, and the system never completely compensates for this distortion.

People, whether as individuals or in groups, hold various assumptions about the environment and their place in it. These assumptions are fundamental views that are taken for granted. Often they are based more on tradition and truism than on objective reality. When shared among members of a group, they affect the way group members understand experience—bringing members closer together while distinguishing the group from organizations with different suppositions. Anyone who has worked with community groups will recall the power of such ideas. Shared assumptions act as prisms refracting all information that enters the group.

Even though consultants see the world through their *own* prisms, a consultant who understands the importance of shared assumptions and recognizes the varieties of cognitive bias

has a significant resource to offer a community group. Suppose
we review some findings from the study of social cognition that
may be useful for the consultant.

Most of the experimental work in social cognition has
concerned the individual. Nevertheless, evidence from various
lines of inquiry suggests that biases in the way individuals think
may be magnified rather than modified by group process. In his
conformity research, Asch (1948) suggested that people interpret the meaning of issues and events to conform to group consensus. A study by Allen and Wilder (1980) supports this position and shows, moreover, that cognitive restructuring leads
people to take more extreme stands on target issues. In "risky-
shift" research, a persistent finding is that group discussion and
information exchange lead groups to make decisions that are
more extreme than those of individuals who compose the
groups (for a review see Clark, 1971). In the literature on attitude change there is evidence that when it is in the interest of a
group to take a certain stand on an issue, the group will engage
in biased scanning of arguments (O'Neill and Levings, 1979).
Janis (1972) came to similar conclusions in his analysis of group
thinking among policy makers. The accentuation of cognitive
bias in a group setting seems most likely to occur when the
group is cohesive, when the issue is of importance to the group,
and when members have access to similar sorts of information.
All these conditions are common in community organizations.

In the community context, then, we would expect groups
to fall victim to many of the cognitive biases that affect the way
individuals think. In fact, such biases might be exaggerated by
group process. Five areas of particular interest are the way in
which valid sources of information are defined, the influence of
past experience, social stereotyping, causal reasoning, and ideal
models of the world.

Information Sources. The significance given to information depends in part on its source. French critic Roland Barthes
(1977, p. 15) pointed out that even a press photograph "can
change its meaning as it passes from the very conservative
[newspaper] *L'Aurore* to the communist *L'Humanité*." The
idea that some information sources are more valid than others is

as old as Socrates, who argued that people should listen to those who know what they are talking about. He offered the example of a young gymnast who should ignore the praise and blame of the public and listen only to his trainer. The validity of expert sources is affected by their apparent bias. Applying tests of expertise and bias to information can provide useful rules for deciding what to believe, but these tests are vulnerable to distortion. People may have inflated views of their own expertise or the expertise of those who happen to share their opinions. They may discount the views of those who disagree with them because of perceived bias, yet they may overlook bias in members of their own group.

The effects of the communicator's credibility on information acceptance are well documented (for a review see Eagly and Himmelfarb, 1978). Classic experiments have shown that people are more likely to believe trustworthy communicators (Hovland and Weiss, 1951); moreover, people tend to redefine the meaning of statements depending on who was supposed to have uttered them (Asch, 1948). In a more recent study, Birnbaum and Stegner (1979) varied the expertise and bias of the source as well as the bias of the person receiving the communication. They found that information was given most weight when the source was an expert, but this effect was diminished when the source was also thought to be biased. The views of a biased source were given greatest weight when the person receiving the communication shared the source's viewpoint; apparently people think that compatible sources are less biased.

Community groups, whether professional institutions such as public schools or single-issue organizations such as Family Planning, are likely to be biased toward information consistent with current assumptions. Group members consider one another to be experts, when compared to lay people, and to be less biased than out-group authorities who hold different assumptions. Teachers can discount the opinions of parents, for instance, assuming that the parents do not know enough about schools to have valid views. Moreover, they can discount the opinions of educational critics on the assumption of bias. Family planners see themselves as experts when compared to mem-

bers of the public. Hence they can discount as biased the arguments of Right-to-Lifers. Because people tend not to recognize
biases that are similar to their own, the views of other in-group
members are likely to be accepted as knowledgeable, unbiased
opinion.

   This way of judging sources of information has relevance
for the three linkages to be detailed in later chapters. In Part
One, we explore the link between consultant and client. One of
the resources that the consultant can offer is an objective view
of the group's problems. But an independent assessment of the
group's situation may clash with its assumptions, and the outsider's credibility may be challenged. The tendency of groups to
overvalue opinions from within the group is an aspect of intra-
system linkage, the subject of Part Two. Finally, the tendency
to discount as uninformed or biased the views of those in other
(sometimes rival) groups affects linkage in the wider community. This question is discussed in Part Three.

   Past Experience. The virtues of learning from the past are
expressed in such maxims as "those who fail to learn from history are condemned to repeat it." But the fact that this aphor-
ism was found written over Jim Jones's chair at the Guyana
Massacre must give us pause; perhaps there are hazards in the
way people draw on experience to inform present judgment.
The first problem is that our own experiences constitute only a
small portion, and hardly a random portion, of events at large.
Not only are our own samples of experience small and unrepresentative, but we may be biased in recalling certain experiences
and not others. Tversky and Kahneman (1973) call this an
"availability bias." They give the example of a clinical psychologist wondering whether a depressed patient is likely to commit
suicide. If he relies on his own experience, his best strategy
would be to recall other depressed patients and see whether
they attempted suicide. But because suicide attempts are more
dramatic and salient than instances of depression, the clinician
is more likely to recall other patients who attempted suicide
and then note whether they were depressed. Since relatively few
depressed patients attempt suicide, the clinician would be making a serious error in judgment.

Another bias in our recall of the past occurs because events that confirm our hypotheses about the world tend to be particularly striking and easy to remember (Jenkins and Ward, 1965). These events are more available when we scan experience to assess the present and try to predict the future. What we learn from history tends to be what we expected to find in the first place.

The capacity to learn from the experience of others, as well as from our own experience, is limited by the tendency to be Monday morning quarterbacks. Decisions are made in an atmosphere of uncertainty. But once the decision is in the past and its consequences are known, we tend to think things *had* to turn out as they did. The lessons that might be learned are dismissed as obvious. Fischoff (1975), who called this a "hindsight bias," found that not only do past events seem fated but we overestimate the extent to which decision makers knew the outcomes in advance. Since we think they should have known, and in fact we assume they did know what would happen, we become biased toward paranoid explanations for the behavior of decision makers who make bad choices.

In the community, group members often share a common body of experience that binds the group together while separating it from those outside. Members of Alcoholics Anonymous share vivid impressions of the effects of alcohol, both on themselves and on others, that are less available to outsiders. Because people are struck by experiences that confirm their hypotheses, community groups are most likely to judge information and make decisions on the basis of remembered experience consistent with their prior assumptions. A consultant with experiences different from those of the client group can make a contribution by offering a different assessment of problems and possibilities.

Social Stereotyping. Just as we simplify the world by putting things in categories, we simplify the *social* world by dividing people into groups. When we know what some members of a group are like, we often think that we know what all are like. Sometimes the characteristics of even one person are generalized to the whole group. When Hamil, Wilson, and Nisbett

(1980) exposed subjects to vivid one-case studies of a prison guard or welfare recipient, they found that the subject freely generalized from the case to larger populations—even when told that the cases were highly atypical. The tendency to generalize characteristics to a whole group is most apparent when members of one group are judging another (Quattrone and Jones, 1980). Group members form complex impressions of fellow members but much simpler impressions, based on fewer factors, of out-group members. This tendency leads to more extreme judgments, whether favorable or unfavorable, of out-group members (Linville and Jones, 1980). Moreover, people tend to exaggerate differences among groups and to minimize differences within a group (Tajfel, 1969).

Our culture teaches us that some characteristics naturally go with certain sorts of people: The English are snobs; the Irish are drunken rowdies. Once such an association is established, people tend to overestimate the frequency of cases confirming their expectations—a phenomenon referred to as the *illusory correlation* (Chapman, 1967; Hamilton, 1981). Every Irishman seems to stagger and fight; every Englishman seems to be looking down his nose at the world. In situations where no correlation actually exists between groups and particular traits, we are struck by the cases that are consistent with popular stereotypes and we fail to notice inconsistent examples (Hamilton and Rose, 1980). Sober Irishmen and humble Englishmen are unremarkable.

The strong and pervasive tendency to apply the categories of "us" and "them," creating in-groups and out-groups, has important consequences for social behavior. People discriminate against out-group members when groups are composed on the basis of trivial characteristics (Tajfel, 1970), even when group composition is plainly a function of pure chance (Locksley, Ortiz, and Hepburn, 1980). We would expect discrimination to be magnified when group composition is neither trivial nor random. The more cohesive the in-group, the more likely it is to denigrate out-groups. When Wilder and Thompson (1980) experimentally increased contact within a group, they found that evaluation of an out-group became more negative.

Stereotypes are plentiful among community groups, whether these be natural groups (blacks, whites, Anglophones, Hispanics, francophones) or formal organizations (police and social workers; pronuclear and antinuclear advocates). We will take up the significance of stereotyping for community consultation in Chapter Six. Experiments in social cognition suggest that as community groups become more cohesive, their views of out-groups become more stereotyped. Counterexamples that might modify the stereotypes are unnoticed whereas particular attention is paid to instances that confirm prevailing prejudices.

Causal Reasoning. We construct causal theories to account for striking events and relationships. Suppose a resident in a community group home for the intellectually handicapped assaults a neighboring teenager who taunted him. Where does the cause lie? If the resident regularly attacks neighborhood youths, without provocation, an observer would tend to blame him rather than the situation. If the observer believes that most people would retaliate in the face of such taunts, the cause is likely to be located in the provocative situation rather than in the resident. If the resident has been taunted often but retaliates only on this occasion, the observer might blame the circumstances—"he was having a bad day."

In Kelley's (1967) model of causal attribution, these types of information are referred to as distinctiveness, consensus, and consistency. The behavior is distinctive if it does not occur in different situations; it is consistent if it usually occurs in similar situations; consensus refers to the belief that others would act similarly in this circumstance. Some aspects of the model have been qualified—such as the way people use consensus information (Nisbett and Borgida, 1975) and the tendency to assign causality to a salient stimulus (Taylor and Fiske, 1978). Nevertheless, considerable research confirms the influence exerted by the sorts of information proposed by Kelley (Orvis, Cunningham, and Kelley, 1975; Smith and Miller, 1979).

This way of assigning causes in everyday situations seems quite reasonable, and no doubt it often produces defensible explanations of events. But it can also lead to errors. People lack equal access to the three sorts of information specified in the model. If they have not seen the actor in a range of situations, or in other situations of this sort, consistency and distinctiveness information are not available. Our understanding of what "most people" would do in a situation is obviously vulnerable to subjective factors. The possibility of bias is intensified by the tendency of people to approach events with preconceived causal theories . . . and then to look for the sort of information that would confirm them. Nisbett and Wilson (1977) point out that cultures transmit implicit theories about causal relationships, and individuals are predisposed to look for evidence of these relationships.

Hansen (1980) induced subjects to read a case with the expectation that either a person or a situation could be considered the cause of events. Subjects were permitted to ask for various sorts of information. One striking result was their tendency to use very little information, only one third of that available, in making causal judgments. Hansen also found that people who were biased toward a person-cause explanation asked primarily for distinctiveness information. (Does the person do this in other situations?) Those biased toward a situational attribution asked for consensus information. (What do others do in such circumstances?)

People with various interests in the community hold different assumptions and will therefore search for different kinds of information to understand events. In our earlier example, neighbors may believe that intellectually handicapped residents of the group home are unpredictable and perhaps dangerous. In explaining the assault, they might look first for evidence of low distinctiveness. ("He's a mean-looking guy, like he's always ready for a fight.") The staff of the group home, with a different assumption about residents, might look first for evidence of high consensus. ("Anybody would fight if they were taunted like that, even I might.")

If this analysis seems to overstate the amount of cognitive distortion taking place, remember that people in different positions have differential access to information. In this example, the group home staff would have consistency information ("he usually never fights") that might be unavailable to neighbors.

Shared assumptions about cause and effect have staying power. They influence our thinking about the world, even when the initial evidence on which they were based is discredited. Anderson, Lepper, and Ross (1980) gave subjects extremely weak data supporting either a positive or a negative relationship between risk taking and success as a firefighter. They then asked some subjects to come up with causal explanations of the relationship. Even when the researchers totally discredited the initial information, people still believed in the causal theories they had invented. In community groups, shared and strongly held explanations may well persist even in the face of contradictory cases.

Ideal Models. Decision making is affected by beliefs about the probability of various events occurring in the future. Often predictions are based on internalized ideal models of the world. The belief in a Just World, for example, might lead us to predict, against much evidence, that good acts are ultimately rewarded and bad acts lead people to bad ends. Laboratory studies offer striking demonstrations of the way a Just World view distorts judgment: People assume that even random rewards must have been deserved (Lerner, 1965), and they blame victims for their own misfortunes (Lerner and Simmons, 1966).

Another ideal model portrays the world as fulfilling our wishes. According to Freud (1955), history is largely determined by people acting out their wishes. He points to statements by nationalists that only their race is capable of culture and cites the widespread belief that "the Messiah will come and found a golden age" (p. 53) as examples of wishes transformed into beliefs. Predictions about social and political events are consistently biased toward optimistic outcomes (McGregor, 1938; McGuire, 1960; Milburn, 1978). In their personal lives people rate their chances as above average for positive events and below average for negative events in the future (Weinstein, 1980).

These are examples of broad cultural assumptions about the ideal world. People also have more circumscribed models—or, in Abelson's (1976, 1981) term, "scripts"—that are used to understand some limited aspect of experience. These models

may be referred to when a person wants to predict how a course
of action will turn out. The prediction is weighted by the extent
to which the event is representative of the ideal model. Kahneman and Tversky (1972) say that when we estimate the chances
that a company will go out of business or that a politician will
be elected, we have in mind models of the business or political
situations. "We evaluate as most likely those outcomes which
best represent the essential features of the corresponding model" (p. 451).

There are virtues in building and using models to understand experience and predict the future. A good part of education consists of teaching models to people and showing them
when the models should be applied. But the process has its inherent distortions. Kahneman and Tversky (1973) note that reliance on representativeness ignores the prior probability of
outcomes and the unreliability of available evidence.

In the community framework, cognitive models of an
ideal world have many ramifications. The tendency to be overoptimistic, to believe in a Just World and a positive future, may
explain why it seems easier to motivate groups to engage in political action opposing negative events than to work to bring
about positive ones (see Toland, 1981). Since the likelihood of
positive events occuring is overestimated, people are led to assume that they will come to pass anyway. Although the probability of negative events is underestimated, once people *are* convinced that danger looms they can be motivated to oppose
threats to their fundamental assumptions about the way the
world should be.

More limited models, and the tendency to base predictions on them, are also relevant in community consultation.
Consultants themselves have models of community processes
and theories of the way consultation should proceed. Although
these models may be helpful in organizing experience, they can
lead consultants to make bad decisions when the future is predicted on the basis of the model without consideration of the
community context.

We have now considered five broad areas of inquiry in social cognition (definition of valid information, influence of past

experience, social stereotyping, causal reasoning, and ideal models of the world) that seem to have particular relevance to community consultation. With our interest in assumptions and context, and our view of the consultant as a resource to community groups, we are ready to look at examples of consultants at work. The first cases bear on the linkage between consultant and client—a territory that must be mapped accurately before the consultant can be of much help with linkages inside the group or among groups in the community.

Part One

~~~~~~

Links Between Consultants and Settings

The first link that must be forged in consultation is that between the consultant and the setting. All other possibilities depend on that link. When the consultant's personal characteristics clash with the features of a unique setting, the consultant is likely to be rejected at the outset. Even when consultants do gain entry, the contracts they establish with clients have profound effects on the success of their interventions.

Jack Glidewell, a founder of community psychology, once commented: "Considering the amount of resistance that consultants regularly encounter, the fact that a consultant will enter in the dark is either a compliment to his courage, a comment on his conceit, or a manifestation of his masochism—or all three" (1959, p. 56). It may also be a testament to certain unavoidable features of consultation. There is almost always ambiguity about who is the real "client" of consultation, about the match of values between setting and consultant, about the most appropriate intervention. Small wonder that Glidewell pictures the consultant as entering in the dark.

How much illumination can we offer? Some, but certainly not enough to resolve all the ambiguous issues. Each consultant is different; every setting is different. Many facts that the consultant would like to know before entering a group only come to light as the relationship develops. But if we cannot tell consultants what they will find in each case, we can at least describe the sorts of things they should be looking for.

2

Matching
Consultants
and Settings

Consultants are outsiders. Their independence, the fresh perspective they can bring to events, is an essential resource for the community groups with which they work. Yet they must become identified with clients, must share their ideals, must even share some of their assumptions, if their interventions are to be of value. We consider this to be the fundamental paradox underlying all consultation. The tension between independence and empathy is inescapable. Although it is manageable, the way it is managed often determines the consultant's ability to play a useful role.

A brief example from the work of Kahn (1970) gives a flavor of the issues that lie ahead. Kahn referred to a common entry problem in the early days of the civil rights movement, when a young, white, middle-class student from a Northern college would arrive in a small rural Southern town. Should the prospective organizer move in with a black family or stay with whites? Moving in with a black family would immediately cut the Northerner off from whites—not only from the white power structure but also from poor whites who might have some common interests with local blacks. But staying with a black family might have a positive and catalytic effect in the black community. Blacks could scarcely trust anyone working with poor whites, let alone with the white power structure.

This problem, although stated concisely, expresses a complex interaction among consultant, setting, values, and strategy. The ecological analogy directs our attention to the position of a Northern white activist in a small Southern town with a tradition that draws sharp lines between whites and blacks. The analogy helps us focus on the clash of values between the consultant and an important segment of the community. However the value dilemma is resolved, the choice of where to live will also be affected by the consultant's model of community organizing. This cognitive model dictates the way the consultant evaluates probable outcomes of different choices.

Much of this chapter is devoted to the fit between characteristics of consultants (including status, gender, and ethnicity) and characteristics of settings. The issues we shall raise will be relevant to different consultants at different times and in different places. But the fundamental paradox of an outsider working on the inside is a generic issue. For that reason we have chosen it as our starting point.

Consultants as outsiders soon discover that every strength entails a weakness. They will probably be regarded as experts— in group process, knowledge of social action tactics, delivering human services, understanding social cognition, or some other areas. The very expertise that catches a group's attention may make it dependent and eager to relinquish its own decision making. If the consultant's advice is hard medicine to swallow it can be discounted. Again the outsider role may be implicated. A group's natural xenophobia may prevent the consultant from gaining access to data needed to make informed assessments. Although accepting the consultant as an expert, the client group may believe that his or her advice is not relevant to local issues: "That character just doesn't understand what we're up against."

Despite these obstacles, the consultant's relative independence and objective view of the group's problems and possibilities are potential resources that cannot be duplicated by someone occupying a permanent role in the group. The problem is to negotiate the outsider role in such a way that the consultant is regarded as a valid source of information.

When we outlined concepts from social cognition that might be useful in community consultation, we noted that the significance of information depends on its source. A credible source is one that is seen as expert—provided the expertise is not tainted by bias. The consultant may be a resource to the group if he or she is seen as knowledgeable in some area relevant to the group's task. The consultant will not necessarily be perceived as unbiased, however. Research cited in Chapter One indicated that people are less likely to perceive bias in someone who shares their own views. By maintaining an independent posture, by confronting a group's shared assumptions, the consultant risks having his or her credibility challenged.

For our first case example, we have chosen an instance in which the outsider role was particularly well handled. Indeed it was the consultant team's independence, more than any other quality, that was deemed to be a resource to the client. Our example is taken from a description of their work by Sarason, Zitnay, and Grossman (1971). Like all other case narratives in this book, we have paraphrased the case rather than quoted directly. This strategy permits us to look at a particular aspect of the example. In this case we wish to examine the external critic role played by the Yale Psychoeducational Clinic in creating an innovative program for the intellectually handicapped.

> The Central Connecticut Regional Center (CCRC) was created with the objective of providing a clear break from some unfortunate traditions in the care of the intellectually handicapped. Larger state institutions, however innovative in conception and however well run, were geographically isolated from major cities. It was difficult for parents to maintain contact with children after the children were admitted. Providing total care for these children took away the responsibility for helping the handicapped from families and local communities. In cases where institutions were able to improve a resident's functioning, geographical distance from the home community made reintegration difficult.
>
> The new regional centers were intended to be small settings embedded in the communities they

served. These centers were to use existing community services rather than duplicate them. The emphasis was to be on daycare, not on providing residential treatment. A major goal of the regional-center concept was to increase the sense of community responsibility.

Consultants from the Psychoeducational Clinic were involved from the outset in planning CCRC. An early decision was to avoid putting up new buildings, even though the state legislature had allocated a generous amount for that purpose. Another early decision was to use residential care as little as possible; beds would be available only for temporary, not custodial, use.

In three years CCRC became involved in three programs. The first was daycare that had been established by local parents. This program continued to be run by the parents' association, but it now had financial backing and staff support from CCRC. Next came the Independent Living Unit, serving a dozen people who were selected because they could learn to work in the community while living in the unit. The objective was to get these people back into the community after a short period in the unit. The third aspect of CCRC was the Family Involvement Program. This accommodated a half-dozen children whose family situation was problematic. Before a child entered this program, an agreement was signed by parents and CCRC specifying length of stay and obligating parents to visit the center and observe the way the child's behavior was managed.

A five-day week was maintained for people in the Independent Living Unit or the Family Involvement Program. CCRC was determined to avoid becoming a total institution with care provided seven days a week. It was recognized that if the center assumed total responsibility for clients it would be difficult to get the community to accept a share of the responsibility.

As CCRC worked to translate its ambitious goals into reality, it used the consultants as external critics. According to the center's director, the consultants could perform a valuable service by keeping CCRC honest; in particular, they could examine the relation between practices and stated objectives and point out discrepancies.

The consultants participated almost daily in the life of CCRC. At no time were there less than six workers (three consultants, three interns) associated with the center. Their commitment kept their advice from being dismissed as mere academic opinion. Yet the fact that they were outsiders with no responsibility for center decisions made it possible for them to see things more dispassionately than regular staff members. The consultants had a stake in CCRC, but they also had the luxury of being independent of it. Their obligation was to participate and respond without needing to conform, ingratiate, or praise.

This role was not without its problems. For example, staff members knew that the consultants communicated regularly with the CCRC director. At times they would try to get their concerns transmitted indirectly through the consultants. This presented a danger that the consultants would become messengers, thereby absolving director and staff members of talking among themselves about troublesome issues. The consultants were aware of this potential problem and worked to avoid it. They emphasized the need for communication and doggedly brought ideological and interpersonal issues to the surface. The occasional difficulties that arose between consultants and center never came close to jeopardizing the relationship.

From an ecological perspective this case illustrates how a concern with side effects can be beneficial in community intervention. The regional center described by Sarason and his colleagues was a response to the unintended side effects of institutional care. The prevailing approach to delivering services for the intellectually handicapped had the unwanted consequence of absolving the family and the local community of responsibility for the person in the institution. Those planning the regional center made some decisions that were intended to have far-reaching consequences. These decisions included turning back the money that had been allocated for buildings and refusing to provide total live-in care. It was anticipated that these decisions would foster local and family responsibility for the continuing welfare of the handicapped person.

Although the consultation team had expertise in the areas of rehabilitation and the creation of settings, Sarason and his colleagues do not emphasize these qualifications in discussing the resource they provided. Rather, it was the balance between independence and involvement that was particularly helpful to the setting. They made a major time commitment to the project, which kept their advice from being dismissed—kept them, that is, from being regarded as utter outsiders. They remained somewhat independent, however, and were less influenced by the shared assumptions and outright myths that develop in a close-knit organization.

According to Sarason and his colleagues, the external critic serves as a check on "organizational craziness" in a setting. This craziness comprises all the intergroup and interpersonal maneuvers, alliances, and conflicts that distort the purpose of the organization. When afflicted by this condition, the lives of those in the setting center around issues of power and influence. Goals and ideals are undermined. In dealing with such craziness, the missionary zeal of leaders often turns them to exhortations, inspirational sermons, or the development of organizational charts, none of which is particularly effective. At this point an outsider who is perceptive, whose advice is respected, and who has the freedom to confront issues directly can be of benefit to a setting.

The weakness of the outsider position may result from the very lack of formal power that helps the consultant to be objective. Consultants take on a wide variety of tasks in host environments; some of these tasks are hard to accomplish without organizational authority. Cherniss (1977) reported a case in which the consultant's role in a community mental health center was constrained by his marginal position.

The consultant held a joint appointment at a university and a mental health center; only a quarter of his time was allocated to the center. He found that despite being progressive in ethos and staffing, the center concentrated on direct service rather than on preventive programs. Little consultation was undertaken by the center. Although it was involved in school-related issues, the center had not initiated any ongoing program for teachers.

The consultant suggested that a program be developed to provide group consultation to new teachers in the public schools. The idea was approved by officials at the center and in the school district. The consultant was put in charge of organizing the program, and he selected five staff members at the center who would lead the proposed teacher groups.

From September through January they carried out the complex tasks of contacting teachers, reassuring them that the groups would not be a form of therapy, and coordinating schedules. By early January the discussion groups were ready to go, but by then two of the original five staff members had withdrawn because of commitments to other projects at the center. A third staff member missed many meetings and found it hard to sustain his involvement. When the consultant discovered it was impossible to recruit others to fill the vacancies, the program was abandoned.

As he considered the reasons for the failure, the consultant concluded that his own marginal status in the center had a great deal to do with the outcome. He spent less time in the setting than did regular staff members, and he lacked formal organizational status. His outsider position affected the ill-fated program in several ways. He could not influence the center's priority setting, an activity that had consequences for the program's viability. Officials and staff at the center paid lip service to prevention, but they put their

emphasis on direct service. One of the five staff members withdrew when assigned to a halfway house; another withdrew because of her increasing load of
counseling. The consultant frequently learned about
administrative decisions, such as redeployment of
staff, only after they had been made. Even without a
decision-making role, the consultant concluded that if
he had heard about decisions sooner he would have
reacted to them more effectively.

The consultant's marginal status also undermined the program because the center saw it as *his*
program rather than accepting full ownership. The
five staff members had a reduced commitment because the program had been organized by an outsider.
Staff members who had to choose between this program and those favored by regular supervisors seldom
chose the one run by the consultant. Two who withdrew actually said that the consultant's marginal position influenced their decisions.

Whether the consultant's independence is seen as a positive
quality depends on the context. In the regional center case discussed earlier, the client group had a commitment to a new approach to rehabilitation. This commitment fitted well with the
interests of the consultants. Although the consultants were independent, their work contributed to a central task of the
group. In the case Cherniss describes, however, the mental
health center had little real commitment to preventive services.
The consultant's focus was on an area that came second to ongoing treatment of clients. In this context, independence was
translated into marginality and the consultant's project was
undermined.

Whether externality helps or hinders consultants depends
also on the sorts of interventions they undertake. In the case reported by Sarason and his colleagues the consultants were asked
to work as advisers. Although they were, in a sense, the con-
science of the project, they had no formal responsibilities. In
the case reported by Cherniss (1977) the consultant was given a
leadership role but found that his marginal status put him in a

poor position to compete for scarce resources with other projects in the center.

Some settings are so suspicious of outsiders that they seem closed to independent consultation. This is particularly true in contexts where social scientists are looked upon as alien and antagonistic. Even in such an environment it may be possible to build a bridge between the consultant and those in the setting and, in so doing, create healthy system change. One approach is to use a team consisting of at least one insider and one outsider. The person recruited from within the setting can help the team read the environment and also confer legitimacy on the team's activities. The outsider brings not only expertise lacking in the setting but also the degree of objectivity that we have associated with outside consultants.

The use of this team approach to an apparently closed institution was described by Gluckstern and Packard (1977). We shall see that a major task in consultation consists in working through the shared assumptions in a client group. In this case, the closed institution was a county jail. The jail staff had well-defined views rationalizing the status quo and stereotyping any outside expert who might argue for change. Rather than confront these assumptions head on, the consultation team worked with groups of staff members and inmates, encouraging them to articulate needs and to take a full share in the planning of change.

> A county sheriff invited a university to help bring reform to the century-old House of Corrections, a notoriously closed institution. It housed eighty inmates, mostly white males, serving sentences for serious offenses such as rape and manslaughter. Prisoners spent their days watching television or doing menial chores. The jail was authoritarian and repressive; inmates had almost no responsibility in running their daily lives. The environment fostered passivity, resentment, and alienation.
>
> The university agreed to work with jail officials to develop a model education program. The intent was to create new educational opportunities for inmates and to change processes within the jail so that

further innovations could be started and sustained in
the future.

The university hired a project director with a
background in counseling, group work, and organizational development. The jail assigned a correctional
officer who had demonstrated initiative and interest
in jail reform. These two worked as internal and external change agents for three years. Despite a commitment to work together, the jail and the university
expressed their mutual suspicion in the way they
composed the consultation team. The university
wanted to hire the project director to ensure that it
would have influence over the program. The jail administration expected its own staff member to be a
watchdog and protect the setting from overzealous
outsiders.

The activities of the two team members changed
over the three years, as did their relationship with one
another. Each had background and skills helpful for
certain tasks. During the first year the outsider diagnosed the system, established her credibility with
those who lived and worked in the jail, and built communication links with subgroups. The insider educated
the outsider to the power relationships in the setting.
He taught her how and when to push for change and
helped her to distinguish between the issues that were
worth fighting for and those that were not. In return,
the outsider taught relevant skills to her colleague:
group work, leadership training, organizational development, and counseling.

The two team members provided support for
one another in the difficulties each faced. The outsider had to overcome the distrust of staff members,
often expressed as cynicism about "liberal do-good-
ers." The insider was alienated from his peers at first.
His fellow correctional officers believed that his new
involvements and activities represented a challenge to
their own values. To gain support from all segments
in the setting, the team formed committees, discussion groups, and task-oriented workshops. Inmates
and officers were encouraged to articulate specific

needs and to help plan programs to meet them. Gradually suspicion and reserve were transformed into acceptance of the new program.

By the end of the first year the team's achievement included an occupational training project, a self-help drug rehabilitation group, a basic learning center, and a degree program affiliated with the university. In the second year the team established a governance board consisting of inmates, officers, and jail administrators. This board was given a mandate to consider grievances and to approve new programs. Creation of the governance board was a decisive moment in the intervention's history. The consultants had gone beyond establishing their own credibility; now they had earned credibility for the process of change itself.

During the third year the external consultant limited her direct involvement and began to function more as an adviser. The insider became interested in taking on similar responsibilities in the wider arena of state corrections. As he readied himself to take on an outsider role, he sought out and trained interested officers in the jail, just as he himself had been trained by the project director.*

A number of ecological assertions stated in Chapter One are relevant to this case. The outsider can learn a good deal about a setting by looking at the way the consultative task is initially defined. In this example, distrust of outsiders and the potential struggle for control were apparent in the very formation of an insider/outsider team. But while this way of beginning the task pointed to problems in relating the university to the jail, it also helped solve them. Once the team was formed, the insider and outsider acted not as watchdogs for their parent organizations but as partners in a common enterprise.

The ecologically oriented consultant has been encouraged

*Reproduced by special permission from *The Journal of Applied Behavioral Science,* "The Internal-External Change-Agent Team: Bringing Change to a 'Closed Institution,'" by Norma B. Gluckstern and Ralph Packard, Volume 13, Number 1, pp. 41-52, copyright 1977, NTL Institute.

to develop the aspects of a setting that can be resources for change. In the county jail, the team used a group approach to give inmates and staff ownership of prospective programs—thus increasing the capacities of various groups to provide indigenous resources. The project developed the inside staff member himself into a systemwide resource, and he in turn groomed another staff member to take on new responsibilities in the jail.

We have urged that the consultant's primary focus is on the system rather than on individual intervention. In the county jail project this orientation was expressed in the development of a governance board that could hear grievances and approve new programs. With membership from inmates, administrators, and officers, this board constituted an important change in the system. It was a change so fundamental to the jail that it could be expected to have far-reaching positive consequences.

In their discussion of this case, Gluckstern and Packard (1977) list assets and liabilities inherent in the outsider or insider position. The insider has greater access to the system and more experience with the way it operates. It is easier for the insider to talk with peers in the setting and to find sources of valid information. The insider has a better grasp of the politics of the system and knows how to respond within the limits of those politics. But the insider is also controlled by the setting because of a need for job security. He or she is vulnerable to peer pressure aimed at maintaining the status quo.

The outsider lacks firsthand experience of working inside the system and does not have alliances with various constituencies that make up the setting. The outsider may lack legitimacy, but he or she also has the advantage of being relatively independent of the setting's rewards and sanctions. The outsider may have a resource base beyond the client system. As the county jail case illustrates, when an insider and outsider can put their skills together in a team and function with a good working relationship, each member can overcome the weaknesses inherent in the other's position.

Most consultants do not have the luxury of belonging to teams containing insiders. They must do their own reconnaissance. This requires that they know themselves, and take their own characteristics into account, while finding out enough about a setting to determine the potential for a good match.

Consultants bring themselves—their viewpoints, backgrounds, and personalities—into all their community interventions. As Si Kahn, an organizer of poor communities in the southern United States, says, "There is a place for organizers who can't live without drugs, Mao posters, left-wing books, Raga rock, beads, and overnight visitors of the opposite sex, but it isn't in rural communities where poor people are struggling for their rights" (1970, p. 10). Or, in the pithy words of Saul Alinsky, "If I were organizing in an orthodox Jewish community, I would not walk in there eating a ham sandwich" (1971, p. xix).

Except for consultants who deal only with selected populations or limit themselves to certain issues, community psychologists must be able to work in multiple and diverse settings; and even a consultant who prefers to concentrate on only one issue or one constituency will find it necessary at times to interact with people of differing social status, attitudes, and lifestyles. Adaptability is clearly useful. But not all a consultant's characteristics are as easily shed as an affinity for drugs, beads, or posters. Community psychologists come in different colors and genders; they come with different levels of status and various institutional ties; they possess different skills and values.

Alinsky exhorted potential organizers to cut their long hair if it interfered with their work (1971, xix); it is more difficult, however, to adjust one's cultural attitudes and deeply held beliefs in response to the perceived needs of a population or setting. Sometimes a consultant can produce the style and skills needed to work with a particular group; at other times the consultant would be wise to find a different environment where the match is better.

Consultant Status and Responsiveness of Setting

One approach to consultant-client fit classifies consultants as having high or low status and categorizes settings as being responsive or resistant. Kelly (1979) defines a responsive setting as one in which a group wants to improve the setting and is willing to work with an outside resource. A resistant setting too involves people who have decided to improve the setting, but they have some ambivalence and are balanced by a group opposing change. In the responsive environment, the visible presence of the consultant tells people a serious effort is under way to improve the quality of the setting. But in the resistant setting the presence of the consultant may cause anxiety and suspicion. Kelly suggests that successful entry into a resistant setting involves supporting those who want change and helping them to acquire new skills and influence without intimidating those who are antagonistic to the changes.

The status of the consultant interacts with the responsiveness of the setting. All four combinations of high/low status and responsiveness/resistance produce possible maladaptive conditions that must be guarded against by the change agent. We shall begin with the combination that might be expected to provide a good climate for consultation: the high-status consultant in a receptive setting. In the first of two cases, the consultant's status was an essential ingredient in his success. In the second, it was implicated in his failure. Walton (1968) has described a brief intervention in which the consultant served as a third party in an interpersonal confrontation between two government officials.

> The dispute arose between two program directors in a large U.S. government agency. The director of Information Systems (IS) had been working for five months to develop a new organizational procedure to be considered for adoption by the whole agency. Systems Research (SR) supplied much of the professional talent needed for this project.
>
> A new director of SR demanded that the project be reviewed, including the role of his staff in assisting IS. The new director made a number of criticisms that disturbed the IS officials, who called in a behavioral science consultant. A meeting was arranged among both directors and the consultant.
>
> The consultant's firm ran workshops that both program directors had attended in the past.

Thus the consultant had established credibility with the two officials, even though he had never met the SR director before the three men sat down together.

At the meeting, the SR director complained that his staff had been given only lower-level technical work on the project and had not been permitted to contribute to the strategic design. He objected to the IS director's supervisory style, which allocated SR staff without involving the SR director. In his turn the other official denied that SR staff was given only lower-level work and defended his own leadership.

In his observations the consultant said the interchange should be characterized as negotiation. He sharpened the issues between the two officials and identified the areas of concern that seemed fundamental. The SR director believed the other official's leadership style was too loose and unstructured. He had his own ideas about the project, but he thought he was not being given a fair hearing. The IS director, said the consultant, felt under attack by the new man's approach. Having seen a display of the interpersonal style of the two officials, the consultant also alerted them to subtle interpersonal issues that might interfere with their future relationship.

This meeting was the consultant's only involvement with the two officials. When it was over, they had scheduled further sessions among themselves and the staff members of their programs. At these meetings they were successful in negotiating a good working relationship.

In reviewing this case, the consultant noted that despite their interpersonal difficulties both officials were receptive to the intervention. Because they had participated in workshops run by his parent organization, the officials had confidence in the mediating process that the consultant would employ. Having a third party present decreased the risk of an abortive confrontation. The fact that the consultant was associated with laboratory training suggested to the directors that he probably had the skills to make the meeting productive. The consultant concluded that his basic function was a passive one constituted by his mere presence at the meeting. The two directors' expectations about his training, background, and neutrality made it easier for them to deal with one another and begin to resolve outstanding issues.

A key issue in this case was the mediation of interdependence between two system components. The two had to work together if the system was to achieve its main goals. In viewing a setting as a series of linkages, a consultant would be alerted to intervention tactics that would improve the interaction between the two groups. Improving the interaction would be consistent with our view of consultation as the facilitation of intended effects—the power of a system to meet its objectives is enhanced by the consultant's intervention.

In his discussion of the case, Walton (1968) noted that in many situations the consultant's effort is aimed largely at establishing his or her credibility. An appropriate role must be found, and the consultant's personal attributes must be presented to the parties. Here the status of the consultant with both parties meant that they could cut through such preliminary issues quickly and go to work on the substance of the matter.

An important factor in such third-party work is the consultant's apparent neutrality or lack of it. Walton refers to the consultant's symmetry or asymmetry in relation to the negotiating parties. There are cases in which an asymmetrical role works best. For instance, when there is a basic power or skill disparity between the two parties, the consultant can offset this by playing a role that supports the weaker party more than the stronger. In other cases, such as that just described, it is essential that the consultant's relationship with both parties be symmetrical. This symmetry requires that consultants be neutral with respect to the outcome, that they be equally close or distant in their previous relationship with the two parties, and that they propose ground rules that do not operate to the disadvantage of either party.

In Kelly's (1980) outline of his model, he warns the high-status change agent in a responsive setting to guard against elitism. The consequences are illustrated in a case reported by Mullin, Blakeney, and Bell (1974).

> An urban citizens' group obtained a federal grant to start a program for adolescents. The objectives were to divert adolescents from the criminal justice system, to assist runaways, to provide counseling, and to develop new ways to locate and help young people with problems.
>
> The group decided to use paraprofessionals to fill the six counselor positions. These trainees ranged in education from high school to master's degree. Officials negotiated a contract with an expert on child and adolescent psychiatry to act as consultant and provide fifty hours of training for paraprofessionals.
>
> The consultant decided that group training sessions would be most effective. Weekly meetings of an hour and a half each were to be attended by the trainees and administrative staff of the program. At these meetings the consultant spoke little. He had a stiff and formal manner. Both his style and his reputation in psychiatry gave the trainees the feeling they were participating in group therapy. They were reluctant to engage in group therapy because they thought it inappropriate, but the consultant's status intimidated them and kept them from confronting him on this issue. The trainees sat back and watched whenever the consultant and the administrators engaged in discussion.
>
> After four months the administrators realized the groups were going badly and stopped attending meetings. Shortly afterward, the trainees approached the administrators and asked that the group sessions be terminated. When the consultant was advised of this request, he admitted that he was clearly not the person for the job and withdrew.
>
> A second, more successful, training program was launched two months later. The groundwork was laid through discussions with trainees about the earlier abortive effort. The next consultant emphasized that sessions were for training, not therapy, and he

excluded the administrators. He was sensitive to the
paraprofessionals' insecurity about their skills and
status. He made it clear that his was to be a helping
role, and the trainees responded.

This brief case provides a good illustration of what can
happen when the resources of the consultant do not match the
needs of a group. Although the setting was receptive, the first
consultant's training and manner prevented his work from being
effective. In fact, to the extent that his methods lowered trainees'
self-esteem and made the path more difficult for the second
consultant, his intervention was actually harmful. The first consultant's status drew him into the trap of elitism. The second
consultant's careful groundwork, including extensive discussions
with trainees about the earlier failure, illustrates the value of reading the environment to understand the unique aspects of a setting.

Kelly (1979, 1980) suggests that the high-status consultant in a receptive environment is in a particularly good position
to achieve long-lasting growth in a setting. This may involve organizing diverse groups for future tasks, creating social structures that can plan future development, translating the setting's
ideals into a plan for daily activity, or helping varied groups in
the setting to initiate new activities where there is no precedent
for such initiation.

These broad opportunities for a growth-enhancing intervention are less available to the high-status consultant in a resistant setting. Much of the consultant's energy is spent dealing
with those who oppose change and mistrust intruders. Settings
may be resistant because they are committed to operating procedures much different from those represented by the consultant.
We have found several examples in the literature documenting
this sort of clash between consultant and client. Consultants
trained in a human relations approach may find their efforts
thwarted in a rigid, hierarchical organization. Such a problem is
described by Bennis (1977) in his report of work by an industrial social psychologist consulting to a large Swiss service industry.

The industrial firm hired a consultant to develop and execute a training course for supervisors. Deciding to use the laboratory training method, he initiated nine one-week laboratories in a mountain resort. The techniques were new to those attending the sessions; nevertheless, the consultant was pleased with the results he was getting.

The company president had visited the training site in previous years and had observed case study and lecture methods with great approval. Now, however, he heard disquieting rumors about the new approach. He decided to see for himself. While laboratory participants were at breakfast, the president walked in unannounced and uninvited. He demanded that he be allowed to observe two laboratory sessions.

He found the proceedings shockingly different from what he expected or wanted in a training program. Supervisors were sitting in a circle; between long silences they would talk about group relations. Occasionally someone would ask what others thought of him. Pressure would build up in the group, and there would be an explosion with everyone talking at once.

In a later interview the president said the whole procedure was inconsistent with his view that training sessions should train key people how to guide their subordinates. He was astonished that the consultant seemed unwilling to have him sit in on the sessions: "I told him that I am used to inspecting courses. I am, after all, the president. . . ." The day after he visited the workshop, the president returned to company headquarters and announced the termination of the project. When the consultant's contract came up for renewal, it too was terminated.

Looking back on the experience, the bemused industry president said, "We Swiss, in our schools and in our land, rarely get any instruction in guiding people. Our main indoctrination, our main orientation, is the army. This is primitive, but at least they come to certain conclusions."

The ecological principle of interdependence, when applied to consultation, asserts that interventions are intended to
be matched with the host environment. In this case the intervention was so at odds with the prevailing philosophy in the
organization that the consultant's work was discontinued. It
would be easy and convenient for consultants to assume that
such a mismatch always discloses a flaw in the setting only. But
as Bennis points out, authoritarian structures are often more effective than democratic structures in task performance: "Although democratic organizations enjoy generally high morale,
there is a real question whether 'closeness,' interpersonal sensitivity, and analysis are functional for bureaucracies" (1977, p.
192). An authoritarian organization may be defending its current level of functioning, not merely dogmatically resisting
change, when it expels the democratic consultant.

This case also illustrates problems that arise when client
and consultant are guided by conflicting theories about how organizations should operate. In our discussion of social cognition
we argued that people can be biased by their own models. In
the example of consultation with the Swiss firm, it is clear that
the consultant was tuned to one ideal model, based on a human
relations approach, while the client had a military model. Shellow and Newbrough (1975) confronted a similar problem in attempting to provide consultation to juvenile officers in an
American police department. Once again the high status of the
consultation team was no guarantee of success in a resistant setting.

> The police inspector hoped that community
> psychologists would offer a series of lectures with
> himself as a participant. The psychologists wanted to
> work in small groups with emphasis on free discus-
> sion. They knew this could best be achieved if senior
> officers did not attend. Superiors were worried, how-
> ever, about maintaining administrative control over
> their men. After much debate a compromise was
> struck. Senior officers would not come to sessions,
> but the sergeant would be permitted to attend.
> At the first session the policemen showed their

discomfort with the consultants' format. Even such commonplace discussion group procedures as putting chairs in a circle made the participants tense. Throughout the seminar series, police officers had trouble relating to the discussion approach. At the last session they seemed sure that here, at last, there would be a lecture—if only to tell what they had learned.

Superior officers too felt threatened by the seminars. Finally the inspector walked in on a seminar unannounced, even though it had been agreed that he would not attend. What he saw did not reassure him, but he permitted the seminars to continue. When the program reached its uneasy conclusion the police officers were eager to discontinue the uncomfortable unstructured approach.

In settings as apparently different as a Swiss service industry and a North American police department, introduction of discussion groups proved so threatening that excluded superiors felt they had to crash into the sessions to see what was going on. Both organizations had rigid, military-style hierarchical structures that resisted a human relations approach. In both cases, the consultants failed to recognize the importance of matching their interventions to the host environment. Instead they proceeded on the basis of their preferred models and ignored features of the client group that conflicted with their approaches. Drawing conclusions from the last case, Shellow and Newbrough (1975) caution consultants to take into account the hierarchical nature of certain organizations. They believe the consultant should not divorce leadership from the intervention but instead must find ways to include it. Without such leadership, a hierarchical organization may become chaotic.

Not all consultants espouse democratic models, of course, nor do all resistant settings react from a commitment to an authoritarian ideal. Sometimes the philosophies may be reserved. An illustration is provided by Crockett's (1977) description of his intervention in the U.S. State Department. Once again the setting was resistant, this time resisting an authoritarian change agent. Once again, too, the intervener had high status. He was sent in by a new administration and given a mandate to make sweeping changes. Although his leadership role puts him outside our definition of the consultant, we have included this brief case description because it shows how a resistant setting can frustrate a change agent, even one with formal authority.

An unknown foreign service officer, catapulted by President Kennedy into one of the top administrative positions in the State Department, immediately sought to introduce major changes. His style was influenced by the new administration. Shortly after the official's appointment, Attorney-General Robert Kennedy called him into his office and said tersely: "The State Department must be made to assume a leadership position in the foreign affairs community. Your job is to make that happen. Do you know how you will make this happen? You will make it happen by giving orders and firing people who don't produce."

Taking this hard line as his touchstone, the official attempted to bring about change with an authoritarian style. Wielding undisguised power, he soon found that while direct orders could alter formal structures, behavior was left untouched. The State Department was so ponderous and bureaucratic that it was referred to as the "fudge factory" by its detractors. Lines of authority crisscrossed throughout the organization, making it difficult for someone who gave an order to discern its implications throughout the department.

The organization subverted all his attempts to create change by command. Finally he realized his approach was a total failure. He took stock and decided to redirect his efforts. He saw now that he had been unconcerned about the human side of the department. His emphasis shifted to trying to work with people rather than against them. He adopted a team approach. He began to involve as many people as possible in his attempts to introduce change. This new style had a positive impact on the department's effectiveness and on the satisfaction people expressed in their jobs.

We have indicated that this case, although instructive for all prospective change agents, is not actually one of consultation. If Crockett had been a consultant rather than the occupant of a formal role, he would probably have left the setting once it was clear that his approach had failed. As a role occupant, however, he had reason to remain in place even though he could not carry out his mandate. He had time to change his approach once he learned what changes might be beneficial. Consultants, though, are unlikely to get second chances.

The Low-Status Consultant

We have presented several short narratives of high-status consultants dealing with responsive or resistant settings. Now we move to the problems encountered by low-status consultants in these two types of setting. Low status may be temporary for the consultant—intern status while learning the craft is a good example. It may also reside in the interaction between permanent consultant characteristics, such as race or gender, and the perspective of those in a certain client group.

In the responsive setting, Kelly (1980) believes, the low-status consultant is in danger of being co-opted. His or her own perspective, independence, and operating mode may be overwhelmed. In this section we present two narratives involving the experiences of consultants working separately in the same setting: an alternative high school. Although this setting had features that resisted certain kinds of intervention, a fact that will become apparent in the two cases, it fell properly in the responsive category. Because staff members prided themselves on providing an alternative to traditional education, visitors of all kinds were welcomed into the school. Those who had something to contribute were free to make their contribution.

In the first case, which we shall give in more detail than those presented earlier, Levy-Warren (1976) found that entry itself was much easier than being an effective consultant. The very philosophy that opened the setting to various visitors made it difficult for the high school to accept the need for consultation that might pinpoint systemic problems or produce systemic change.

The High School in the Community (HSC) was an attempt to create an alternative educational experience within the existing public school system. It was founded by a group of teachers, students, parents, and school board members who had become disenchanted with many characteristics of traditional high schools. The goals of HSC included increasing teacher involvement with students, developing a true sense of community, and creating a setting where students and teachers could meet on equal footing.

The school's structure was designed to advance its goals. All school policies were formulated by a policy council made up of parents, teachers, and students. A facilitating unit composed of four teachers had responsibility for administrative procedures. The community orientation program placed students in community settings where they could learn a range of skills.

The school had a relaxed atmosphere. Staff and students called each other by first names. All rules applied to teachers and students alike. Staff and students frequently could be found mingling in the halls and outside the buildings smoking, talking, and playing games.

Teachers at HSC tended to be liberal or radical in their politics. They were firmly committed to non-hierarchical school structures. They performed multiple roles, working on personal and interpersonal problems of students as well as teaching academic subjects. This extra load meant that they worked longer hours than teachers in traditional schools. Despite the hard work and constant insecurity of federal funding support, teachers maintained considerable enthusiasm for the experiment.

The history of HSC, and the principles that guided it, presented problems for anyone entering the school as a consultant. The school was created as a reaction against the educational establishment, and staff members tended to think that anyone coming from a university would not have much to say.

A practical problem for the consultant was to differentiate herself from the many visitors who spent time in the school: evaluators commissioned by the city, school board members, students from other schools, volunteers from the community. This constant traffic made the school somewhat chaotic. Staff members tolerated the influx of outsiders because of their commitment to connecting HSC to the community, but they had no reason to think outsiders had much to offer.

The consultant, who was not an evaluator, school board representative, or community volunteer, had to find ways to establish an identity. She did this by demonstrating that she had a commitment to the school which extended beyond that of temporary visitors. She maintained high visibility, came in contact with all staff, and attended the school's various after-hours activities as well as being in the school on a regular basis.

A more basic problem was to convey to staff members that she shared the guiding ideas which sustained the HSC experiment. Opportunities for proving herself were often thrust on her. She found herself barraged by questions about the local community, political issues, previous work situations, and personal relationships. While such questions might seem too inquisitive, the consultant knew that teachers were trying to measure her compatibility with the school's values. She was able to make it clear that she supported such ideas as the lack of formal school hierarchy, peership among staff and students, lack of role boundaries, and community involvement.

Even when she was accepted by school staff, there were barriers preventing full use of her consulting skills. The ethos of the school specified that since it was created as a reaction against institutional arrangements in other high schools, it must not itself have any institutional problems. All difficulties had to be defined as the responsibility of individuals. The school per se could thus have no need for a consultant. Staff members who asked for help were clearly displaying a problem of their own, not one created by the system.

Naturally this orientation made it somewhat

hard for teachers to admit their problems. The consultant had to busy herself on her own to demonstrate her competence. She drew up statistics on attendance, followed up students who were frequently absent, and initiated conversations about these students with their teachers. She visited classes and volunteered comments about classroom process to staff members. After the consultant had spent two months on such projects, a teacher finally sought her opinion about how to deal with some disruptive students in her class. Word circulated that the consultant could make a positive contribution in this area, and gradually she found herself being used as a resource by teachers.

The cognitive approach to community consultation emphasizes the role of shared assumptions in client groups. The ecological analogy directs our attention to the fit between these assumptions and those carried into the setting by the consultant. In this case, the consultant found herself tested in many ways by people in the setting. Were her politics compatible with theirs? Was her view of society the same? Did she have compatible views on education? Before she could do any worthwhile work, she had to *show* that she shared the important assumptions of those in the school.

If she accepted *all* of the group's assumptions, however, she would have been frustrated. One set of beliefs in the school was that because it was an alternative to traditional education, it could not have the systemic problems found in traditional schools. Accepting this view would mean abandoning a focus on the need for system change and development. She would indeed, as Kelly (1980) puts it, have been co-opted.

Another shared assumption in this setting was that HSC did not have, and could not have, racial problems. The liberal philosophy of those teaching at the school was weighted toward equality and tolerance. Any inquiry or intervention that posed the possibility of looking at racial issues was threatening, as Gooden (1977) found when he did an internship in consultation at HSC. Again the consultant was in a student role and faced the possibility of being overwhelmed and co-opted by a responsive setting. And in this case the setting was particularly responsive because the consultant was a black male and many of the students were black. But this initial receptiveness did not mean that those in the setting were willing to look at racial issues in the school.

At HSC most of the students, but only a few of the teachers, were black. The school staff recognized that this was a problem: There were few blacks to teach courses in black history, few black counselors, and few role models for black adolescents. Although black students were generally happier at HSC than they had been at other schools, they felt less supported than the school's white students because of the racial imbalance in the staff.

Teachers hoped the consultant, as a black man, could give help in an area where it was much needed. But they were also somewhat threatened at what a black consultant might discover about race relations in the school.

The consultant's major project was to try to establish a series of workshops for teachers concerning the problems of inner-city adolescents. This goal would be consistent with his own role definition, because it would offer consultation rather than the sort of direct service provided by the teachers themselves.

He found that the teachers lacked enthusiasm for the project. They failed to take any responsibility to get the workshops organized. It seemed to the consultant that staff members believed that the very existence of the proposed workshops would indicate there were racial difficulties in the school.

His next tactic was to involve himself in the school's attendance problem. He expected that after he had surveyed the scope of the problem by talking to students, he would make recommendations for an approach that could be implemented by the school as a whole. But again there was little enthusiasm for this idea. Instead, his contact with black students about absenteeism was seen as an end in itself. He was praised for his work with these students and gradually found himself cast into a direct-service role which, though valuable to the school, undercut the broad consultation function he might have provided.

Kelly (1979) makes it clear that settings are never purely responsive, and probably only rarely are they entirely resistant. Usually consultants face a mixture of attitudes. In the case described by Gooden the alternative school had several reasons to be receptive: It valued the consultant as a black male, and its innovative philosophy predisposed it to welcome new ideas. But there were undercurrents of resistance, such as the fear that the consultant would find racial problems in the school. Ultimately the setting was willing to accept the consultant only if it could subvert his consultation role.

A setting that might be characterized as openly resistant offers serious challenges to consultants with low status. Much of their time may be spent merely surviving and looking for resources to maintain some role integrity. When the resources are not found, the likely outcome is alienation (Kelly, 1980). A case described by Huang (1976) illustrates how resistant settings deal with consultants. As in the previous case the setting was a high school. But this was not an alternative high school with a commitment to innovation; rather, it was a traditional school with strong commitment to managing problems in ways that left the status quo intact. In the previous case the consultant's internship status was partly offset by his race—a valued characteristic in the setting. In this example, however, internship status was compounded by the consultant's gender, reducing her status in the eyes of the clients.

The consultant was invited to do her internship working in the resource program of an inner-city high school. State law required that all schools have resource programs to serve students with histories of school failure, troublesome behavior, or truancy. The school had little commitment to its resource program. The staff consisted of a male resource counselor and a female outreach community worker. Both were cut off from the mainstream functioning of the school and lacked direction.

Although this situation opened up possibilities for a system-centered consultation, the intern found that barriers created by her age, gender, and neophyte status kept her from playing this role. Instead she was guided into direct-service functions and was strongly reinforced whenever she engaged in these activities.

Gender seemed to pose problems. In her contacts with the resource counselor, the consultant found herself listening to more and more personal material. She was being cast as a confidante rather than a professional. The resource counselor, who proclaimed himself a "liberated male," insisted on relating to the consultant in a social manner while treating males in a businesslike fashion. When he introduced her to school staff, he always omitted any mention of consultation.

The consultant's low status in the eyes of school staff was one factor undercutting successful intervention. The other had to do with the school's attitude toward change. There was a commitment to keeping things just as they were. Students had to adapt to the demands of the system, and the resource center was there to see that they did. As it happened, the resource center was quite unsuccessful in meeting this objective. Most students who were referred to the center failed to make the necessary adaptation and continued to cause trouble or dropped out of school.

In all three of these high school cases there were pressures on consultants to avoid a systemic focus. One consultant found that to look for systemic problems in an alternative high school would threaten the staff's assumptions about the value of their innovative work. Another consultant discovered that any attempt to investigate sources of racial tension in the alternative school would violate assumptions about the tolerance in the setting. Finally, in a much more traditional school, the consultant was guided toward direct service and away from any

work that might threaten the status quo. This was a school in
which diversity among students was not valued. Those who
could not adapt to a narrow range of acceptable behavior were
labeled as troublemakers and dealt with individually by the
school's resource center. The setting resisted any attempt by the
consultant to define the problem differently.

If being an intern were the only cause of low status for
consultants, it would simply be something to survive on the way
to a professional identity. This is not the case. Often relatively
inexperienced consultants, even students, can do productive
work. And consultants often find themselves in low-status positions with their clients, even though they may have ample professional credentials and experience. Gender, which contributed
to the discounting of the intern's status in the previous case,
may create obstacles for experienced consultants as well. Frederick, Fretta, and Levin-Frank (1976) point out that women are
often seen as "cutie pies" or "women's libbers" when they attempt to intervene in community settings. But as they indicate
in the following case, even in a somewhat resistant setting such
issues may be negotiated successfully.

> A group of judges from the county courthouse
> asked the local mental health center to help them by
> providing an intensive consultation program. Two
> women with consultation experience in a variety of
> community settings were chosen by the center to set
> up the program. The judge's chamber hall in the
> courthouse had a conservative, male-dominated at-
> mosphere—in fact, it resembled a men's club. The
> only females accustomed to entering the hall were
> two clerks who served coffee, delivered snacks and
> lunch, and took dictation.
> Although the judges had requested the service,
> there was much evidence of resistance and denigra-
> tion of the consultants. A judge, on first meeting one
> of the consultants, gave her a loud "Hello, sugar!"
> Other comments ranged from the remark that wom-
> men's liberation was just a passing fad to sexually sug-
> gestive references.

The younger of the two women found it particularly difficult to negotiate a professional role with a judge who was her partner in family interviews. While families were present, the judge was appropriate but somewhat passive. He seemed to expect the consultant to provide legal as well as mental health advice. She was aware of this and took care not to accept any legal decision-making responsibility. At the end of each session, when the family had left, the consultant and the judge were supposed to engage in case discussion. At this point the judge became more talkative, making many personally charged comments. The consultant tried to handle these uncomfortable interchanges with humor. She kept a tight rein on her temper, even though she resented being trapped in a situation requiring so much control.

After working with the judge for several weeks, the consultant found that her interpersonal strategy was working. He stopped making suggestive remarks. "Sugar" disappeared from his vocabulary. He became more sensitive in discussing cases and even admitted feeling helpless when assisting a family that had a difficult emotional problem. Gradually the consultant was able to overcome the difficulties created by the client's denigration of her status.

Consultants must understand the traditions of the settings they enter if their interventions are to have real effects. In this case, the tradition was that of a male-only group of judges who was dubious about the value of advice from women. The consultants were not only women but they lacked legal training. Which factor—background or gender—caused them to be denigrated? Apparently gender was the salient factor, since the most difficult judge wavered between discounting a consultant and inappropriately asking her to make decisions on legal issues. She had to counteract the judge's stereotype and, moreover, create boundaries that would permit her to deal with mental health rather than legal aspects of cases.

Traditions may change slowly, but they do change. No doubt the women who had difficulties with some male judges would not even have been invited into chambers a few years earlier. And, a few years later, the entry process would be easier with women judges in chambers. The succession principle in ecological inquiry emphasizes change over time. At any point a setting is, to some extent, a product of its history. The responsiveness of a setting to intervention by a particular consultant may shift. In fact, settings may need different sorts of consultants at different times. Goldenberg (1971) made this point in his account of the development of an innovative residential youth center. His leadership role in the center probably varies somewhat from our view of the consultant as someone who occupies no permanent role. Nevertheless, we think the case is particularly useful as an illustration of how a person's background, professional status, and style can be effective at one point but might interfere with the setting's development at another point. Goldenberg foresaw this possibility and built transition of leadership into the nascent youth center.

> The Residential Youth Center (RYC) was funded by the U.S. federal government as a demonstration project. Its goal was to evaluate whether a neighborhood-based residential youth program could facilitate the growth and rehabilitation of poor adolescents and their families.

> The first twenty adolescents to be served by RYC were youths from families characterized by chronic unemployment, social disorganization, and severe interpersonal conflict. Most of the families had a history of welfare dependency. Seventy percent of the adolescents had been arrested at least once; one had a dozen arrests. Only three had never spent time in any kind of institution.

> The center had nine staff members. Essentially it was a nonprofessional staff. The initial director was a university professor, but most staff members had high school diplomas. Among them were a former automobile mechanic, policeman, and baseball player.

> The demonstration project was structured horizontally. Each staff member, regardless of formal job description, carried a case load. Having a case load

meant assuming total responsibility for all decisions and interventions involving a resident and his family. No other staff member, regardless of status, could make decisions in another person's cases. Horizontal structure also meant that duties traditionally associated with certain jobs were shared among all staff. For example, everyone was expected to live in and cook on occasion. RYC's goal was complete interchangeability of roles.

The program promoted ongoing relationships among staff members, residents, and their families. The objective was to help residents and their families become employed and learn to deal with social and psychological problems that were standing between them and a satisfying life.

During the day residents were usually out of RYC at work. Staff members took this time to go to the work site or visit families. At night and on weekends RYC was used for special programs open to residents, their families, and eventually the general community. Parents were encouraged to visit any time of the day or night. Residents paid rent and were free to go home any time they wished.

Such a setting goes through life cycles involving changes in conceptions, goals, and processes. At least four such phases could be identified in the life of RYC. The first was a period of innovation during which the setting was developing its own ethos. The second was a period of implementation when the basic philosophy was translated into specific internal processes and patterns of conflict resolution. In these phases the first director saw his most important function as creating conditions for staff to relate to one another as sources of help, support, and growth.

The second major task of the initial director was to create the conditions for his own replacement. RYC was designed to demonstrate that a helping setting could be successful without guidance and control from a professional. From the outset it was understood that the staff member who served as deputy director would become the leader after six months.

When the transition had taken place, the new
leader faced tasks defined by the next two stages in
the setting's evolution. One of these was a consolida-
tion phase, during which the regularities that were established could be questioned and reassessed. Then
came a renewal stage resulting from a period of intense reevaluation.

The youth center described by Goldenberg is typical of
a trend toward involving the community in issues such as youth
services, treatment of the intellectually handicapped, and rehabilitation of prisoners. In this project there was a strong emphasis on conserving and developing community resources. The
youths served by the center were, of course, among the potential resources that might be lost to their communities without
intervention. We have said that an ecological approach encourages an appreciation of diversity among people. Such diversity
was positively valued in the youth center. It was assumed that
people with different backgrounds would have different things
to offer. A former baseball player, policeman, and auto mechanic
worked with common purpose as staff members at the youth
center.

The healthy respect for diversity also led planners to
project leadership change after the formative period. A professional got the setting started, and a staff member without
professional credentials took over after the first six months.
Goldenberg, looking back on the RYC experience, says it is
not necessary for one person to be an organization's man for all
seasons.

Respecting Diversity in Settings

Some failures in consultation can be attributed to the
consultant's difficulty in appreciating, and valuing, diversity in a
community. At times the whole community is utterly alien to
the consultant's experience. He or she may approach the community with neither understanding nor respect, discounting local people as potential resources. Alinsky (1946) points out that
it requires empathy to appreciate the dilemma of local people

confronted by an outsider telling them what their problems are. Since consultants, including community organizers, are essentially outsiders, they must approach this problem with tact. When the intruder lacks empathy the results are often disastrous, as Alinsky indicates in his description of the organizing of a poor community.

> Muddy Flats was described by the local police chief as a place where rats, men, women, children, lice, dogs, and pigs existed and died. The poverty-stricken people lived in shacks with no indoor plumbing. They suffered from malnutrition. Most parents had watched their children go through typhoid fever and smallpox as if they were ordinary children's diseases. On a hill above the squalid community, residents could look up at the fine homes and well-kept lawns of the owners and executives of the only local industry.

> For years, attempts to organize the people had failed. All organizational drives emphasized the fact that people on the hill were to be blamed for the misery and suffering in the community below. Organizers would come into the community and say, "Look, don't you understand the reason you are suffering all of this poverty and disease is because of the way the people at the top of the hill are treating you?" Residents would agree.

> Then the organizer would say "We're going to have a meeting next Friday night and we want all you people out there so we can organize." People would nod, but few would come to the meeting. After several attempts each group of organizers would conclude that the people were too broken and demoralized to stand up for themselves, and they would leave.

> The organizers did not recognize that their approach put the local people in a dilemma. Of course residents knew that the people on the hill were the cause of their problems. But they also said to themselves, "That smart outsider must think I'm dumb— I've lived here for forty years in all this mess and that

guy has to come around to tell me why . . . he thinks
I'm too dumb to know the reason for my trouble,
and at the meeting he's going to show me he's smart
enough to do something about it. If I go, I'm showing
that he's smart and I'm dumb."

Finally, however, an organizing campaign was
successful. The organizers used the simple procedure
of listening to what local people were saying. Then,
when local residents invariably pointed to the people
on the hill as the source of the problem, the organizers would use the residents' own analysis to help
them get together. People were given room to define
the problem, and the organizers helped them to articulate it. Soon people were demanding that an organization be formed to do something, and the organizers
took on the task of bringing people together.

In Alinsky's view, the organizers who used a heavy-
handed approach and failed to gain local support were really
demonstrating that they had little respect for residents. Organizing succeeded when outsiders were prepared to listen,
to help people come to their own formulation of the problem,
and then to assist them when they decided to bring an organization into existence. The case also shows the value of a resource-based approach. From an ecological standpoint, the
consultant is a resource to the community. The unsuccessful
organizers in Alinsky's description saw themselves as effectors
rather than facilitators of change. People in the setting are resources too. But the style of the unsuccessful organizers denigrated local people and made them more hopeless about their
situation. Organization was possible only when the community
was permitted to pose the problem itself and use the outsiders
as resources in its own project for change.

If consultants have so much trouble understanding the
views and feelings of people in their own country, it is much
more difficult when consultation is cross-cultural. Westermeyer
and Hausman (1974a) have outlined some of the problems involved when ethnicity is a barrier. They note that in consultation the client is not always identical with the target of inter-

vention. One group may sponsor consultation with another group. Various ethnic combinations are possible, each with its characteristic problem.

The consultant and client may be from the same ethnic group, but the target population may be from another group. There are no cross-cultural communication barriers between consultant and client, but the client may have a paternalistic relationship with the target group. Consequently the client may try to structure the way the consultant relates to the target group, perhaps choosing "representatives" of the target group and limiting the consultant's interaction to those people.

The consultant and target population may be from one ethnic group, the client from another. A government agency administered by whites may hire a Native Indian consultant to work among Indians, a Hispanic to work among Hispanics, and so on. The ease of communication between consultant and target group may be impaired by the nature of the consultant's contract with the client and by suspicions the target group may have about one of their own who works for the majority group.

Seldom do the consultant, client, and target group all come from different ethnic groups. But when they do, Westermeyer and Hausman suggest that potential problems multiply geometrically. The consultant must try to understand a client and a target group from cultural backgrounds different from that of the consultant. The consultant needs to understand the relation of client to target group and to assess communication problems in that relationship.

A common cross-cultural relationship involves client and target group from one ethnic background and consultant from another. This situation can result in considerable confusion. The consultant may assume that the client can provide an orientation to the problems of the target group, but this may be an illusion. Although they are of the same ethnicity, the client may differ from the target group in various important ways including social class, norms, and values.

As an illustration of cross-cultural problems, Hilliard (1974) has reported a case in which two agencies, representing the American and Liberian governments, arranged to have a

university-based group of American educators consult to educators in Liberia.

A U.S. government agency with little awareness
of local conditions arranged to help Liberian educators set up a school district with semiautonomous administration and policy formulation. In a country
that had a centralized national system of education,
the plan called for the reorganization of schools in
the capital city. A school district would be created
along North American lines, with a school board, a
superintendent, and supporting administrative and instructional staff.

The project had been proposed by foreign aid
technicians who lived in the local setting for only a
short period. Because of the nature of nation-to-
nation contacts the project had to be fully specified
in advance. There was no room for details to flow
naturally from a developing relationship between local educators and American consultants.

A team of fifteen consultants was involved
with the project during the eight years it took to re-
shape the capital city's school system. The team
found that the whole notion of a semiautonomous
school district was alien to local society. Each step required adjustments in power and prestige. The consultants were always struggling against contract demands
and bureaucratic procedures that undermined true
collaboration with the Liberians.

Some of the problems could be attributed to
difficulties in developing a satisfactory helping role in
a foreign country. The consultants tended to foster
dependency in local officials. They tried to make
themselves more necessary rather than less so. Frequently they evaluated the Liberians as "not ready"
for some responsibility and were reluctant to turn
over decision making, even when the transfer was explicitly mandated.

At first the Liberians either accepted a dependent role or found ways to avoid the consultants. But
gradually they took charge and insisted on making

their own decisions. The Liberians had to grapple with two problems: how to introduce change in their own community when that change included new and unfamiliar institutions; and how to incorporate a group of foreign consultants. The American team gradually realized that with sufficient resources the Liberians could handle most tasks without the help of outsiders. Nevertheless, the Liberians had to accept the fact that resources were contingent upon the presence of well-meaning consultants who knew little about local conditions.

Often the consultants found that their value lay not in the advice they gave but in the clout they gave to the ideas of local people. One Liberian school principal was determined to keep his consultants even after the contract period had expired. He knew that his own proposals were given more serious consideration by his superiors when they believed the Americans had contributed to them.

Consultants must have a healthy respect for the evolution of settings if they wish to have any long-term beneficial impact. In the case described by Hilliard, the project was created in a vacuum. The traditions that had led Liberians to develop the school system as they had were considered irrelevant. Implanting an American model of education, whether it matched the host setting or not, was of prime importance. The consultation team found itself tied to this inappropriate model and unable to change the ground rules. This is another example of failure to respect diversity by those embarking on an intervention scheme: Since the Liberian system was different, it was therefore subject to change. Even though the thrust of the project was flawed, it had some positive side effects. One Liberian school official, for example, wanted continued consultation because his superiors would accept his ideas if they thought the ideas came from outside experts.

The problems of cross-cultural consultation can be encountered without crossing national borders. In countries with significant minority ethnic populations (the United States,

Canada, and Great Britain are all examples), consultants often
find themselves working with people who have different cultural backgrounds. The Liberian experience shows that outsiders sometimes intrude without understanding the local people;
similarly, in their own country consultants may not appreciate
the problems of a minority group or the way group members
see the world. King, Cotler, and Patterson (1975) described a
case in which consultants offered behavioral consultation to a
school that primarily served Chicano children.

> In an elementary school located in a Mexican-
> American community, the primary problem was ab-
> senteeism. The consultants drew up a behavior modi-
> fication program that would reinforce children and
> their parents when children had good attendance rec-
> ords. Three groups were created: an experimental
> group with reinforcement; a control group in which
> parents were urged to send children to school but
> with no reinforcement; and a no-treatment control
> group. The program was conducted in three segments
> of fifteen days each. Children in the experimental
> group received reinforcement every day they attended;
> parents received prizes at the end of each fifteen-day
> segment.
>
> At the beginning of each period, letters were
> sent to parents in the experimental group and one of
> the control groups emphasizing the importance of at-
> tendance. In the experimental group, children were
> rewarded each morning at school with two-cent can-
> dies, praise, and a star placed by their names on a
> chart. Parents could receive an enlarged photograph
> of their child, a five-dollar gift certificate, or a sub-
> scription to a Spanish-language magazine.
>
> At the end of the program it was found that
> there was no difference between the experimental
> group and the group in which parents were simply en-
> couraged to send their children to school. Both groups
> had significantly *worse* attendance records than did
> the no-treatment control group.
>
> In explaining their unexpected result, the con-

sultants noted that the reinforcements were relatively trivial. For children who find school aversive, the experience is not likely to be much improved by two-cent candies. In fact three children in the experimental group, after receiving reinforcement for a few days, refused to leave their classrooms to go to the cafeteria where the rewards were given out.

The consultants realized later that they should have been more familiar with the needs and problems of the community in which they were operating. They noted that the Chicano experience with the Anglo community has not inspired trust. The consultants considered themselves naive to expect that infrequent and trivial rewards would overcome a history of abuse and discrimination from Anglos.

The program also ignored the major reasons for low school attendance in this community. Children often were needed at home to look after younger siblings while parents worked; or they were needed to work in the fields. There was much greater payoff for families in having children perform this work than in any reinforcers the consultants had to offer.

This example differs from the Liberian case in various ways. In scale it was a much smaller project. It took place in the change agents' home country, even though it involved cross-cultural issues. It was planned by those who did the project, rather than being negotiated among government agencies and being presented to the consultants ready made. Nevertheless there are also some similarities, and these made important contributions to problems encountered by the consultants. In both cases, not enough attention was paid to characteristics of the host communities. Interventions are most likely to be successful when they are designed to match the environment. In both cases, important aspects of the community, including the traditions of the people and the reasons for current circumstances, were largely ignored.

We have argued that consultation is most effective when the objective is system change rather than individual change. In the case just presented, this systemic focus was lacking. Characteristics of the school and the classroom that might discourage school attendance were ignored. Conditions in the community that rewarded absenteeism were disregarded.

Many behavior modification projects, with their emphasis on immediate reinforcement, tend to omit the larger context of behavior. Yet there is nothing in the behavioral approach per se that rules out consideration of context. By neglecting the wider environment the consultants actually settled on highly inappropriate reinforcers while ignoring factors that maintained behavior. Regardless of the model that informs the consultant's action, a systemic focus seems desirable for achieving any change and it is *essential* for long-term change. This is apparent in an intervention reported by Andolfi, Stein, and Skinner (1977). A multilevel systems approach was developed to work with schoolchildren, their families, and their teachers.

> The intervention focused on eighth-grade children in a school in a low-income section of New York's Bronx. The consultants wanted to bring together parents, children, and teachers to work on problems that appeared in the school. They began with fifteen children who lived in the same neighborhood and would be together in school for at least five periods a day. This program maximized the possibility of involving peer relationships in the program.
>
> In the first phase consultants met with children in a group each week. These meetings promoted peer relationships and emphasized the children's responsibility to solve problems. In another weekly meeting the consultants brought together teachers and guidance counselors to build a mutual support group. Once a month consultants went to a neighborhood location to meet with parents. The objective was to promote understanding and mutual support. Occasionally the consultants went on home visits; sometimes parents came to observe in classrooms.
>
> In the second phase consultants continued their meeting with children and added a weekly meeting between children and teachers. Finally, teachers and students joined monthly evening meetings with

parents. The objective of these sessions, and of the program as a whole, was to involve the community in school problem solving.

Andolfi and colleagues (1977) note that few interventions with children include peers, school, and family as well as the target child. The traditional approach is to deal with a child's problems individually. Sometimes lip service is paid to the importance of environmental variables, but rarely does the change agent try to intervene at that level. Indeed, an ecological approach suggests that one go further than the program outlined above. Poverty, overcrowding, and discrimination are all community characteristics that affect children. Problems expressed in the classroom may well be consequences of such social conditions.

Several cases that we have presented were striking for the failure of consultants to assess the setting thoroughly before planning an intervention. Sometimes the actual consultation team had nothing to do with project planning, as in the Liberian school district. Sometimes the consultants were misguided by a narrow interpretation of their theoretical model, as in the Mexican-American school. Whatever the reason, when the consultant does not understand the setting the intervention is unlikely to be helpful. Sarason and colleagues (1966) take this point into account when they negotiate entry into schools. These consultants tell teachers at the outset: "We do not view ourselves as people to whom questions are directed and from whom answers will be forthcoming. Life and the helping process are not that simple. We have no easy answers, but we have a way of functioning that involves us in a relationship with the teacher and the classroom" (p. 61). They stressed that they were not experts, and would not pretend to know how to solve the school's problems. It takes considerable finesse and some fortunate circumstances to be able to set up a contract that will allow extensive assessment before the consultant even proposes an intervention. This is one of the most common problems in negotiation with a client group, and we examine it further in the next chapter.

To conclude the present discussion of consultant-setting fit, we turn our attention from the client back to the consultant. If it is difficult to assess a new setting, it should not be hard for the consultant to take his or her own characteristics into account. After all, consultants should not be strangers to themselves. But consultants do disregard the importance of their own characteristics.

Sarason (1971) has offered a striking analysis of the way consultants can focus on the setting while ignoring their own backgrounds. He refers to the example of a university-based expert entering and judging the public school system. Sarason pictures the hypothetical consultant as keenly aware of deficiencies in the public schools but blind to similar characteristics in the university.

Consultants find school textbooks and curricula dull and out of date; they see teachers as poorly grounded in their subjects. But the teachers, taking a look at the university environment, might well complain that professors teach but have no teacher training and in fact seem uninterested in teaching when compared with activities such as research. The consultant may fault the schoolteacher for failing to make learning stimulating and exciting. But teachers remember university courses as dull affairs, with students sitting in large lecture theaters taking down every word uttered by the lecturer. The consultant sees teachers as trying to "pour" information into students, rather than helping them learn for intrinsic rewards. The teacher recalls, however, that the needs, interests, and curiosity of college students seemed of little concern to the university.

Consultants find school systems to be overorganized and top-heavy with supervisors and administrators who stifle the creativity and initiative of individual teachers. They do not see that for those involved in public education, universities are tradition-bound; they have elaborate hierarchical structures and seem unresponsive to the needs of the surrounding community. Consultants seem surprised when their pronouncements meet with resentment. The failure to see parallels between the schools and their own institutional homes makes their advice suspect to teachers. Observers frequently see with a keen eye the irrationality of the settings they seek to change; yet they are blind to similar characteristics in the settings from which they come.

The tendency of consultants to ignore their own unique contributions is mirrored in the paucity of literature on the topic. Much more effort has gone into discussion of techniques than into looking at consultants' characteristics. This bias may give the illusion that when techniques are mastered, they can be used effectively by anyone in any setting. Further, more has been written about settings than about consultants. Kelly (1979) notes that community psychologists tend to focus on the external environment rather than on the psychology of the individual. Traditional psychologists have chosen to explore personality factors while ignoring social forces and the impact of settings. Community psychology marks a turning away from this mode of explanation in favor of examining the impact of environment on behavior. This attempt to correct a long-standing imbalance is healthy for the discipline; but the tendency to deemphasize personal factors can lead to a failure to consider the person of the consultant in the process of consultation. In Kelly's opinion, "We have avoided those features of ourselves, including our foibles, that in fact emerge as central defining elements when out doing work and as pivotal elements when conceptualizing what to do" (1979, p. 246).

Research in social cognition suggests some reasons why consultants tend to overlook their own characteristics as important causal agents. We noted in Chapter One that naive theories of causality are built on questions like these: What do most people do in this situation? What does this person usually do in similar situations? What does this person do in other situations? In Harold Kelley's (1967) covariance model, the information sought by these questions is referred to as consensus, consistency, and distinctiveness information.

One of the most frequent findings in the literature is that observers attribute the causes of behavior to internal dispositions of actors, whereas actors tend to blame the situation (Jones and Nisbett, 1971). Actors and observers have different opportunities for gaining the information that would answer the consensus, consistency, and distinctiveness questions outlined by Kelley. Consultants have lifetimes of opportunities to observe variation in their own behavior and to observe many different reactions to their personal characteristics. Because there is so much variation, consultants may discount the importance of factors they bring to the consulting situation. People also tend to attribute cause to the factor that is particularly salient in a situation (Taylor and Fiske, 1978). Because consultants live their lives with themselves, they may take their own characteristics for granted. Their attention is tuned to the environment; situational features, including the acts of others, are especially salient.

In the cases we have discussed in this chapter, it was much easier for American consultants in Liberia to see the dependence of Liberian educators than it was for the consultants to recognize that they were fostering dependent behavior. Community organizers in Muddy Flats assumed their failure to organize people was a function of the defeated spirit of the community rather than their own condescending manner. A newcomer to the State Department saw its resistance to him as a demonstration of its ponderous bureaucracy; only later did he appreciate the importance of his authoritarian style.

Successful cases all involved awareness of the characteristics of the consultant. Women consulting to judges had to recognize and then overcome the difficulties that resulted from reactions to gender. The professional who helped develop a residential youth center had to recognize that as the setting evolved it would be better served by someone with less professional status. An intervention in the county jail, a closed and xenophobic institution, made use of a consultant team with members from inside and outside the facility to maximize strengths and compensate for potential weaknesses.

If consultants have insight into their own characteristics, including personal style, and if they can overcome the attribution bias that blinds them to the importance of these characteristics, they will have good information with which to assess the consultant-setting fit. Getting reliable data on the setting may take longer and will involve more guesswork. In the next chapter we explore the structure of the consultant-client relationship. One aspect of this relationship is the degree to which it permits the consultant to learn about the environment before embarking on specific interventions. Another aspect involves the way in which consultant and client discover and clarify one another's values. Still another aspect is the importance of unwritten (and often unspoken) expectations the parties bring to the process of consultation. Although many complications will arise as we explore more cases, we conclude this chapter knowing that one important aspect of consultant-client relationship is the match between consultant and setting.

3

Consultant-Client
Contracts

Finding a match between consultant and setting is useful, but a perfect match is neither necessary nor sufficient for successful intervention. If it were necessary, little consultation would be done. If it were sufficient, consultation would be so straightforward that we would need no books to discuss it. Consultants make their best guess about whether they can be helpful in a particular context and then engage the client in a process of negotiation over defining the problem and their own role in the setting. Negotiation may continue, in some form, for the duration of the intervention. The negotiation may be formal and even result in a written contract. More often it proceeds by inference and implication; in this case the contract is no more than the sum of remembered comments and unspoken assumptions.

Even when a formal written agreement exists, the relationship between consultant and setting will remain somewhat ambiguous. There are always unwritten expectations that set boundaries on the scope of intervention and the consultant's function. A formal contract may be negotiated with someone in authority, but the consultant will quickly become involved with others in the setting. These people will have their own ideas about the setting and its problems, about the usefulness of outsiders, and about the consequences of welcoming *this* outsider into their territory. We shall see cases in which a firm, formal agreement at the outset helped consultants to facilitate change in settings. But in other cases such agreements are so removed from the needs of the setting and the real possibilities for change that they become irrelevant or even hinder intervention. Whether a contract will help or hinder depends on the context.

In this chapter we are concerned with the process of negotiation between consultant and client and with the way that negotiation structures the consultant-client relationship. In the concept of structure we include all the agreements and understandings between the consultant and those in the setting. This structure influences and sometimes wholly determines whether the consultant can be a significant resource.

Some factors that determine the success of intervention only become apparent in the process of mutual discovery between consultant and setting. Two factors of particular importance are the values that motivate consultant and client and the assumptions each holds about the other. It might appear that questions of value are paramount in consultation. Many of our ecological assertions, such as the importance of cultural diversity and the need to focus on system change, are statements of value. Although such matters are of great importance, they can seldom be seen clearly before the consultant is already engaged in the negotiation phase. We shall return to the problem of value discrepancy, but first we must consider some of the ways in which different assumptions between consultant and client affect the intervention.

The initial relationship between consultant and client is affected by perceptions of what the setting needs, what contribution the consultant can make, and how dependency issues will be negotiated. Glidewell (1959) points out that all consultation is based on several assumptions: The consultant has something to offer to the setting (although that something is likely to be more helpful to some people than to others); the needs that the consultant will meet are temporary or can be taken over by existing roles at some point in the consultation process; and the consultant has the personal qualities and skills to meet the setting's need.

Certainly the consultant-client relationship will be affected by the extent to which client and system agree that an immediate need exists. A school superintendent may believe there is a need for consultation, but the teachers might not share this view. Those in the system may agree that the need exists but disagree about its importance to their basic values. A police department may respond to public pressure by permitting consultants to introduce human relations training while doubting that the consultation will contribute to their primary objective of keeping the streets safe.

The client's perception that consultants have something to offer can be separated into two issues: Are the needed resources really unavailable in the setting at present? And does the consultant really have the skills the setting lacks? The consultant's effectiveness will also be determined by the equitable distribution of the resource he or she represents. Will the consultant be available to different subgroups and individuals. Will all those in the setting benefit equitably from new ideas or skills developed in the consultation process?

Dependency issues too can be perceived in advance, and their negotiation at the outset will clarify the consultant's role later. Glidewell points out that there will always be tension about these issues. There is always a fear of becoming dependent—particularly on someone who is fulfilling a valuable role but only temporarily. An outsider's perspective on the setting cannot avoid being evaluative, perhaps prompting withdrawal or defensiveness. Recognizing these issues in advance and attempting to face them during the entry process will increase the probability that the consultant can in fact be a resource.

A difference in the assumptions that consultants and clients bring to intervention may create divergent definitions of the problem. The cognitive approach directs our attention to the way in which ideal models shape our perceptions and expectations. A teacher who adopts an individual-pathology model will have different explanations of disruptive behavior than a consultant who relies on systems theory. Police officers who believe that stricter laws are a panacea will see citizen complaints in a different light than the consultant with a human relations approach.

Typically the client, not the consultant, has the first chance to define the problem. Although the consultant may see the problem differently, either at first or after a while in the setting, it is the client who must eventually legitimize a new problem definition. Sometimes the consultant's own model immediately offers a different perspective on the problem as defined by the client. To draw an analogy with clinical practice, when the family declares that a child needs treatment, the systems-oriented therapist sees at once that the problem requires intervention in the dynamics of the family. The only issue is how to bring the family to this new perception of the problem. There are also situations in which the consultant accepts the client's view at least as a working definition of the problem, perhaps to be modified as work proceeds.

Gordon (1975) described a case in which the initial problem description skirted more serious issues. The setting was a telephone crisis line for young people that was staffed with a few regular staff members and many volunteer phone aides.

Volunteer phone aides at the hotline expressed a number of difficulties they were having with callers. This problem prompted the founder and coordinator of the service to bring in a consultant. The first suggestion was that the consultant might give some basic lectures on psychopathology and diagnosis. The consultant suggested that the best way to find out whether he had the appropriate resources would be to talk with the people who did the work.

When he met the entire staff of the hotline, the consultant learned that phone aides were eager to have the consultant lead group meetings at which many topics could be covered, including problems with callers, personal difficulties, and psychological theory. The consultant agreed. In these meetings a feeling of closeness seemed to develop among phone aides. They began to exercise more influence on the operation of the hotline. The consultant was able to build a bridge between phone aides and the paid staff. When they met together, the two groups were able to resolve issues that had divided them. An important precondition for this problem solving was the recognition by aides and paid staff that the same principles that guided their work with clients should be applied to their own interpersonal and intergroup relationships.

In his presentation of this case, Gordon notes that the real problem—a status difference between paid staff and volunteer aides—was quite different from the problem initially presented to the consultant. Nevertheless, as he responded within the initial guidelines, his groups provided a means for redefining the underlying issues.

Another important aspect of problem definition concerns the degrees of freedom left to the consultant. Given that the client will probably define the problem at the outset, it is essential that the definition does not completely define the solution. A teacher who tells a psychologist "I'm having trouble with Johnny—I want him tested and then placed in a special class" is leaving no room for consultation. In fact, the teacher who says "I'm having trouble with Johnny and I want him tested" is seriously restricting the possibilities of intervention. When those in the client setting present problems in such a way that only one response is possible, they are specifying a role definition that is not consultative. A short case, reported by Brockbank (1968) as an illustration of failure in consultation, points up the difficulty that occurs when the client specifies both problem and solution.

A team consisting of two psychologists, a psychiatrist, and a cultural anthropologist were working with the San Francisco branch of the Bureau of Indian Affairs. The director of the branch had identified the problem as one of serious interstaff conflict. The staff was divided into two teams to meet with consultants twice a week.

The goal of consultation was to help staff members work more effectively with one another and to increase their ability to help clients. Early in the process it became apparent that there were many reasons to invite the director to attend the session. Staff problems in the bureau clearly involved the director; some staff members felt alienated from her and others blamed her for a variety of difficulties.

The director, however, insisted that meetings be held without her. She argued that the sessions should provide opportunity for staff to vent their frustrations about her and be honest about their interpersonal difficulties. She claimed they would find this difficult to do with her present. Reluctantly the consultants continued the sessions without the director. The staff meetings led to an irreparable break between director and staff.

Toward the end of the consultation period, an administrative decision was reached between the director and the Washington office to close the San Francisco branch. This decision was made without discussion with staff or consultants.

Frequently authorities will ask for intervention that has as its target those of lower status in the setting. A superintendent asks a consultant to work with principals and teachers; a principal defines the problem so that the intervention focuses on teachers; the teachers argue that the problem is the children. Those excluding themselves from the change process often have elaborate and convincing rationales. In the Indian Affairs branch, the director would not attend staff sessions because she might inhibit those who needed to voice their frustrations. In Brockbank's view (1968, p. 273): "If the consultant accepts this seemingly rational and magnanimous attitude without question and proceeds accordingly, he is often met later with criticism that he added to staff criticism rather than helped to resolve it."

Brockbank's warning against uncritically accepting clients' rationales brings us back to the question of values. Consultants and clients may have trouble perceiving value discrepancies because people so often cloak their actions in high-sounding explanations. This is as much a problem for the client as for the consultant. Glidewell (1959) notes that an important problem associated with entry into a new setting is the need for social systems to make the behavior of newcomers predictable. The system does not need to know exactly what the newcomer will do. In fact the consultant's utility may lie in the fresh perspective he or she brings, entailing a certain amount of surprise. What the social system does need to know is that whatever consultants do, their actions will be consistent with the basic values and goals of the setting. Much of the initial fencing that consultants encounter in a community group can be interpreted as an attempt to ensure that the consultant's intervention will be consistent with these values and goals. When statements of motive are censored to make them socially appropriate, it is more difficult for the parties to see how their values clash.

The basic problem is not so much that people hide their motives from others, but that they also hide them from themselves. Argyris (1975) points out that people often believe they are operating according to one set of principles, but after observing their behavior for some time a perceptive observer would conclude that different principles underlie their behavior. He distinguishes between espoused theories and theories-in-use. Espoused theories are those that people say guide their actions; theories-in-use can be inferred from the way people actually behave. Argyris notes that while people are often blind to the discrepancies between their own espoused theories and theories-in-use, they are able to see clearly such discrepancies in others.

This analysis suggests several problems that may confront consultants. They may agree to intervene because their own values are congruent with those espoused by clients, only to find that the clients' theories-in-use are much different. Or consultants may misread their own motives and fail to see discrepancies between their espoused theories and theories-in-use.

In his consulting work, Argyris has identified a theory-in-use that seems to account for much organizational behavior. This theory, which Argyris calls Model 1, prompts people to work according to four values: to achieve their purposes as they define them; to win and avoid losing; to suppress negative feelings; to emphasize rationality. The underlying behavioral strategy for achieving these aims consists of trying to gain and maintain control over others while protecting oneself at all times. People who program themselves to follow Model 1 tend to be manipulative, controlling, and competitive. They are defensive in their interpersonal and intergroup relationships. They mistrust others, value conformity, and put a higher premium on diplomacy than on honesty. Since they are afraid to take risks, their freedom of choice is reduced. Organizations consisting of people and groups governed by Model 1 are characterized by organizational entropy, which results in ineffective problem solving and a decrement in performance.

Argyris offers Model 2 as a contrast. The strategy of controlling others is rejected. People are encouraged to talk about their purposes and goals and urged to invite others to confront their views. Every significant action is put to this test: Does it help the individual to generate valid and useful information and to solve problems so they remain solved? Sharing of power is valued. Arranging encounters so there is a maximum of face-saving and a minimum of honesty is rejected as a defensive activity that undercuts learning.

Argyris's Model 2 may provide a touchstone for consultants judging their own work and evaluating client organizations. But since Argyris believes the majority of organizations operate according to Model 1, a clash of values will be built into consultation much of the time. His prescription would be to help an organization see the contradiction between its espoused theory and its theory-in-use and, further, to understand how the contradiction blocks achievement of goals.

Value Clashes in Imposed Consultation

Value questions are particularly important when the client, or an important segment of the client system, does not really want the consultant in the setting at all. To draw another analogy with clinical psychology: A therapist may favor criminal court diversion programs that provide resources for young offenders rather than locking them up. But what does he do when a young man convicted of robbery is sentenced to therapy rather than to jail? There is serious doubt, of course, whether the client is genuinely motivated for therapy. Yet for therapists to wash their hands of such cases might undercut a humanitarian alternative to traditional justice. If judges know they cannot sentence young offenders to therapy, they may go back to sentencing them to prison.

In community consultation, the consultant often enters a situation as a result of outside pressure on clients. It would be unrealistic to tell consultants they ought not to be in such settings unless clients have a genuine need for them to be there. In two cases involving consultation with police departments, to be detailed in a moment, different approaches were taken by consultants with different consequences. But in both cases the consultants would not have been involved at all except for circumstances that put pressure on the clients to accept some form of intervention. The important question, then, is not whether there are value discrepancies between consultant and client but how they are handled.

Each of the two police cases presented consultants with ambiguity about how to define the real client. When the consultant is being paid, it might seem obvious that whoever pays the piper calls the tune. This is true to the extent that consultants who ignore the wishes of those who sign the checks often (but not always) have their contracts revoked. Nevertheless, consultants frequently use formal sponsors to provide them with the means to work with those they consider their real clients. The community organizing of Saul Alinsky got a boost from Gordon Sherman, president of Midas Muffler, who contributed a half million dollars. Alinsky commented, "All I knew about him was that he was a big corporation executive in town whose hobbies included playing the oboe, raising rare birds and orchids, mountain trout fishing, and the United Jewish Appeal" (Saunders and Alinsky, 1970, p. 72). The only conditions attached to the money were that it be used in Chicago, where Sherman lived. If there had been other conditions, presumably Alinsky would not have accepted. If an attempt to set conditions had been made after the money changed hands, Alinsky would have rebuffed it. The clients of the organizer were the disadvantaged people with whom he worked, not the sponsor whose money helped make the work possible.

Usually consultants think of themselves as consulting to settings, and a setting has a broad definition. According to Sarason (1972, p. 1), a setting is "any instance in which two or more people come together in new relationships over a sustained period of time in order to achieve certain goals." His definition includes instances ranging in scope from marriages to national governments and revolutionary movements. A setting cannot sign a contract, though. Someone in the setting (or out of it) may seek help, ostensibly on its behalf, but those in the setting may greet the consultant with different levels of enthusiasm.

In the two descriptions of consultation to police forces, all these elements of ambiguity about client definition were present. In both cases, intervention was possible only because of a public outcry about police behavior. In neither case did the police themselves initiate consultation. Once consultants were involved, both police departments had opinions about the process that differed sharply from those of the consultants. In each case consultants found themselves insisting that their own values must be expressed in the interventions. The first case, reported by Reddy and Lansky (1975), involved consultants in human relations training for police recruits. Not only were the police reluctant participants, they also were not the group paying the consultants and hence felt little ownership of the project.

> The arrest and detention of the pregnant wife of a white minister during a civil rights demonstration in a large northern city precipitated intervention in the police department. Human rights organizations approached police officials about the allegation of police brutality in this case, and they emphasized the need for better human relations training on the force. After four months of negotiation, the police department reluctantly agreed to add two weeks of human relations training for the next recruit class. Human rights groups agreed to find and pay consultants to carry out the training.
>
> A group of community psychologists affiliated with the local university was asked to take part in the program. They requested a meeting with top police

officials, particularly those in the training sections, so that an agreement could be worked out. The request was refused. Instead they were told to meet with a sergeant in the training section to explore the proposed program. The sergeant told the psychologists that police regarded the proposal as an unnecessary imposition on the training schedule.

A few days later, one of the consultants received a call from a high-ranking official in the training section expressing anger that the emerging proposal seemed to be moving "out of the hands of the police division." He called the consultants to a meeting. At this session, a police lieutenant colonel and a captain in charge of the training section made it clear that they were only considering the proposal because of outside pressure. They demanded that it be limited strictly to recruits. The consultants argued for a broader program but finally gave way.

The police officials demanded as much structure as possible in the program. They wanted, in advance, an hour-by-hour outline of the program. They had difficulty accepting the consultant's strategy of diagnosing, planning, and designing the intervention in response to the reaction of the recruits. The consultants, too, limited the intervention. They failed to learn more about the police through informal contacts and passed up the opportunity to observe the police in their day-to-day work. Looking back on the experience later, they felt that their own stereotypes about the police prevented them from doing this potentially useful groundwork.

The consultants soon discovered that with a reluctant client, what seems to be a clear contract may lead to misunderstanding. Two days before the workshop was to begin, a police lieutenant colonel called one of the consultants to insist that an "objective observer" be present during all workshop sessions so that a "good evaluation could be done." The consultant rejected this demand. While evaluation was important, he explained, a nonparticipant observer would limit the effectiveness of the workshop.

The day before the workshop, the consultants received several calls from the training captain explaining that he could not spare an observer to participate fully in the workshop. He wanted his staff to supervise by walking in occasionally to "check up on things." The captain was firm: He was the one responsible for his men and his program. Finally, after a good deal of discussion in which the consultants pointed out the harm this would do to the workshop, it seemed that there was an understanding and no supervisors would be walking in.

At the opening of the workshop one of the consultants told the recruits that anyone coming into the program would be asked to participate. The training captain, standing at the rear of the room, turned to another consultant and said, "That's not the way it's going to be." A few minutes later, away from the recruits, the consultants had a heated exchange with the captain. They insisted that the matter had been resolved the day before; he refused to budge. When the consultants threatened to terminate the program immediately, the captain went to telephone his superiors. Without further negotiation with the consultants, they decreed that a training sergeant would spend the entire time participating in the workshop. The consultants agreed to continue.

The consultants had planned a workshop learning experience that departed in a number of ways from the traditional, structured, classroom experience with which the recruits were familiar. Rather than having information come from "experts," it was expected that information would be developed from the social environment, including the learner's experience in the workshop.

In the traditional approach to learning, problems are defined by the experts and the emphasis is on solving known problems. The consultants' approach emphasized the role of the *learner* in defining issues, forming hypotheses, and collecting data. Instead of treating problems only on an intellectual basis, the consultants hoped to treat them as laden with feelings and values. They wanted to establish the fact that feelings and values have consequences in action.

These goals were seriously compromised by the context in which the workshop took place. The recruits had been told that the workshop was initiated by the community. It was not a police program but a response to public pressure. Veteran officers told them the whole idea would be a waste of time. The recruits were near the end of their twenty-two weeks of training; now they had to endure another eighty hours, postponing graduation for two weeks. All these circumstances made the training program less than the consultants had hoped.

Even receptive settings can be expected to greet consultants with some apprehension. As Glidewell (1959) suggests, social systems have a need to make the intruder's behavior predictable. The system needs the security of knowing that whatever the consultant does will be consistent with its values and goals. In a resistant setting this security is hard to come by. Because the intervention is prompted by external pressure, those in the setting have good reason to doubt that outsiders' values are consistent with their own. The setting may adopt a strategy of limiting the consultant's impact. Whatever the consultants do, whatever their motives may be, at least the potential damage can be contained. This strategy was apparent in the case reported by Reddy and Lansky (1975). Police officials confined the intervention to police recruits, made it clear to recruits that the program was illegitimate in the eyes of the police department, and attempted to watch over everything that occurred.

Even when the problem definition is, to some extent, imposed on the client, and the intervention occurs more through external pressure than client motivation, consultants can do useful work. This point is demonstrated in the next case taken from an account by Sherwin and Renner (1979). Again a police department was the reluctant host and consultants had to overcome resistance to enter the setting at all. Once entry was established, the consultants insisted that their own values guide the intervention—which meant refusing to do precisely what the police command thought was necessary.

In a midwestern city, members of the black community complained that some policemen were using excessive force in dealing with the public. The police command rejected the charges. They also rebuffed suggestions than outside help was needed, arguing that they investigated all complaints vigorously.

A psychologist found an approach that did not require initial cooperation from the police command. Every entry on the court docket over a four-year period was examined, and all cases where citizens were charged with resisting arrest were noted. If resisting arrest were a characteristic of the person being charged rather than the police officer, then each officer on patrol should have an equal chance of coming up against an unruly citizen. But when actual frequencies were computed for specific officers, they departed significantly from chance. In fact, three officers had one chance in ten thousand of running into so many citizens who resisted arrest, and one had only one chance in a billion. Once this information came to the attention of police officials they saw that social science might be relevant to their problems after all. They were prepared to sanction an intervention.

As the consultation team negotiated entry, it became clear that there were divergent views on what sort of intervention would be acceptable. Police officials were prepared to make police records available so that consultants could find out which officers were not doing their jobs properly. There would be no consultation with the officers or with the community.

The consultants declined to participate on such terms. They reasoned that such an intervention would be aimed at deviant individuals rather than at systemic causes. With an individual focus, any good that was done by the project would last only as long as the consultants were involved. The police officers who would be the unwitting and unwilling participants would be harmed rather than helped. To the extent that the consultants' activities became known by police officers, they would lower morale and produce changes in reporting techniques rather than in actual behavior.

The consultants wanted to intervene in a way that would benefit the police officers themselves. They wanted their activities to be perceived by the officers as in their own best interests. One violent officer can make community conditions difficult for the whole force, so any work that would reduce antagonism between police and citizens should benefit the entire force.

A process was created in which the police-community relationship could be examined, information could be made public, but individual officers would not be pinpointed. Each officer used a code number and could see where he stood on any distribution. But individuals were not identified to the command. All foreseeable consequences were thoroughly discussed with officers. With this approach, the consultants were able to work cooperatively with the police in a nonpunitive atmosphere.

The case reported by Sherwin and Renner is a good example of action research, in which information is gathered to explain social phenomena and as a way of intervening in social problems. In much research, value issues are unacknowledged. In action research, however, they come to the surface. Sherwin and Renner were guided by the belief that research should be done *with* people rather than *on* people. People should be treated as ends not means. Subjects should benefit from the research in which they participate, not merely serve the researcher's personal goals or the special interests of a funding agency. This was the context of values that prompted the consultants to reject the way the police command wanted to shape the intervention.

One of the values we have drawn from the ecological analogy is that of designing and implementing interventions so that they can be matched with the host environment. In Chapter One we argued that interventions should be specifically responsive to the unique aspects of the setting. Sherwin and Renner were aware of police morale, alienation of police officers, and the tendency to alter reporting techniques rather than change behavior. They took these factors into account when designing their intervention. But in the earlier case of human relations training with police recruits, the consultants had a packaged approach to change that ignored the unique aspects of the setting. They even avoided opportunities to observe the everyday life of the officer on the street, which might have given them a better picture of the environment.

The Flexible Contract

When discussing the consultant-setting fit we noted that many aspects of a system are hidden from outsiders. Often the consultant can learn the landscape only through involvement with it. If it is of value to design interventions so they suit certain settings, then the consultant must negotiate a contract that permits some exploration before the actual change process is fixed. Many consultants find this to be the most troublesome aspect of striking an agreement with a client group. A system needing to make the behavior of intruders predictable tries to gain this security by having the consultant specify a definite course of action. Consultants try to leave room to find out more about the setting before committing themselves. The tension created by these conflicting motives is nicely described by McIntyre (1969), who served as consultant to two elementary schools in a New England town.

McIntyre's experience makes the point that even when the consultant believes that a fairly loose contract has been negotiated, the client may have a different view of what will occur. In fact, the client may believe that the consultant really knows precisely what tactics he or she intends to use, and failure to state those tactics at the outset is just part of the consultant's plan. The consultant who insists that he or she has much to learn about the setting may simply not be believed by the client who overvalues the omniscience of experts.

A psychologist assigned to work in two elementary schools in a small Connecticut town met with the superintendent of schools, who had requested services. This initial meeting, which was intended to provide the consultant-client structure, also involved the principals of two elementary schools. The superintendent had been told that the primary interest of the psychologist's clinic was in researching the school's culture. This goal required that the consultant keep the initial contract as loose as possible so that he could learn about the setting before undertaking any important intervention.

The superintendent opened the meeting with an informal monologue affirming the value of psychological services in the schools. He emphasized the experimental and unpredictable nature of the proposed consultation. The consultant would have to spend a certain amount of time simply observing in classrooms and getting to know the teachers and children before offering definite help. As the superintendent talked, it seemed that he understood the need for a flexible contract. The consultant felt reassured.

When the superintendent finished his speech he sighed and folded his hands. Then, as though getting down to business, he asked the consultant to give concrete details on what he planned to do. The consultant quickly learned that the superintendent was able to proclaim the need for flexibility and even give reasons for it without believing them. The consultant protested that he was as ignorant of schools as he had claimed to be and that he really would need time to decide what sort of intervention would be appropriate. He found himself saying exactly the same things the superintendent had said earlier. He was relieved to find that his words now were apparently accepted by the three school officials. There was instant agreement, and the subject was changed.

But a few minutes later another attempt was made to spell out what the consultant would be doing. The superintendent approached the matter with some delicacy by asking the consultant's position on psychological testing. It was obvious that the superintendent hoped that this was a concrete service that the psychologist would be unable to dodge, since intelligence testing is traditionally identified with psychologists. The consultant explained that although testing was within his scope, he worried about the danger of being tied down to a testing schedule. He recommended that the schools maintain their usual resources for testing. He thought he noticed a shadow of disappointment on the faces of all three school officials, but they did not object.

The trio now took a different approach in an attempt to make the consultant be more specific. The superintendent asked the two principals if they had any ideas about how they could make use of the psychologist's services. The principals apparently viewed this question as a test of their professional worth—no principal ought to be caught without a stock of good ideas. One principal vigorously presented ideas about definite services. He felt the consultant undoubtedly was a competent person who had a great deal of knowledge to offer teachers, and there was no reason why he should hesitate to offer it. He envisioned a kind of crash program of teachers' seminars during which the consultant could let teachers know quickly and directly the latest scientific principles of effective teaching and management of children. Again the psychologist turned this approach aside, remarking that he was not well enough acquainted with the teachers to know what should be presented to them. He also expressed doubts about how well the teachers would react to such instruction from a man who had never taught a class in his life. Finally, he said he was not even sure that there was anything like a Latest Scientific Approach to teaching on which there would be general agreement. The principal agreed that of course the consultant must have the freedom to proceed as he wished, but remarked that he did not have much confidence in the ability of teachers to respond to the "gentle" approach.

All attempts to tie the consultant to a specific

program had now, apparently, failed. The school officials turned to working out the technical details of
the psychologist's entry into each of their schools. Although the meeting ended cordially, the consultant
had the nagging feeling that this display of good fellowship might not mean that they all understood one
another on the same terms.

Over the next few weeks the consultant carried
out the program that he had described. He tried to
become familiar with the schools; he attended classes,
talked to teachers, found his way to places where the
teachers relaxed and talked to one another socially or
about work. He found there was growing acceptance
of his presence and that he was learning a good deal
about the ecology of the school.

He discovered, however, that there were still
lingering assumptions about his work that contradicted
the flexibility with which he was attempting to operate. He received a message from the superintendent
summoning him to another meeting to discuss his
progress—his entry into "Phase II." The consultant
had no idea what was meant by "Phase II"; and he
had no opportunity to find out, since he was informed
only a day in advance of the meeting. He was somewhat annoyed because he had not been asked whether such a meeting would be helpful; he had not finished observing in all the classrooms or even meeting
all the teachers.

The two principals said little during the meeting; clearly they were attending only because they
had been told to come. Although the superintendent
was pleasant, he spoke with an authoritarian under-
tone. He seemed to feel that the consultant's functioning, like that of everyone else, should be marked
by clear-cut purpose. In his comments the superintendent implied that the initial familiarization (Phase I)
of the consultant's involvement had come to an end.
It was time for the consultant to be launched into
Phase II—in effect, to get down to serious business. It
seemed that he envisioned this phase as one of firm
and decisive action, in which the consultant would

give a series of hard-hitting and dramatic lectures to teachers.

Once again the consultant explained that the process through which he and the school staff were coming to trust each other was a continuing one. Whatever help he might be to the system or to particular people in it would involve a great deal of give and take and would be a product of the emerging relationship. When he tried to explain this and tell the superintendent the progress he had made, his explanation was met by shocked silence. He felt like a small boy who had been caught neglecting his chores. His assertion that "Phase I" would probably never come to a clear-cut end seemed incredible to the school officials. The consultant left the meeting feeling as though he had been loitering on a virtuously busy street of life and was being allowed to continue this life more out of pity than out of rationality.

Looking back over this excruciating experience in developing a contract with a client who had different assumptions about consultation, McIntyre (1969) reflected that subcultures build certain ways of responding to organizational necessity. The traditions that develop in the system, and the value patterns that evolve, are moral in nature. As such, they do not allow an easy discussion of different options. His own approach to consultation was so radically different from the superintendent's notion of what constituted efficient behavior in the school system that the psychologist found himself treated as one who had advocated an alien way of life.

In this case the consultant was clearly assumed to have expert status; after all, he had professional training and came from a psychoeducational clinic with standing in the field. Therefore the idea that he really did not know precisely what he was going to do was simply beyond belief. The consultant's professed ignorance must be part of some obscure technique. When the superintendent asked for clarification, he was only asking the expert to set aside this mysterious technique long enough to provide a better idea of his real plans. In many settings the presumed expertise of the consultant may lead to similar problems.

Disagreement over what should occur in a consultation is often masked by apparent agreement and cordiality between consultant and client. In the case described by McIntyre, each time the consultant argued for a flexible contract he seemed to receive approval from the assembled officials. Only as the consultation progressed did he discover that the initial agreement was hollow.

In some contexts it is useful to develop a structure of consultation that permits thorough exploration of the setting and a gradual building of relationships. But in other contexts there may be no time for such a gradual process. If the consultation task is to give advice on the best way for a program to be developed, the situation may require a written report and constrain the time available for its preparation. Consultants may need all the clarity they can get at the beginning of their work. A contract with clear guidelines and precise information may mean the difference between success and failure.

Westermeyer and Hausman (1974b) have reported two cases of time-limited consultation. Although the cases were similar in many respects, one represented a clear success and the other a failure. Ambiguity about the client's expectations of the consultant was cited as a major cause of the eventual outcome.

> Two projects involved development of programs for drug abusers in minority populations. The consultant's task in each case was to study the problem and produce a report with recommendations in less than two weeks.
>
> In the first project the goal was defined broadly; in fact, the consultant was unable to get the client to articulate a goal more specific than simply to help the addicts. In the second project the client spelled out the problem in detail and specified the resources available.
>
> In the first project the consultant had to work entirely with local bureaucrats. A powerful leader who made the major decisions remained unavailable.

In the second project the consultant had access to top policy makers. Contact with the target population was confined to large, formal meetings in the first case; but in the second the consultant was able to discuss the proposed intervention with members of the minority group on a confidential basis.

The results of consultation were very different. In the first case, officials ignored the consultant's warnings and included in the project many aspects he had advised against. The project had elements that were poorly thought out and represented political compromises. In the second case, the consultant was able to be specific in his treatment recommendations and the government implemented most of his ideas.

In the two cases involved here, the consultant was the same and the settings were similar: Both were tribal societies with drug problems that had proved intractable to religious, legal, and medical approaches. The differences lay in the structure of the consultant-client relationship. According to Westermeyer and Hausman (1974b), consultants in such situations ought to have access to those who are making the big decisions. They also need informal contact with representatives of the target group. Finally, consultants will be seriously handicapped if they do not get a clear idea of what the client expects.

A comparison of the time-limited cases just described with the earlier narrative of a consultant in a New England school system illustrates the wide variety of activities and contexts covered by the term *consultation*. One situation required the consultant to write a report as a basis for action; the other involved the consultant in an emerging relationship with those in the setting. One intervention was a response to a pressing problem; the other focused on the growth potential of the setting. One had an extremely tight time schedule; the other permitted a long-term relationship. Despite these differences, both examples meet our criteria for consultation: The consultants intervened, whether by presenting written advice or by working directly with those in the setting; the interventions were temporary, whether they lasted two weeks or for a school year; any

advice given by the consultants could be accepted or rejected
—they had no mandate to give orders. And, finally, in both
cases the focus was on the system—in one instance, the functioning of public schools; in the other, delivery of federal drug
programs.

In the case of consultation to two schools reported by
McIntyre (1969) a major source of tension between consultant and client was the consultant's need to keep his initial
contract flexible. Although this problem confronts many consultants, we have qualified it by pointing out that when the intervention must be completed in a very short time, vagueness in
the contract may ensure failure. Another qualification is that
firm and decisive action by the consultant will be needed when
the setting is in crisis. The consultant who has to bargain for
time and room in a functioning system may need to develop an
early plan of action in a system that lacks direction. Reppucci
and colleagues found themselves in a situation of this sort when
they agreed to work with a new youth camp in a New England
prison system (Reppucci and others, 1973). Their experience
suggests that in some contexts a consultant who takes a wait-
and-explore attitude will be defined as irrelevant by the setting.

A newly appointed state commissioner of corrections announced that he wished to introduce many
innovations in the correctional system. When a group
of university-based consultants expressed an interest
in helping with the process they found themselves involved with a new youth camp for adolescent offenders. This camp was located on a mountain in the midst
of a dense forest five miles from the nearest private
residence. The program, which had the stated goal of
treatment rather than punishment, was still in its formative stage. When the consultants first became involved there was a staff of twelve for only six inmates.
The psychologists agreed to work with this new program even though they had some misgivings. They
were above all concerned that no permanent director
had been appointed to the camp; there was no one in
authority to whom the consultants would relate.

In their early contacts with the youth camp the consultants deliberately kept their role vague so they could buy time to decide what activities would be mutually beneficial. For example, they rejected a suggestion by the head counselor that each consultant see an adolescent in individual therapy. They explained that this would commit them to offering traditional psychological services, and it might also infringe on the work of the counselors. Members of the consulting team believed their role was to provide suggestions and interpretations rather than give direction or offer clinical services. They did not want to be seen as "experts" by the staff. They chatted with staff members and inmates informally over coffee, dinner, or games.

Only much later did the consultants realize how difficult it was for the staff to accept the advice offered by the consultants. They had no previous experience with consultation of this sort. In the past people in authority had provided them with guidelines. Having no other framework, the staff members related to the consultants as if they were visitors from the front office. Staff members were polite but ignored the consultants' ideas whenever the psychologists were not actually present in camp.

The consultants had stressed to the corrections department that a permanent director was needed as soon as possible, but a director did not arrive for three months. During this period the camp was adrift. Staff members knew they were to innovate, but no one could say specifically what these new approaches were to be. The temporary leaders were naturally unwilling to take chances or set policy that might be rescinded when a permanent director arrived. The leadership vacuum was destroying staff morale.

After several weeks of familiarizing themselves with the camp, the team of consultants decided to collect systematic data. They wanted to find out how staff members felt about such issues as delinquency, the role of correctional settings, and their own expectations about the way the camp might develop. Such introspection might promote growth among staff members and ultimately improve the functioning of the camp.

These interviews highlighted the general lack of ideas on how to develop a rehabilitation program. Most staff members assumed the camp would be successful if it had clear guidelines and received the "right kind of boys." (No one knew precisely what the right kind would be.) The consultants also learned that they themselves were thought to be irrelevant. The gap in leadership was affecting all aspects of camp life, and the consultants were not filling that gap. When the interviewing did not produce immediate and obvious changes, the staff's feeling about the consultants was reinforced.

If the staff was pinning all its hopes on the arrival of the permanent director, the consultants had now fallen into the same trap. They had come to believe that the arrival of the director would be the appropriate time for them to intervene actively. They felt it was imperative that the new director, not the consultants, be the one to show strong leadership. Later the consultants realized that by going into a holding pattern they had reinforced the staff's fantasies about how things would improve when the new director arrived. Moreover, they probably discouraged the staff from taking initiative in the search for solutions. By the time the new director arrived, the consultants found that relationships had become rigid. When they tried to begin active intervention, the staff had no faith in the effort.

"Active intervention" by the consultants included trying to improve the relationship between the camp and the community (agencies and families of inmates); conducting psychological assessments to determine the scholastic ability and the personality profiles of incoming adolescents; and holding meetings to improve the poor relationships between counselors and security staff.

The meetings were successful in building cohesion within each group. But when the consultants attempted to introduce a general meeting format involving the permanent director, they found that his need for an authoritarian structure interfered with the kind of open communication they hoped to achieve. The staff was not particularly interested in the community contacts offered by the consultants. They did not care about the testing program, either, and correctly perceived that the consultants themselves did not have a great investment in this traditional psychological service.

The consultants, realizing that the early relationships they had established at the camp were resistant to change, had an overwhelming sense of futility, even impotence. The staff now perceived them as, at best, Monday morning quarterbacks. In the eyes of staff members, the consultants were outside experts who neither shared the load (such as working individually with inmates) nor isssued firm guidelines to help run the camp during the long period when leadership was needed. The consultants wrote a report on their experience and then withdrew.

An important issue in the structure of the consultant-client relationship is the question of how much actual leadership the consultant should assume. Sometimes the very expertise that makes a consultant valuable to a community organization also encourages others in the group to expect the consultant to be a director rather than an adviser. To cite just one example of a leadership dilemma, often the consultant will discover a problem or come up with a suggestion that requires a meeting between the consultant and members of the client system. Who should call the meeting? Is it necessary for the consultant to convince someone in authority that a working session is needed? Would such a maneuver really maintain the consultant's nondirective role? If the consultant calls meetings is he or she jeopardizing the advisory function? If the consultant calls meetings will members of the client group who are summoned really take responsibility for what occurs? There are no answers to these questions that will apply in all situations. However they are answered in a specific case, the simple issue of who should call a meeting brings the consultant back to the issue of leadership.

Reppucci and colleagues (1973) saw leadership as a central issue in the failure of their consultation at the youth camp. From their experience they drew the lesson that there are contexts in which consultants will have leadership thrust upon them. If they retreat from the challenge they may be of no further use to their clients. In the youth camp the consultants wondered later whether their efforts might have been more fruitful if one of them had offered to be interim director of the camp. Such a move might have posed many other difficulties, but Reppucci and his colleagues noted that they never even considered such an option.

Decision makers often have blind spots when they consider options. Nor are consultants immune to cognitive bias in making decisions. Tversky (1972) refers to one of these biases as "elimination by aspects." The decision maker weighs options by considering some crucial aspect and then ruling out choices that fail to meet the standard. Another aspect is then selected, and another, until only one option remains. The bias involved in this procedure is that options eliminated in early rounds are not reconsidered and tested against all decision rules. Reppucci and his colleagues valued the principle that consultants do not direct —they facilitate. Taking this aspect of consultation as their first decision rule, they eliminated the leadership option so early in the process that the issue was never seriously considered. Only later did they realize that when all aspects of the situation were considered together, reasons for taking a leadership role might have outweighed the principle against it.

In retrospect, the consultants in this case noted how difficult it is to change early relationships in a setting. In an earlier case we saw a consultant working to keep his role flexible in the early stages so that he would not become locked into activities that would constrain him later. Reppucci and his colleagues also tried to maintain flexibility while waiting for the arrival of the youth camp's permanent director. But in this case they found that the very style that was intended to maintain flexibility actually fixed them in a role considered irrelevant by the hard-pressed client group.

Rigidity in the Consultant-Client Relationship

Once clients perceive the consultant in a certain way, the consultant will not find it easy to take on a new role or different activities. Actually, the consultants were aware that this would be a problem when they began consulting to the youth camp. This led them to reject offers to undertake traditional psychological activities such as individual counseling. They did not want to be associated with clinical activities. But the flexibility they gained interfered later with their attempt to become more active and forceful.

The tendency of roles to become fixed has been discovered with regret by consultants who hoped to move gradually into a true consultative role during the course of consultation. A client system may deal with prospective consultants by asking them to become involved in traditional activities such as psychotherapy or clinical testing. Consultants may feel it is necessary "just at first" to play the game by the client's rules. They may intend later to develop a role with a systemic rather than an individual focus, but such changes are often hard to negotiate. Coiner (1977) has given an account of such an experience in the context of school consultation.

> In a school district that had a contract with the mental health facility to provide consultation, Smokerise was a very traditional elementary school setting. With the exception of two team-taught classrooms there were few educational innovations. When she was assigned to Smokerise the consultant was warned that this was a closed setting resistant to the notion of a team approach to consultation—the approach favored by the consultant herself. She entered the school firmly committed to an indirect-service model that emphasized the promoting of teachers' skills rather than individual work with children by the psychologist.
>
> Smokerise was bitter that it had not yet received its share of consultation time in the past. When the consultant asked the school guidance counselor what Smokerise would do with its share of consultation time, the counselor said she wanted help with the

many referrals she got from teachers. She seemed to
have in mind psychological testing and individual
work with problem children. The counselor warned
that her own experience with teachers in the school
indicated that they did not favor a team approach. Although in theory there were six teams, only one actually functioned. There were four teachers who
seemed interested in looking at the social and emotional aspects of education, but they were on separate
teams.

Despite the warning signals, the consultant did
not try to switch schools but treated the situation as
a challenge. She formulated a hierarchy of possible
modes of consultation. Ideally she preferred to work
with teams of teachers in a case-discussion format.
The objective of consultation would be to increase the
teachers' own skills in handling the general student
problems represented by particular cases. The second
option in her hierarchy would be to aim for the same
target—improving skills in dealing with problem children—by meeting with teachers individually over specific cases. A third possibility would be special team
meetings called to consider particularly difficult cases
that were worrying several members of the team.
Near the bottom of the consultant's list of prefer-
ences was the possibility of assessing specific children
and then meeting with the whole team to discuss the
child. Finally, and most undesirable if the whole team
could not meet, the psychologist might do assessments and meet only with the referring teacher.

With this hierarchy in mind, the consultant attempted to negotiate a role for herself in the school.
But when she met with the principal, he produced a
typed list of twenty names of children referred by
teachers in the first weeks of the school year. When
he proposed that the consultant follow up these cases
individually, she replied that she would prefer to
work with teams of teachers.

At that point the guidance counselor arrived
and announced that she wanted to pass along to the
consultant the really difficult cases that had been re-

ferred to her. The consultant offered to discuss the cases with the guidance counselor and help her develop plans for dealing with teachers and parents. The guidance counselor said that while this might be useful, it would not reduce the sheer number of referrals with which she had to cope.

It was becoming clear to the psychologist that "handling a referral" really meant testing. Because she had the background to administer and interpret tests, she found it difficult to refuse. She proposed that even if she did an assessment, it would be important to meet with teachers and observe the children's behavior in the classroom.

On her first working day in the school, the consultant was handed two referrals. Immediately she attempted to broaden what was in danger of becoming a narrow assessment function. The consultant went to the teachers of both children to get background information, but the encounters were brief. One teacher could only spare time during a class change; the other supplied a few hurried details while children were cleaning up the classroom after an activity. By her second day in the school, the consultant was engaged in routine psychological assessment.

Despite being trapped in a role she did not wish to play, the consultant still had fantasies of transforming her activities and undertaking the kind of consultation that interested her. But her attempts to do so met with limited success. In one case, a team consisted of a female teacher who had referred a child for assessment and two male teachers who saw no problem with the boy. The two men said there was no point in sitting down with the woman teacher to discuss that case or, for that matter, any other case. They preferred to give the consultant their observations individually. Another team pointed out that different release times made it almost impossible for the three teachers to meet.

By the end of the academic year, the consultant's persistence had helped her make a number of contacts that were consistent with the indirect-service model. She was gratified too that some teachers seemed to be applying principles from one case to similar cases. But the consultant knew she had failed to gain acceptance for the kind of role she had hoped to play in the school. Activities that came close to her favored hierarchy had never been endorsed by the principal. Teachers regarded their talks with her about children as peripheral benefits that psychologists sometimes offer, not as components of a legitimate role.

In her reflection on this case, Coiner (1977) emphasizes the need for prenegotiation in contract setting. There is groundwork that can be laid before the consultant discusses a specific contract. Coiner suggests that soon after the initial discussion between consultant and client, the consultant should meet with those directly affected by the intervention to identify objectives. The consultant may discover that those in the client system are unsure or misinformed about the skills the consultant has to offer. The consultant must bridge the gap, learn about the setting and those who work in it, and develop a relationship.

In the case described above, Coiner notes that it would have been important at an early stage to learn why the setting wanted consultation at all. Sometimes the key motive springs from a common commitment to improve the system's functioning and delivery of services. But often the motive reflects external pressure to meet certain standards—for example, to comply with legal statutes. The consultant must understand the source and effect of external pressure. If there is a law requiring the school system to provide diagnosis and assistance for the learning disabled, how does that law affect School X and how does the school respond?

Coiner's experience reinforces the point that initial consultant-setting relationships are resistant to change. But as the next case illustrates, in some circumstances the consultant can be moved from direct service to an indirect, skills-enhancing role. Briggs (1973) took advantage of concurrent system changes to break out of a direct-service role as psychologist in a school setting.

In an urban junior high school serving 1,700 students the psychologist had been assigned the traditional direct-service role: Teachers made referrals, and the psychologist provided testing. When a new psychologist was assigned to the school, she decided to adopt a consultative role.

Conditions in the school facilitated the change. The school was in its third year of a major reorganization emphasizing a team approach. Teachers who shared the same students met around a conference table three times a week. These meetings were supposed to facilitate communication among team members, increase joint planning, and permit the exchange of information about students. At first the new psychologist was an uninvited guest at these team meetings, but soon she found herself accepted as a team member.

The psychologist actively sought out opportunities to fraternize with teachers, guidance counselors, and administrators. She knew, however, that she would not transform her role unless she found some way to take care of the large number of referrals requiring direct service. Because the school was located in an urban area there were psychological services available outside the school. Instead of testing children herself, the psychologist served as a liaison linking school problems with appropriate community services.

The psychologist was also active in extending services to areas where none had been requested or offered in the past. She discussed childrearing practices with home economics students, told health classes what psychologists do, and consulted with reading teachers regarding cases of poor reading ability. By the end of her first year, the consultant found that she had indeed transformed the image and activities of the school psychologist in her setting.

In the case described by Briggs (1973) the role change was facilitated by the fact that it was undertaken by a new role occupant. No doubt it is much easier for those in the client system to accept new activities from a new person rather than from someone they know. She made many moves that could be recommended, but again the context was particularly important. Since the school itself was going through a major reorganization, a change in the psychologist's role seemed less arbitrary or unusual. Teams of teachers, holding regular meetings, provided the appropriate setting for a consultative approach. The existence of external support services that could handle referrals removed a potential source of pressure on the consultant to provide direct service.

We have presented cases in which, for the most part, the consultant's contract offered legitimacy for his or her activity in the eyes of those throughout the client system. Thus teachers might be expected to accept someone whose contract was arranged with school administrators, correctional staff would cooperate with a consultant whose preliminary discussions were with correctional officials, and so on. But there are also cases in which a consultant works among warring factions. A contract negotiated with any group makes the consultant suspect in the eyes of the opposition. Such a situation requires considerable skill in finding a port of entry without losing one's autonomy. Our final case in this chapter illustrates this problem. Wedge (1971) has described the delicate entry process, using as an example his work as an intergroup consultant at the height of U.S. intervention in the Dominican Republic in 1971.

The consultant had previous experience working with opposing factions in several international conflicts. His working model had five stages: Establish contact with each party to the conflict while presenting oneself as an interested outsider; define the interests of each faction, including areas of mutual interest; bring opponents together on neutral ground; help to develop cooperative programs; then, once the programs are in place, withdraw.

It was this model that Wedge used to guide his intervention in the Dominican Republic crisis. In April 1965 there was a power struggle between senior and junior military officers; at stake was the right to govern. In four days of civil war, at least seven hundred citizens were killed. After the initial fighting had ceased, but while tensions were still high, the consultant received a telephone call from an official of the U.S. State Department in the Dominican Republic. The official asked if the consultant would be willing to go to the island to see whether communication could be established between the revolutionary Dominican Youth Movement and the U.S. diplomatic mission. The youth movement represented thousands of idealistic young people who were frustrated by the direction their country was taking. They were also extremely suspicious of the intentions of the United States, which had sent troops to the country in a highly controversial foreign policy move.

The consultant accepted the invitation, provided he could act with complete independence. He negotiated a contract with the State Department that ensured he would not represent the U.S. government; nor would he be under official control. He would not be required to identify his informants either in the U.S. mission or in the youth movement. He rejected a suggestion from the State Department that he travel on an official visa. But the consultant was aware that while it is one thing to be independent, it is another thing to be *perceived* as being independent by warring factions.

> The consultant arrived in Santo Domingo a few minutes after the deposed president of the Dominican Republic had returned from exile. It was a day of great tension as crowds moved from one demonstration to another. After the consultant had established himself in a hotel near the demarcation line, he walked among the tense crowds for several hours until he was approached by young people who demanded to know his identity.
>
> He presented himself as a visiting scholar interested in the political psychology of revolution. When his views were tested by the young people, he indicated that he was willing to listen and talk, though he might not always agree with their position. It was natural that members of the youth movement would suspect him of being a CIA agent. Because it was pointless to try to disprove the accusation, he simply pointed out that even if he were an agent it still would be in the interest of youth leaders to outline their

position to him so that he would transmit it back to
Washington. After all, they believed the Americans
did not really understand them.

Over the following three weeks the consultant
met with many people on both sides of the conflict.
He found a point on which the youth movement and
the U.S. mission agreed: the need to strengthen the
Autonomous University with which most of the
youth leaders identified. The youth movement knew
that if radical reforms were to succeed in Dominican
society, technical help would be needed. They were
willing to have this help provided by the United States
if it was on Dominican terms. The consultant focused
on this area of mutual interest, urged the State Department to assist the Autonomous University, and
later helped to recruit internationally known experts
needed by the university.

The success of Wedge's intervention rested heavily on his
neutrality and perceived independence. The biggest challenge
was the need to maintain his credibility even though he could
not share each faction's stereotypes of the other side. Participants in the conflict seemed to recognize that the consultant's
neutrality was of value, and this perception helped overcome
hostility aroused by the consultant's failure to accept the shared
assumptions of each group.

The consultant was struck by the fact that stereotypes
were not based on ignorance. In fact, each side had very accurate information about the other. Officials in the U.S. mission
were correct in their assessment that some of the youth leaders
were communists who sought radical changes in the political
system. The revolutionaries had good information about sup-
posedly secret Pentagon contingency plans calling for drastic action. Despite the accuracy of the information, the inferences
drawn from it were exaggerated. Neither group seemed to consider that there were powerful situational restraints that would
check the behavior of extremists on both sides. The stereotypes
that develop in such conflicts cannot be discounted as mere
propaganda or brainwashing. In his observation of the youth

movement, Wedge found no clear authority structure. A process of consensus had been developed. "Every succeeding event was discussed widely until an interpretation and a position were agreed upon—sometimes in hours, sometimes over several weeks —after which the decisions reached became a permanent part of the group belief system, and deviation led to isolation of the deviant" (Wedge, 1971, p. 740). This is a concise account of the process that goes into the development of shared assumptions in a group. Much of the tension in consultation with community groups is created by the consultant's need to maintain an independent position without being rejected by the group as too deviant to be of help.

The cases discussed in this chapter have illustrated some of the issues facing consultants as they negotiate relationships with clients in community settings. Our approach to these issues differs significantly from earlier theories of consultation. The difference can be drawn sharply by contrasting our view with the influential model of psychiatrist Gerald Caplan (1964, 1970). He tells consultants to negotiate formal contracts with specific people, to be responsible only to those people, and to quit when faced with a clash of values. In our view, obtaining formal contracts is sometimes impossible or even undesirable, the consultant's responsibilities are always ambiguous, and value clashes are hard to recognize in the entry phase.

In Caplan's model the person seeking consultation is referred to as the *consultee* whereas the term *client* is reserved for those affected by what the consultee does. Caplan (1964, p. 233) is very clear about the consultant's responsibility: "The consultant should attend to the needs of influential members of the institution. . . . Sanction must be continually maintained. It is important that the consultant keep the upper echelons of the authority system informed of his activities and solicit their suggestions for modification." On the other hand, the consultant is thought to have no responsibility whatever for clients, even if they are affected in important ways as a result of the consultant's work. Caplan justifies this stand by noting that no one is obliged to accept the consultant's advice.

We agree that the person seeking help is free to take it or

leave it. But we do not agree that this absolves the consultant of responsibility for what happens to others in the setting—those people whom Caplan calls clients. Consultants are responsible for the effects of their actions, whether those effects are intended or unintended, direct or mediated by others. We use the word *client* to include all those the consultant hopes will benefit from an intervention. This broad use of the term accurately expresses the ambiguity found in the real world. Moreover, it keeps issues such as the need to define responsibility and to assess side effects high on the consultant's list of priorities.

Caplan tells the consultant to obtain sanction in the form of an agreement establishing common perceptions of problems and role expectations. "The sanction of the consultee institution should be by written contract" (p. 233). We do not share Caplan's confidence that all important issues can be settled at entry and codified in a contract. Cases in this chapter indicate that precise, formal contracts, setting the boundaries on the consultant's activities, can be helpful, harmful, or irrelevant depending on the context. In time-limited consultation, where the consultant may have a few weeks to write a report with recommendations for action, a clear agreement with precise information from the client is essential. In cases where the intervention will emerge from the relationship between the consultant and various people in the setting, a specific contract can be unnecessarily restrictive. The initial agreement may be irrelevant if the true needs of the setting prove to be quite different from those set forth by the client during the entry phase.

Formal contracts may raise as many issues as they resolve. They always leave gaps that must be filled before intention can be translated into action. Suppose a school consultant has a contract that specifies meeting with teachers to help them with classroom management. When will the teachers meet with the consultant? Will it be on their own time, or will they be released from other duties? Will the meetings give them credit for in-service training? These questions may sound trivial, but this chapter and the previous one have described cases in which the consultants' preferred team approach depended on negotiating this issue. Failure to solve this problem often led to failure in consultation.

Certainly there is one definite advantage of a clear contract: If it sets forth appropriate activities for the consultant, he or she can use it as a justification for maintaining a preferred role. If the contract says "no direct service," it backs up the consultant's refusal to provide the service. But if the contract includes inappropriate activities, it may lock the consultant into an undesirable role. Sometimes early relationships can be changed. In Chapter Two we reviewed a case in which a State Department official was able to change his approach and convert failure into success. In this chapter we referred to Briggs's (1973) account of redefining the role of a school psychologist. But there were fortunate circumstances that made these transitions possible. In Briggs's case, they included a change in consultants, a major reorientation of the school, and availability of outside resources to pick up direct-service functions. The fact that so many factors contributed to role redefinition suggests that a successful transition is the exception rather than the rule. The experiences of Coiner (1977) in a school and Reppucci and his team (1973) in a correctional setting are eloquent testimony to the difficulty of changing established relationships.

Often a consultant must make a clear break with the client's notion of consultation. If the initial agreement says what *will* occur, the consultant may need to be explicit about what will *not* occur. In the case described by Sherwin and Renner (1979) the consultants had to flatly refuse the police command's request that they provide information about the job performance of individual police officers. Only this refusal gave them the necessary room to introduce an intervention consistent with their own values—and their understanding of the setting's real needs. In a case described in the previous chapter, a new facility for the intellectually handicapped established its innovative approach by rejecting money that had been allotted for new buildings. Whatever the project attempted, it would not invest in a set of buildings that would identify it as just another institution. Another example of starting with what the consultant will *not* do is offered by Sarason (1976, p. 318) in his description of the founding of the Yale Psychoeducational Clinic, a pioneer venture in community psychology: "We were not clear about what services we could provide. . . . If we had said we were going to provide diagnostic and therapeutic functions, life would have been easy. But the one thing we were clear about was that we did not want to provide these services."

A break with current expectations about intervention is often useful because it provides a means to confront the client's assumptions. In our discussion of cognitive concepts in Chapter One, we said that assumptions which guide behavior are often based on internal models about aspects of the world. The notions people have about what will occur, including their predictions of consequences of various plans, may be biased by reference to these models. People may give too much weight to possibilities that conform to their ideal models while giving too little weight to unique features of the situation. Kahneman and Tversky (1972) refer to this weighting bias as the use of a representativeness heuristic: Outcomes are considered likely if they are representative of strongly held theories.

In this chapter we have seen that internal models do affect the structure of the consultant-client relationship. The effect can be positive: Briggs's (1973) consultation model gave her the assurance to undertake the formidable task of redefining the relationship between school psychologist and setting; Sherwin and Renner (1979) had a particular model specifying acceptable intervention procedures, and their reference to this model enabled them to design a successful intervention with a police force. Wedge's (1971) theories about conflict resolution gave him a much needed procedure when he found himself working in the midst of a civil war.

But, as Kahneman and Tversky (1972) have found in controlled experiments, the representativeness heuristic can be a source of cognitive bias. We have seen cases in which reliance on internal models distorted the consultant-client relationship and limited the success of intervention.

Sometimes the problem is caused by the client's internal model. McIntyre (1969) found that his freedom to assess the setting thoroughly was compromised by the client's "omniscient expert" model of consultation. Sometimes the consultant's model is the source of trouble. Reppucci and colleagues (1973) failed to consider the option of being more directive in a leadership vacuum because that avenue was inconsistent with their model of the consultant as facilitator.

Consultants and clients may both have fixed models of consultation, and we might expect that when these models differ the relationship will be jeopardized. In a case reported by Reddy and Lansky (1975), consultants adhered to a human relations model while the police force operated on the basis of a military command model. This divergence had serious implications at every step of the consultation process. In Coiner's (1977) consultation with a resistant school, she was never able to overcome the contradiction between the school's direct-service expectation and her own model of skill enhancement through a team approach.

We are not implying that consultation is only successful when there is complete congruence between the assumptions of consultant and those of the client. We are suggesting that the recognition of divergent assumptions, and the way the divergence is handled, will have important effects. Glidewell (1959) has categorized some of the ways in which consultants and clients may differ in their perceptions.

The consultant may differ from the client in substantial ways: about the need for consultation, the availability of resources in the system, whether the consultant has something to offer, and the way in which resources brought by the consultant are to be distributed in the system. The two cases of consultation with police described in this chapter illustrate such incongruence. When consultants offered to provide human relations training, they were in conflict with clients who doubted that the intervention was needed and, moreover, doubted that the consultants had resources that would contribute to law and order. In the other case, police officials differed with the consultants about how resources were to be distributed in the system. The command wanted data that would identify police officers who were not doing their jobs. The consultants insisted on keeping data anonymous and designing an intervention that would be of particular value to the officers themselves.

When the conflict is fundamental, Glidewell (p. 56) recommends that consultation begin with a period of observation that permits the parties to size up each other: "Observation is threatening to the system, to be sure, but less potent than the active consultant role." The consultant uses this period to gather information bearing on whether intervention is in fact possible, and he or she shares information freely with those in the setting so they can make their own decisions about furthering the relationship. Once again we refer to the two police settings. In one case the consultants avoided opportunities to become acquainted with the setting in an informal way, choosing to press ahead with their preferred intervention. In the other case, preintervention observations were made through inspection of court records. Sharing this information with police led the command to see intervention as useful. The positive outcome in this case shows that initial conflict between the views of consultant and client can be overcome.

There may be agreement between consultant and client on the need for consultation, leaving open questions such as whether the necessary resources already exist in the system, whether the consultant's own skills are relevant, and how the resources of consultation are to be distributed. Wedge's (1971) work in the Dominican Republic crisis is an example of this level of congruence. All parties in the conflict realized that some assistance was needed, although it was not clear at first that they knew what sort of intervention would be helpful, or that the consultant had the necessary resources, or how such resources should be used.

Glidewell points to increasing levels of congruence between consultant and client, but he warns that to expect complete agreement on all important issues at the outset is unrealistic. The various people who might be affected by an intervention will not have resolved all their conflicts about authority and dependence before the consultant sets foot on the threshold. In fact, congruence on all issues may be undesirable. As we have noted throughout these first chapters, the tension between the perceptions of an independent observer and the shared assumptions of the community group may help redefine important problems and possibilities for the setting. In Glidewell's words, "The more congruence of perception needed by the consultant

as a basis for entry, the fewer are the opportunities for change"
(p. 57).

We now have completed our survey of the issues that confront consultants as they seek out settings for their work and negotiate with clients to create a structure in which their work will be productive. Structure requires content. Once entry has been accomplished and the consultant is equipped with some sort of mandate, the next step is to fashion an appropriate intervention. In Part Two we look at interventions that focus on the links among people and among subgroups within a client system.

Part Two

~~~~~~

Links Within
Community Groups

The consultant must have something to offer. Kelly (1971, p. 899), describing the qualities needed by a community psychologist, comments that he or she must be able to do at least one thing clearly and well: "Without a recognizable competence there are few opportunities for the community psychologist to be in a position to solve genuine problems in the community." Kelly suggests further that consultants seek out settings where their skills can be displayed.

In Part One we described cases in which consultants demonstrated competence in various areas—program development, human relations training, action research, conflict resolution—but we dealt with these skills only as components of the consultant-client relationship. Now we focus directly on these skills as they are employed to improve the links among components of community groups. Internal linkages have major implications for interpersonal relationships and communication patterns, for decision making and problem solving, and for the development of resources in a setting. Depending on the consultant's philosophy, status, mandate, and the characteristics of the setting, he or she may work within an existing structure or work for structural change. In either case, the overall objective is to permit the setting to use the consultant's skills in order to achieve its objectives while being responsive to its members.

113

4

Improving Group
Problem Solving
and Decision Making

The principle of interdependence in ecology asserts that a system is a series of reciprocal processes. The way groups and individuals interact with each other has implications for the harmony and effectiveness of the system and its members. An emphasis on interdependence turns the consultant's attention to the way persons, roles, and ideas are linked in a setting. How interdependence is mediated determines whether people can work together to develop norms and goals, and it dictates what sorts of people emerge as adaptive members of the setting.

A classic formulation in attitude theory, according to Smith, Lasswell, and Casey (1946), is "Who says what to whom and with what effect?" This is also a useful starting place for the consultant who wants to understand the linkages of a client group. In a daycare center where administrators and staff members work together in the same building, the consultant may find it significant when directives from the administration reach the staff only through parents. Information flow is an important aspect of interdependence. A setting may have formal rules limiting certain kinds of communication. Lawyers and judges who interact with one another, sometimes socially, are constrained from talking about pending cases. Usually there are

115

also unwritten norms governing information flow—norms that can be inferred by listening to the sorts of conversations that occur among groups. The principal of a school may encourage her teachers to come to her with personal problems that could interfere with their work, but she might think it improper to unburden herself in the same fashion.

The way decisions are made in a setting is another aspect of interdependence. Who decides what for whom? In a community group there are frequently different areas where decisions are made in different ways by different people. In a daycare center, for example, teachers may have authority to determine policies in their own units, perhaps using consensus as a decision-making method. But budgetary matters may be the prerogative of the administration. Later we present a case showing that some dilemmas are ambiguous even when there is common agreement about these spheres of decision making. In many situations, a setting has problems determining not only *what* decisions should be made but *how* they should be made and *who* should make them.

The way in which interdependence is mediated gives a setting its unique character. It sets the context for consultation and determines what side effects, beneficial or otherwise, will accompany an intervention. Understanding the importance of reciprocal processes and diagnosing the state of those processes in a setting will enable the consultant to be a resource for improved problem solving, decision making, and communication flow. An example of the consultant working with this focus is provided by Richard MacGillivray. We have paraphrased MacGillivray's (1980) account, previously unpublished, of his work with a troubled daycare center.

Robin Hill Daycare Center had been in operation for a year before the community psychologist became involved. Much of the center's structure was mandated by the government. The law required a Board of Directors composed of parents and other interested members of the community, with parents having at least 50 percent of seats on the board. Most children came from the lower socioeconomic group; 65 percent were from one-parent families. All parents paid at least some portion of their children's fees and the government made up the remainder. The $7.05 per-day rate allowed by the government was much too low, however, to cover the center's expenses. From its creation Robin Hill had been in financial difficulty, salaries were low, and staff turnover in its first year was 85 percent.

The ten staff members included an administrator and her assistant, five full-time teachers, two part-time teachers, and a cook. The preschool unit served twenty children; the after-school unit served forty-five. Most children were in the normal range of intelligence and developmental maturity, but a few had special needs: children with cerebral palsy, low intelligence, or mild emotional difficulties.

The consultant entered the setting with no clear role definition. He had experience in the child-care field and graduate training in psychology, giving staff members the impression that he might be helpful in solving problems with difficult children. But the first case that was presented to him illuminated problems in the center that went beyond any particular child.

Erik, a child in the preschool program, had cerebral palsy. He was diagnosed as deaf, although he seemed to follow some verbal instructions and he liked to sing. His singing presented a problem, however; it was much too loud and seemed to make no sense. In a group singalong he was very noticeable and his peers ridiculed him.

The Christmas Concert was approaching. Staff members felt a commitment to work with all the children, including Erik, and rehearsals for the concert were proceeding—if somewhat discordantly. One day Erik's disappointed parents told the teachers they had been informed by the administrator that Erik would not be allowed to participate in the concert. The administrator and her assistant, concerned that the concert be a success, had reluctantly decided Erik would not sing. They had not communicated this to the staff members, however, and the angry teachers turned to the consultant for support. Rather than give an opinion on the case, the consultant used the issue to diagnose ways in which the center seemed to be dysfunctional; the case also provided a starting point for improving such areas.

It was not surprising that with children like Erik the administration and the teachers had different priorities. Staff members worked with the children every day. Although they had to experience the problems Erik presented, they felt keenly the need to provide for such children and to integrate them into the group. The administrators, who also cared about the children, were somewhat removed from daily programming. They had more responsibility for the welfare of the center generally, including its public relations. Apart from the positive experience the Christmas Concert might offer individual children, the administrators saw it as a public relations event.

There was little empathy between staff and administrators for the other's viewpoint. This lack of empathy had much to do with poor communication— the staff heard about the decision from the parents rather than from the administrators who worked in the same building. Despite the small staff, it was not easy to hold staff meetings. Since the center could only afford to pay teachers for the time they spent working with children, holding group meetings meant asking hard-pressed and underpaid staff members to give up one of their free evenings.

Communication, clearly part of the problem, did not exhaust the difficulties. If the administrators had made the same ruling and communicated it properly, the decision itself would still have been challenged. Staff members questioned whether such a matter should be determined by the administrators.

Who *should* make decisions involving the welfare of the center? Was there one sort of issue that was properly dealt with by the administrators and another sort that should be settled by majority opinion?

These questions seemed crucial to the center's functioning, but the consultant learned that precedents were unclear over the center's one-year history. Staff had been permitted to decide on programming in each unit and administrators usually made decisions that affected the whole center, such as those dealing with budget. But there were borderline cases. When staff members were having difficulty getting parents to send their children properly dressed, they maintained that the administration should set some policy with parents. The administrators resented having the issue thrust at them. They believed the matter involved teachers' abilities to provide a program; in this case, they said, it was up to the staff to talk to parents.

On another occasion, one of the teachers had planned to present a progress report on a child to the mother. The administrator intervened, however, and instructed the teacher not to give the report because the parent had not paid her bill. Staff members saw this as an intrusion by budget-conscious administrators into the important relationship between teacher and parent concerning a child's progress.

Then there were cases like that of Erik, in which both administration and teachers had legitimate concerns—concerns that would lead to different decisions. Was this primarily a case of programming for a child with special needs and thus to be made by staff and administrators together? Or was it primarily a public relations issue to be settled by the administration and communicated to the staff?

There was general agreement when the consultant suggested that this was a matter of sufficient importance to warrant a full meeting. Once the staff members had the opportunity to express their strong views about the need to include Erik in the group, staff and administrators were able to reach a consensus that he should participate in the concert. Without ignoring the problem of Erik, the consultant used the meeting to put the issue in a broader decision-making context. The session ended with recognition of the need for better communication, although many difficulties would remain because of the constraints imposed by the nature of staffing. The consultant pointed out the areas that seemed to have been implicitly agreed as suitable for participatory decision making and those that properly fell to the administration. It was agreed that this and other broad topics would be the subject of another meeting.

The initial meeting went well but the second did not. Having given ground in Erik's case, the administrator now seemed defensive. She acted as though the staff had called the meeting to threaten her position. Teachers who had been vocal when advancing their arguments about the Christmas Concert now were curiously quiet. This surprised the consultant, since he was well aware that every teacher was concerned about the way the center functioned. With the meeting a failure, the consultant had to decide what he could do to improve the way that staff and administrators dealt with issues.

The staff seemed to need support to bring their concerns into the open. The consultant thought that teachers might not realize how many of their complaints were shared by others. Although staff members had come to him with opinions, and although most teachers had the same opinions, all wanted them kept confidential. He urged teachers in each unit to find time to hold unit meetings. With the administrators absent, teachers were able to express their concerns and found they were not alone with their complaints. Morale seemed better.

This procedure also created new problems. As common resentment toward the administration became the focus of discussion, anger built on anger, particularly against the administrator herself. Intragroup solidarity was developed at the expense of moderation and objectivity. The units were now eager to have another big meeting, but the consultant was nervous about the prospect. There had been tension in the center before the consultant began working with the units, but it had been a general tension without factions or focus. Such tension was, no doubt, partly responsible for the high staff turnover in the previous year. Staff no longer considered quitting, but they now wanted changes in the way the center functioned. The consultant feared that a new meeting at this time would create an explosion.

The consultant turned his attention to the administrator, who would need support to be less defensive. He hoped to facilitate solidarity in the administration, but when he met with the administrator and her assistant he found they did not present a common front. The assistant was unwilling to support the administrator, even though they often had similar views. The assistant had only recently been promoted from teacher to his new post and still taught part-time. He thus had a foot in both camps and was well liked by staff. His contacts with teachers alerted him to the anger directed at the administrator. He was unwilling to risk his popularity, which had recently been demonstrated in his election to the board as staff representative. If the administrator lost her job, moreover, he was the likely beneficiary.

The consultant knew that he must provide support for the administrator himself. But the woman felt that tension was increasing and suspected that the consultant was responsible. The new group feeling among teachers, and their willingness to complain, coincided with the consultant's arrival. It was therefore natural for her to pinpoint him as the cause of her troubles.

The consultant held several meetings with the administrator to suggest the issues he thought were important. Since he was careful to cast these observations in systemic terms rather than as matters of personality, it was easier for the administrator to accept problems without feeling threatened personally. Using this approach the consultant thought the administrator was much more willing to face the staff without being defensive. With the consultant supporting the legitimate concerns of the administrator, the assistant was more willing to identify himself with the administration. This made the administrator more secure.

But the consultant was still concerned that there might be such a load of complaints, delivered with such heat, that even an open and receptive stance by the administrator would be insufficient to make the meeting constructive. He had one more card to play.

When he first entered the situation, the psychologist had been asked to give the center a report of his view of its operation. He agreed, provided the report would be available to staff, administration, and board members—and, through board members, to parents. Now he revived this dormant request, announced that he was working on his report, and suggested that he distribute it in time for it to be discussed at the forthcoming meeting. He took considerable care with the way he stated issues in the report by providing support for all those involved, including the embattled administrator. He tried to assess the various things that might go wrong in the meeting and to head them off in his report.

Several days after the report was distributed, staff and administrators met. This time the teachers were more vocal in expressing their complaints. The administrator was also much more open than she had been at the previous meeting. When the consultant supported the legitimate concerns of the administrator, the assistant administrator tended to take a mediator's role. Both the assistant and the consultant worked to find common ground when conflicting positions were advanced.

The meeting distinguished the areas where the decisions would be made by staff from those where staff opinions would be sought in administrative decisions. All recognized that there would still be issues in which the appropriate mode of decision making was unclear, and the group agreed to keep lines of communication open so that these issues could be debated. The resolution of Erik's case provided a model for future debates.

The psychologist's role as consultant ended when he was elected to the center's board of directors. He had not sought election, but he agreed—somewhat reluctantly—and hoped that his new vantage point would enable him to work on the strained relationship between the board and those at the center, both staff and administration. This change in status posed problems, however. While he was consulting, teachers had offered opinions that would not have been shared with a board member. He had to be sure that during his tenure on the board these confidences were not abused.

In learning to read a setting, the consultant should look for people who connect with others on different levels—including levels not suggested by formal role definition or job description. Sarason (1976) has made this point in his discussion of community networks. He recalled how he had discussed with a student their common lack of access to a certain state politician; only when the student had left did Sarason realize that his own secretary was connected to the same political network as the politician. He suggests that we tend not to think of people as members of numerous networks; yet it is by understanding such links that the consultant can appreciate new possibilities for creating new links in a setting.

In the case described above, MacGillivray found that the assistant administrator was someone with overlapping group memberships. His job description placed him in the administration, but the needs of the center were such that he was still functioning, on a part-time basis, as a teacher. He was also a member of the board of directors, and the fact that he had been elected to the board as staff representative was a testimonial to the complex way in which he was perceived. At first this complexity posed problems for the consultant. Because he wished to maintain his popularity with teachers, the assistant was unwilling to associate himself with the unpopular administrator. Thus he isolated the administrator and made her take any criticism as a threat. But the assistant's various links in the center were also a resource; when tapped in the right way, this resource was useful in bringing all components to a better level of functioning.

The consultant who approaches a setting expecting it to

conform to its organizational chart may be in for some sur-
prises. Formal role designations often suggest that certain people should have common viewpoints and interests, but as
MacGillivray indicates, people often identify with aspects of
the setting other than those suggested by their titles. The assistant
administrator wanted to maintain his popularity with teachers
and was likely to break ranks with his nominal boss in a confrontation. Because he was next in line to take over the center
if the administrator faltered, he had a pragmatic reason for
maintaining his distance.

The daycare center described here also illustrates how a
setting socializes the outsider. We have pointed to the need for
consultants to keep their roles flexible so they can diagnose the
key difficulties in a setting before becoming locked into a specific intervention. But this flexibility is threatening to those in a
system; they want to fix consultants in place so they can find a
safe way to deal with them. Consultants may find themselves
human Rorschach blots—each person in the setting perceives
them differently and perceptions shift at each stage of their involvement. MacGillivray was first defined as someone who
could help with certain problem children; when he redefined
the problem posed by one child so that it took on a systemic
focus, he was in danger of being regarded as a troublemaker by
the administration and as an agent of the administrator by the
staff. The fact that the consultation led to his unexpected election to the center's board of directors shows how varied are the
ways in which a setting socializes consultants.

Understanding Communication Problems

The person who intervenes in an unproductive process
need not expect that hidden motivations and conflicts will always be at the root of the difficulty. One needs *skill* to hold
meetings, ensure group input in decisions, and set priorities.
Sometimes those who must coordinate these organization processes simply lack the necessary knowledge to get the task done
efficiently. Mill (1974) made this point in his account of adapt-
ing industrial consultation to mental health settings. In one case

the consultant found that meetings were unproductive because they were poorly run. He was able to have an impact after attending only three meetings.

> Regular meetings of community mental health directors and administrators in a state mental health region were notably unproductive. The regional director, who chaired the meetings, had tried to encourage maximum participation in decision making, but the meetings drifted aimlessly and degenerated into bickering. Members showed great reluctance to make any decisions.
>
> When the consultant attended a meeting, he found that a great deal of time was taken up with discussing minor matters while important issues were passed over quickly. And when decisions were made, no one assumed responsibility for seeing that they were carried out. The participants hardly knew one another; these meetings provided their only contact. The regional director kept the agenda in his own hands, and members never knew the issues they would have to confront or how to rank issues in terms of importance.
>
> The consultant decided the main task was to give the group some basic training in how to hold a successful meeting. The regional director was encouraged to enlist the help of group members to build a public agenda at the beginning of each meeting. The group identified the items that were most pressing and formed committees to do preparatory work on the main issues between meetings. These committees produced information for the whole group when the issues came up for discussion and decision. The group learned to specify how decisions would be implemented. By the third meeting the consultant observed marked improvement.

Many other issues could have been raised by the consultant. In a traditionally authoritarian structure, the regional director was voluntarily experimenting with participatory decision making. His desire to change formats was being undercut, however, by his need to control the situation. He was maintaining the major mode of control available to him: the agenda. His failure to make the agenda public, and to include group members in its creation, showed his ambivalence about changing operating modes. The consultant decided that the best way to improve the situation was a straightforward set of prescriptions for holding successful meetings rather than delving into hidden issues. Since the regional director and other group members were willing to follow these prescriptions there was rapid improvement.

In the case reported by Mill, a major problem in the work of the group was a tendency to overestimate the importance of trivial or improbable events at the expense of crucial issues. This is a common occurrence in groups that lack a clear procedure for setting priorities—not only in small groups, but in large systems making major social decisions. Jervis (1976) offered a number of striking examples from the history of international affairs illustrating the tendency to waste time and effort on unlikely possibilities: In 1933 the British navy and air force were drawing up contingency plans in case of war between Britain and France; the year before, the United States staged an elaborate war game in the Pacific in which the presumable enemy was a coalition of Britain and Japan; in the 1920s the only war plan possessed by the Canadians provided for the "threat" of an armed invasion by the Americans.

At the community level, a mental health association deciding where to locate a new home for handicapped children may spend an inordinate amount of time on whether or not the street in front of the home has too much traffic. This matter may be studied exhaustively: Members of the association may trade stories about handicapped children endangered by traffic; they may deal at length with staffing needs to prevent an accident and liability if one did occur. Meantime they may neglect such crucial issues as raising a mortgage for the home and persuading neighbors not to oppose rezoning.

Kahneman and Tversky (1979) have pointed out that this problem arises not merely because people tend to *overestimate* the probability of unlikely events, although they do. Even when people are told explicitly what the probability is, they still give too much weight to the unlikely, whether good or bad. Kahneman and Tversky speculated that this concentration on low probabilities may contribute to the attractiveness of both insurance and gambling. At any rate it is one of many cognitive factors that should be kept in mind by community consultants.

A major function of communication is to permit a group of people to coordinate their work on a task. Even though members of a team may have common goals and know how to achieve them, their efforts may be sidetracked in the absence of discussion. Nixon (1975) has provided an example from consultation on a pediatric ward.

A fourteen-year-old boy was admitted to the hospital with severe ulcerative colitis. He was depressed and withdrawn, refused to eat, and appeared passively manipulative. The medical team asked the psychologist to give the boy an evaluation because of the apparent psychological problems that were contributing to a deterioration in his condition.

The psychologist soon reformulated the problem. His first contact with team members indicated that they were experiencing extreme frustration in dealing with the case. It was the fourth recent admission of a child with a potentially life-threatening condition that was not responding to treatment. Moreover, the team was having problems with the boy's family.

Mother and grandmother continually complained about every aspect of the hospital, especially the food. Grandmother kept telling the patient, "They put those tubes in your arm to torture you." There were frequent fights between family members in front of the boy. Mother and grandparents often joined him in bed. Family members were constantly requesting information, and the team was in a general state of confusion about who said what to whom.

When he met with the whole team, the psychologist pointed out that family members were engaged in warfare for the patient's attention, and staff members had permitted themselves to get involved in the conflict. The team was too involved with the family and had lost the objectivity needed to deal firmly with family members.

At this meeting the team members were encouraged to discuss their objectives and decide on the action needed to meet them. Once they paused to talk things over, it was apparent the team knew what had to be done and possessed the resources to do it. The group defined the areas of conflict—such as sporadic information given to family members—and established boundaries between the team and the family on the one hand and the patient and his family members on the other. Following the meeting the team expelled grandmother from the hospital, ruled that only the patient was allowed in his bed, ordered the patient's mother not to bring him food, and used privileges to reinforce participation in occupational therapy and physiotherapy and to reward other appropriate behavior.

In this case, like the one reported earlier by MacGillivray, a major constraint on communication was a simple lack of time. In the daycare center all paid hours were spent with children. If staff members wanted to discuss problems, it would have to be on their own time. Because the work was demanding, it was not easy to ask people to give up free hours to remain at the center and lengthen their day. In the setting described by Nixon, the medical team working with children simply failed to encourage group discussion of management issues. Once this norm was instituted, the staff found the solutions to their own difficulties.

Communication problems often have a more serious basis than the simple lack of a forum for discussion. The consultant would be wise to get a reading of the dynamics in a setting to determine why communication has broken down. This point is illustrated in another brief case that is superficially similar to that just reported. The setting was another hospital, these patients too were seriously ill children, and the difficulty seemed to be a lack of communication among staff members. But now, in addition to the lack of a convenient structure for discussion, there were other constraints. As Drotar (1975) indicates, one barrier was the professional fragmentation of the health team and another was the deep feelings aroused by work with dying children.

Staff members in a pediatric hospital were finding it hard to cope with the deaths of young patients. This difficulty expressed itself in denial and in the inability of medical team members to help families deal with their grief.

A thirteen-year-old boy, critically ill with cystic fibrosis, was well known to the staff after many admissions. Now his condition had deteriorated. Although nurses knew the boy was ill and his prognosis was grave, there was little recognition that death was imminent. Staff members were troubled by the boy's statements that he was "going to die" and disturbed by his agitated behavior. Approaches to him were highly inconsistent. Some staff members valued his exploration of feelings about death; others tried to get him to participate in normal activities and "stop being so anxious."

The boy's parents had another child with cystic fibrosis, who had been discharged recently in much improved condition. The family was having considerable difficulty coping with the situation. The mother tended to maintain a vigil over her children and found it almost impossible to leave the hospital room. Under the strain of these illnesses, the mother and father had drifted apart. Staff members, although they were concerned about the parents, had not been able to help.

The psychologist recognized that certain issues might benefit from discussion among the staff. The institutional barrier, however, was departmentalization of staff members: Nurses tended to meet in their own professional group, as did doctors and social workers. Nevertheless, the clear difficulties the staff members were experiencing in this case created the conditions that permitted a meeting of the whole team.

At this meeting the consultant encouraged staff members to talk about their understanding of the patient's condition and their reaction to it. It was apparent that some had more information than others. Although the boy's own physician believed that this trip to the hospital was the boy's last, house doctors and most nurses did not realize the situation was so grave. But this gap in technical information was not the whole problem.

The consultant recognized the difficulty staff members were having in facing the deterioration of a well-liked young patient. They did not *want* to know how serious his condition was. When the psychologist said it was apparent that the boy was going to die very soon, one nurse exclaimed: "I really hate to put it that way." In fact, the child died the day after the meeting.

A key factor in the reluctance of staff members to recognize imminence of death was the feeling of powerlessness it produced. Doctors admitted that when they had done all they could, medically, they found it difficult to communicate further with parents, even though they might have been able to help family members accept the situation.

Once this feeling of powerlessness was confronted directly by the group, the staff members were able to take a more constructive approach. This involved providing an atmosphere in which young patients could talk about dying and, ultimately, helping family members deal with the death of a child.

The need for accurate reconnaissance of a setting is pointed up in the two brief cases just described. Although they were similar in a number of ways—both involved communication problems in medical teams dealing with seriously ill children—there were also differences that had a bearing on the intervention strategies. In one case it was sufficient to get staff members together to discuss difficulties. In the second case underlying problems—including professional fragmentation and emotional involvement with dying children—had to be dealt with before effective communication could take place.

Communication Can Be Dangerous

Often consultants, particularly those with training in human relations, overvalue communication as a solution to organizational difficulties. We have described cases in which communication was therapeutic; there are also cases in which it is risky or even counterproductive.

Like most tactics consultants use, bringing people together to talk about problems has both positive and negative sides. O'Neill and Levings (1979) have demonstrated how easily groups fall into biased scanning of arguments and information. They carried out research on a problem with serious implications for the host community: There had been an explosion of anti-French feeling by English-speaking residents in an area in Nova Scotia where Francophones were in the minority. Ironically, this was the same geographical area from which the English had expelled the Acadian settlers two hundred years earlier, an event made famous by Longfellow in his poem *Evangeline.* At the height of renewed anti-French feeling, the researchers conducted a study in which small groups were asked to debate the merits of bilingualism. O'Neill and Levings were able to arrange rewards so that groups would look at both sides on the issue with a consequent change in attitude. But in the absence of manipulation there was a strong tendency for groups to become more and more biased in their discussion and views.

We have seen an example of this biased scanning effect at work in the Robin Hill Daycare Center case described earlier in this chapter. MacGillivray recognized that staff members at the daycare center were not communicating enough to know that they shared common concerns. He thought the first task was to arrange meetings of staff who had similar problems and views. This strategy had the desired effect of promoting solidarity, but it also produced biased scanning of issues and resulted in a hardening of opposition to the administration. As we have seen, the consultant had to be especially careful and creative in his next steps in order to keep his intervention from making the situation worse.

Group discussion that involves people with shared perceptions of a conflict is always vulnerable to biased scanning effects that may harden positions and make views more extreme. The consultant who is aware of this pitfall can provide a counterbalance in group discussion by suggesting how the issue may look to those not attending the meeting. A good example can be found in the work of Sarason and colleagues (1966). Their team held meetings with elementary school teachers—meetings in which there was a danger that teachers would stereotype and denigrate parents. The verbatim dialogue taken from the consultants' notes gives a rich illustration not only of biased scanning in group discussion but of the way it can be handled.

A team of consultants working in the public schools found that much of its time was taken up with efforts to help teachers revise ways of doing things they had learned in their training or in the first few months of teaching. Their experience with new teachers led the consultants to form teacher discussion groups. All new elementary teachers in one school system were invited to participate in the groups over a ten-week period. Participation was voluntary, contents of the discussion were determined by the teachers, and proceedings were kept confidential. It was anticipated that the project would help the teachers understand that the problems they faced in the classroom were common issues for new teachers. By helping one another, they could develop a valuable source of social support. The groups were largely successful in meeting these objectives.

There was a danger that teachers would gang up on out-groups, making it easier to externalize problems and find a convenient scapegoat. For example, teachers tended to blame problems on parents and the family background. In one discussion session, these were among teacher comments about parents:

"We had this American Education Week, and

the parents were supposed to come in. I had exactly three parents out. So they didn't come to see me. Monday I started going to see *them*. I sent little notes home and I called. In some places, mama went across the street or to the store at the hour I was scheduled to come. So it worked out beautifully. They don't want to see me."

"The parent has a very definite influence on the child. . . . They may say *I* was like this when I was a little boy. And the parent is really taking pride in the kid acting up."

"It is an apathetic feeling that some of these parents have."

These and similar statements were reinforcing a stereotyped perception of parents. Teachers had little empathy for the parents' position; what empathy they had was being rapidly submerged in a tide of angry comments. To provide a moderating influence, a consultant tried to present a more balanced view of parents:

"I am just wondering if it is more than mere apathy. For the most part, you are drawing from a population where the parents are relatively uneducated, where their experiences in school were by no means happy ones, where it was a situation of relative failure and frustration to them. Why should it be easy for them to come to school? Let's ask that question. Just imagine a situation where it is your child going to school. Would you feel any hesitation about going to school to talk to the teacher?"

When consultants tried to enter emotion-charged discussion offering an external point of view, they did not have instant success. Some teachers reacted against the intrusion by the consultant. One noted that the consultant seemed to be worried about what made parents uncomfortable in the school; but, complained the teacher, parents ought to come to school even if they are uncomfortable and simply "sublimate what happens to them."

Despite more attempts by teachers to continue the diatribe against parents, the consultants kept put-

ting the issue in a different light. In one instance, a
member of the team struck the right note when he
compared the relationship between parents and teachers to that between teachers and the school administration:

"Let's go back to some of our earlier sessions.
. . . You were describing problems that you were running into with administration. . . . You were more or
less saying 'Look, who the hell is interested? Who is
really putting out for us?' . . . You know what it added
up to, that you were alone, and there wasn't anybody
who was really interested in what was happening to
you and what you needed and the like. . . . I am wondering if this is not true for a lot of parents that we
are discussing now. I mean, given their own lives in relation to these schools, their previous experiences
with the schools, whether they don't start off with
the assumption—for which in many cases there may
be good grounds—'What is the sense in getting mixed
up in this?' Now I'm sure that if we had sessions like
this for the administrators, they would be talking a
great deal about what they really want the teachers to
do and to feel and to think. . . . Somehow or other
there wasn't a meeting of minds [between teachers
and administration]. What I am asking is, may this
not be the case between yourselves and the parents
you are dealing with?"

The example seemed to have meaning for the
teachers, so the consultant elaborated it: The reluctance of parents to come to school and meet with
teachers was compared with the difficulty these new
teachers were having in meeting with administrators.
Gradually the discussion turned to ways in which
teachers could do more to make parents feel accepted in the school, changes in the sort of notes that
were sent home, and so on.

The verbatim record of teacher discussion groups provided by Sarason and colleagues (1966) offers glimpses of consultants improvising solutions to many different problems. We
have referred to only a small portion of that record to illustrate

how a consultant can deal with biased scanning in groups. There are times, however, when the risks associated with bringing people together far outweigh the potential gain. Reddin (1977) has reported a case that makes this point concisely. Reddin was consulting to the president of a Canadian fish-packing firm who was having difficulty with his trawler captains. Members of the competing Russian fleet cooperated with each other; the fact that his own captains did not was causing a loss in productivity. Reddin's initial suggestion was to hold team-building sessions with the trawler captains, but this notion was quickly vetoed by the president of the firm.

The client told the consultant that under Canadian maritime law the trawler captains and crews were not employees but merchant co-adventurers. "Each was an independent businessman. Not only the legal system but the existing community structure and a long local history supported this view. He said that it would be farcical to imagine that much could be done by a seminar demonstrating that cooperation optimizes the system but does not necessarily optimize each individual in it. It would be rather like rearranging deck chairs on the *Titanic*. The clincher was the president's report of the first, and last, Christmas Eve party that the executive committee had arranged with the captains. It had to be on Christmas Eve, because that was the single day of the year when all trawlers were in port. The trawler captains used the occasion to announce their first strike. Their spokesman apologized for the timing but explained that it was the first time the captains had all been together" (Reddin, 1977, p. 33).

We have often mentioned the biases that can result from referring to an ideal model of consultation at the expense of reading the setting. The model may be so salient to the consultant that it obscures variation between situations. In the example reported by Reddin, the consultant's background in organizational development led him to propose a tactic that was entirely inappropriate for the situation. He assumed that cooperation among fleet captains was the norm when in fact it was ruled out by law.

This example turns our attention, once again, to the ecological principle of interdependence. Elements of an ecosystem are interdependent. In this case, the difficulty in coordinating activities of the trawlers had an effect on the fish-packing firm and consequently on the trawlers themselves. But merely knowing that groups depend upon one another, while useful as a guiding principle, is insufficient to give the consultant much help in a specific setting. The consultant must learn *how* interdependence is mediated. In Reddin's case, the mediation process was complex. Although the fleet captains depended on one another, tradition and law dictated that they must compete among themselves.

In many systems there are norms or payoffs for both competition and cooperation. The complexities of these systems have been discussed by Hardin (1968) in his classic paper "The Tragedy of the Commons" and in Schelling's (1978) book *Micromotives and Macrobehavior.* Their treatment of paradoxes in social behavior shows how mixed motives in groups can lead to irrational and self-destructive behavior patterns. Moreover, Edney's (1980, 1981) reviews and analyses of commons dilemmas are recommended reading for consultants who would appreciate the issues that confront groups struggling for a share of scarce resources.

Not all clashes among and within groups center on competition and conflicts of interest. Sometimes they arise from contending ideas. We have suggested that shared assumptions bind together members of community groups. When factions in a group have different ways of perceiving reality, cohesion is threatened. A group may continue to function, perhaps uneasily, as long as those subscribing to different assumptions are not forced into a confrontation. Here lies the risk in a consultation tactic that encourages communication. Getting different factions together may precipitate a crisis in the group—sometimes a crisis the group cannot survive. MacFarlane (1978) found this to be the situation when she was consulting to a volunteer Rape Relief organization in a Canadian city.

Rape Relief had only four members when it was founded. Two years later it was registered as an official society, having the objectives of providing rape victims with support, information, and counseling; educating the public about different aspects of the issue; working to get better treatment for victims; debunking myths about rape; and thereby decreasing the tendency to blame the victims.

By the time the consultant became associated with Rape Relief its membership was large enough to permit the operation of six committees, all working to advance one or another of the group's objectives. A representative from each committee also sat on the steering committee, which attempted to coordinate diverse activities. A group with four members is likely to be spared the communication problems that can develop in an organization fragmented into six committees.

The consultant worked with several committees, including the one concerned with educating the public about rape. She agreed to develop guidelines for committee members to use when they went to speaking engagements in the community. It was a source of concern to the organization that speakers were taking very different approaches, possibly creating confusion rather than providing information.

In her initial assessment, the consultant thought one difficulty might be the fact that the committee rarely met, and when it did meet not everyone attended. She discovered this problem when she was unable to organize a full committee meeting to make a start on her task. A superficial analysis might have suggested that simply getting the committee of potential speakers all together for a discussion might bring about coordination and consensus.

But as she talked further with individual committee members, the consultant became convinced that the problem went a good deal deeper. The failure of committee members to meet together was more a symptom than a cause. There were significant philosophical differences dividing members of the committee; one faction included those who saw rape as an aspect of male-female relationships in society and used the speaking engagements as a forum to present this

feminist perspective. The other group thought of rape
as an aberration and educated the public about the
characteristics of rapists and the problems of being a
victim of sexual assault. It was the latter group that
felt the need for a set of guidelines, apparently to
keep the former group in check. Those who used the
rape issue as an opportunity to present a feminist perspective on sexuality were threatened by the consultant's activities.

The consultant had to predict whether the difficult task of getting the committee members to meet
and discuss the issue, even if it could be accomplished,
would do more harm than good. She decided against
provoking such a confrontation. Instead she met with
all members of the committee separately or in self-
selected groups and prepared a set of guidelines that
might be followed by those with either of the conflicting orientations. Obviously many issues could not
be addressed in guidelines meeting this broad objective. But the guidelines provided material that should
be in any informative talk given by members of Rape
Relief, and committee members found them useful.

Some months after her involvement with the
group, the consultant learned that its work was seriously disrupted by confrontation between those with
different philosophies, and Rape Relief soon broke
into fragments.

In the case report by MacFarlane, the consultant could
only speculate on whether she might have made a contribution
by forcing the issue earlier, at a time when she was working in
the group, and used herself as a mediator.

We have suggested several factors that may lead a consultant to adopt or reject the tactic of bringing people and groups
together to discuss issues that divide them. One factor is the
consultant's intervention model. The danger is that this consideration will outweigh others. Another factor is the consultant's
skill. If the consultant is adept at facilitating communication,
the tactic will probably be relied upon extensively. A third factor, and one that demands more attention than it gets, is the
unique character of the setting.

Consultants who make careful assessments of settings discover times when tactics are more or less useful, whether or not
they are prescribed by consultation models and regardless of
their congruence with the consultant's own competence. Kelly's
dictum—that those working in the community should be able to
do at least one thing well—does not mean that they should do
that one thing in every situation. They must avoid the infamous
law of the instrument: Give a small child a hammer, and everything needs bashing. Kelly himself (1971, p. 899) qualified his
suggestion about skills: The consultant "seeks out the setting
where his competence can be displayed and works hard to learn
new ones."

Increasing Client Competence

Another important mode of nonstructural consultation
involves increasing the client's competence and adaptability.
Usually clients occupy social roles that have a specific impact
on the lives of others. When the consultant acts as a resource to
help clients such as teachers or police officers develop new
skills, one can expect a radiating effect on others in the client's
sphere of activity.

This approach to consultation is well illustrated by the
work of Chris Keys and his colleagues, who develop the interpersonal competence of those working in the criminal justice
system. Their method is marked by precise interventions with
clear objectives and by the use of sound research designs to
measure outcomes. In one such project, Fuehrer and Keys
(1978) sought to help deputy sheriffs working in courtrooms to
change their role identity.

In recent years there have been changes in the role requirements of those in the criminal justice system. Citizens have
become increasingly vocal in demanding that police treat them
more humanely and with more interpersonal skill. Fuehrer and
Keys (p. 2) point out, however, that the role of those in law enforcement has not changed to keep up with the new requirements: "Often, police have continued to emphasize action, viril-
ity, and toughness, not interpersonal effectiveness." There is a
component of machismo in the role identity of officers in the

criminal justice system that prevents effective work with the public.

In the courtrooms of Cook County, Illinois, deputy sheriffs have the task of maintaining order and supervising prisoners and jurors. They must be able to communicate effectively with spectators, witnesses, lawyers, and defendants. Pretesting identified three important components of the role identity of deputy sheriffs: evaluation, potency, and machismo.

Evaluation reflected the deputy's concern with presenting a positive public image and included such items as honesty, intelligence, and fairness. Potency expressed the deputy's need to be self-confident. Initiative and leadership were valued. The potent deputy sheriff would be able to take decisive action in a crisis. The third factor, machismo, reflected the emphasis on masculine toughness. It included such items as aggressiveness and dominance; emotion and flexibility were negatively weighted. The macho deputy would regard expression of feeling and signs of flexibility as indications of weakness. It was this machismo that was most out of phase with the emerging interpersonal requirements of the job of deputy sheriff.

The consultants developed a two-day interpersonal skills training program for deputy sheriffs. They specified the skills that might be particularly useful for deputies—including style of responding, basic sending and listening techniques, methods for giving feedback, and teamwork. Groups of eight to twenty-five people participated in small-group exercises, discussions, and role-playing sessions.

The program was intended to modify the machismo component of the deputies' role identity by increasing their awareness of the interpersonal aspects of the job. During training they were told that flexibility is important in managing a courtroom and that to be effective they would have to respond in accord with the situation. They were encouraged to recognize their own emotions and those of others. Emotions were presented as powerful and legitimate fac-

tors affecting the outcome of many courtroom interactions. The deputies learned that if they were to respond appropriately to emotional situations, they
would have to be less aggressive and dominant and
give more attention to the needs of others.

The laboratory training method provided many
opportunities for the deputies to practice new skills
in a low-risk context. The consultants used role-playing situations that simulated actual courtroom experiences. At each opportunity, deputies were encouraged
to discuss on-the-job applications of the techniques
they were learning.

The consultants pretested and posttested the
deputies, asking them to describe themselves in their
jobs, to describe the average deputy, and to describe
the ideal deputy. Some of the deputies were given
only a posttest to control for effects of pretesting;
there was no difference between the posttest scores
of those who received the pretest and those who did
not. The workshop did not affect evaluation or potency factors, but as intended it produced a change in
the machismo factor. After the workshop, participants saw the average deputy as having the same machismo, but they rated themselves and the ideal deputy significantly lower on this factor.

The project described by Fuehrer and Keys (1978) was
aimed at a cognitive factor that impeded effective job performance. The way people think about themselves and their role
can lock them into maladaptive behavior patterns. Deputy
sheriffs saw their ideals as well as themselves as highly macho.
This view of role identity could be expected to interfere with
the deputies' ability to understand and deal with emotional factors in the courtroom. Fuehrer and Keys showed that even a
short workshop can bring about significant changes in the perception of role identity.

The last three cases to be discussed in this chapter all involve consultation that was undertaken with teachers in order
to increase their competence in dealing with children. Problems
of outcome measurement are noted in all three. One of the ma-

jor measurement difficulties is the need to show that consultation with teachers has had an effect on their students. A model
of consultation which suggests that interventions will have a rippling effect, like pebbles tossed into a pool, ought to demonstrate that someone other than the teachers has been affected.

The complexity of measuring such outcomes is illustrated
in a report of consultation by Schmuck (1968). In projects carried out in Philadelphia and Detroit schools, the consultants attempted to help teachers work more effectively with group processes in the classroom. The projects were guided by the notions
that teachers influence group process, that improved group process provides a more supportive learning climate encouraging
more diffuse patterns of friendship and influence, and that diffuse friendship patterns should increase self-esteem of students
with beneficial consequences for learning.

In one project, consultants held regular discussions with
teachers aimed at increasing their competence in dealing with
the social and emotional aspects of the classroom. The discussion groups tended to move through phases—first blaming problems on external forces, then looking to the consultants to solve
problems, and finally relying on one another in mutual problem
solving. Several techniques were used to evaluate the intervention. The consultants kept notes on the groups, and these suggested that positive change had indeed occurred. Teachers were
also positive in their evaluation of the experience. But when students of these teachers were compared with students of teachers
who were in a control group, expected differences were not
found. The consultants concluded that behavior changes reported
by the teachers were apparently short-lived and that positive reports were motivated by a desire to please the consultants.

Schmuck reported more success on the next try. He hy-
pothesized that teachers will be more effective in dealing with
classroom groups if they have had some sensitivity training.

Teachers were placed in three groups, receiving
information and sensitivity training, information
alone, and a no-treatment control.
The sensitivity training included six-hour labo-

ratory experiences daily for four weeks in the summer. T-groups were supplemented with theory presentations and skill exercises. Discussions centered on the classroom as a human relations setting. All participants developed at least one practice exercise that they intended to use with their students, and at the end of the laboratory they made specific plans for implementing these techniques.

When school began, teachers who received sensitivity training continued to meet twice a month until December. During the fall, teachers in the no-training group received the same information as the others, including relevant research findings, diagnostic techniques, and group exercises that might be employed in the classroom.

In their assessment of outcome, the consultants found that those who received sensitivity training had stronger group identity, communicated more frequently with one another to discuss teaching issues, and visited socially more often. Students of the teachers who received sensitivity training were found to help one another more often and to show a more diffuse friendship pattern than students of teachers in the other two groups.

Schmuck (1968) points out that the apparent changes teachers report in their behavior do not guarantee changes in the classroom. A model that predicts a rippling effect should include some measure that assesses whether the intervention had an impact on those affected by the people with whom the consultants work directly.

In another attempt to bring change to classrooms through consultation with teachers, Rogeness and colleagues (1977) found many barriers to good outcome measurements. These consultants worked with a different psychological model than that outlined in the case just reported. Instead of a human relations emphasis, Rogeness and his colleagues took a behavioral approach. But in terms of intervention strategy, both efforts were guided by the belief that intervention with teachers would radiate to practices in the classroom.

An epidemic of negative behavior in classrooms prompted the principal of an elementary school in the inner city to seek consultation. A team including two psychologists and a psychiatrist set up a program to help teachers get better control of classroom behavior. Consultants met with teachers in groups to discuss behavioral techniques; then teachers met with children in their classes and helped them identify the behavior that interfered with learning. It was expected that this procedure would produce more appropriate behavior and result in achievement gains. Teachers who received the intervention were to be compared with a control group to measure the effectiveness of the intervention.

The program was structured so that it would require only a few hours a week of consultant time. In the first phase, each consultant was to meet with a group of teachers. Behavior that inhibited learning was to be specified. Teachers were to be told about the conditions that reinforced desirable and undesirable behavior.

In the second phase, teachers were to train their own students to be aware of behavior that promotes or inhibits learning. Discussion groups led by teachers in their own classes would be modeled after those in which the teachers had participated. In the third phase, teachers were to work with children to help them change behavior. Teachers would model appropriate behavior, encourage the class to praise children who behaved appropriately, and hold regular meetings with students to assess the progress of the class toward its behavioral objectives.

This ambitious program ran afoul of the realities of life in the school. Teachers were unwilling to talk about the general issue of behavior in the classroom; instead they were determined to tell anecdotes about particular children. They expected the consultants, as mental health experts, to produce solutions to these individual problems. Moreover, one group tried to gain the consultants' support for its complaints about the principal.

To save the program from almost immediate extinction, the consultants decided to make themselves individually available to all the teachers in the intervention group. By bringing specific problems to these sessions, teachers could take pressure off the group sessions. Instead of a few hours a week, the consultants were required at the school every day, but at least they were able to get the group sessions focused on classroom behavior as originally intended. Phase I was completed.

The next two phases, where the teachers were to work with their own classes, were carried out only sporadically and inconsistently. The project was also hampered by a teacher's strike, which created bitter divisions among teachers, including those in the discussion groups. Trust and open communication, which had always been problematic, were devastated by the strike. Despite all these difficulties, the consultants kept the project going through a second year.

Various sorts of evaluation data were gathered on classrooms, including a behavioral problem checklist, measures of students' anxiety and impulse control, and a locus of control interview. The validity of the results was compromised by a host of problems. In the first year, half the teachers volunteered for the program, leaving the remainder as a control group. This raised the possibility that experimental and control groups were different. Although the principal rated teachers in each group as about equal in ability, the consultants could not control for the possibility that unknown factors causing teachers to volunteer would be responsible for differences between the groups later. In some ways the experimental and control groups were demonstrably different. Since no eighth-grade teacher volunteered for the program, there were eighth-grade classrooms in the control group but not in the treatment group. Since both regular sixth-grade teachers volunteered, no regular sixth-grade classroom was included in the control group. Control and intervention classes in first through fourth grades were not equivalent; they were formed according to ability, and teachers with the most able students volunteered for the program.

Another threat to the experimental design was the shifting of students during the program. Some upper-level classrooms had as much as a 30 percent turnover. After pretesting, one fourth-grade classroom was closed with consequent reorganization of upper grades. Some students in the lower grades too were moved during the program, meaning that a number of children at various grade levels were supposed to be in the control group but were actually in the intervention classrooms and vice versa.

In the second year of the program, almost the entire faculty participated. This response indicated the acceptance of the program by school faculty and was consistent with the consultants' view that interventions should affect as many people as possible. Unfortunately, the lack of a control group made it impossible to rule out factors other than the intervention that might have occurred during the school year and affected pretest–posttest differences.

With understandable caution, the consultants reported their findings. In the first year there was some evidence that the intervention-group students were doing better than students of control-group teachers on measures of anxiety and impulse control and on the behavioral checklist. During the second year, with no control group, the consultants looked at changes from fall to spring. They saw no improvement that could be attributed to the program.

In reviewing their difficult consultation effort, the consultants concluded that for their model to have worked, the situation would have required all of the following: a good working relationship between principal and teachers; a positive relationship among teachers; a feeling of mutual trust and cooperation among the faculty; open communication among faculty members; the teachers' belief that they had control over what happened in their classrooms and in the school as a whole; the teachers' ability to define problems and behavior significantly related to the general program; their ability to hold classroom discussions with pupils; their ability to talk with children in a way that promoted undefensive communication and increased understanding; their ability to see the value of the overall project and desire to try out the procedures; and, finally, the ability of staff members in the school to develop a relationship of trust with the consultants. The consultants noted that few elementary school teachers could be expected to have most of these qualities.

Reviewing such a case, we might judge the consultants as naive to have expected their intervention to work when it required such an ideal set of preconditions. But what seems obvious in looking back over a completed effort is much less clear at the planning stage. Often consultants do not realize all the preconditions that are necessary for an intervention to succeed. If they do, they still may misread the situation and assume that each precondition is more likely than reality will dictate. Finally, when a plan has a number of steps or conditions, and when each is necessary for success, the consultant may be reasonably accurate in assessing the likelihood of the separate components yet overestimate the probability that the whole plan will succeed. Tversky and Kahneman (1974) have called this the tendency to overestimate the probability of conjunctive events. In the prosaic language of Murphy's Law: If something can go wrong, it will.

Consider the list of preconditions recorded in hindsight by the consultants in this case. Suppose that a consultant actually put rough probability values on each precondition in advance. As an optimist, the consultant might assume that the probability of each is 90 percent (with the exception of the likelihood that the principal's relationship with teachers is good, which might be rated at 50-50). What is the probability that all these preconditions will exist and hence that the project will have a chance of success—even with the best efforts of the consultant? Few would assume that the whole plan has a 90 percent chance, since that ignores the precondition that was rated at 50-50. Recalling that *all* preconditions must exist for

success, the consultant might conclude that a chain is no stronger than its weakest link and decide there is only a 50 percent
chance that the plan will work. But even this is considerably
overoptimistic; with the probabilities outlined, the plan has
only one chance in five. Chains of this sort are much weaker
than their weakest links!

When the probabilities are set forth as clearly as they are
in our illustration, the answer may seem obvious. But in the
planning stage, or in the midst of a program of action, consultants may fall easily into the presumption that when each part
of a plan is likely to succeed, the plan itself should succeed.
This source of cognitive bias is compounded by the fact that all
the preconditions needed for success are seldom apparent in advance, and some steps that do not seem essential at the time are
found to be so in retrospect.

The case described by Rogeness and his colleagues shows
how difficult it is to implement well-designed outcome research
in a natural setting. First these consultants were plagued with
a nonequivalent control group; then they had no control group
at all. Such problems do not stem from lack of research knowledge. Rogeness and his team knew what was required if they
were to make confident conclusions, but reality conspired
against their design. Emory Cowen, one of the preeminent researchers in the field of community psychology, has testified to
the many problems in collecting valid data while intervening in
natural settings. Cowen, Lorion, and Dorr (1974) have described
in hair-raising detail the "natural hazards" that researchers face
in the community—ranging from program instability to the pro-
action and anti-research stance of many community program
personnel.

Turning from the measurement problem back to the actual intervention described by Rogeness and his team, it is clear
that the teachers were initially resistant. Only half of those in
the school volunteered, compared with all the teachers in the
second year. Among the volunteers, it was difficult to proceed
with the first stage of group discussion. Teachers avoided the
issues that were to be the focus of the groups and instead told
anecdotes. Even when they had learned techniques to use in the

classroom, they were inconsistent in applying the program with their students.

Perhaps this resistance flowed from the manner in which the program was developed and presented to teachers. The consultants came to the school at the request of the principal, bringing a ready-made program to solve a problem that *he* had defined. It is not surprising that teachers, especially those in conflict with the principal, reacted to the consultants with suspicion. Instead of bringing in a package, the consultant might encourage teachers to generate their own ideas about what sort of help is needed. The disadvantage is the relatively long period that consultants must spend in the setting—observing, being available, marking time until teachers formulate their requirements. Entering with a package and getting right down to work may seem attractive when the consultant's time is considered; but as Rogeness and colleagues found, the economy of time can prove to be an illusion. In a case described by Broskowski (1973) the consultants committed themselves to considerable time at the outset because they put a high priority on specific requests being initiated by teachers.

> A consultation team was asked by the principal of a racially mixed junior high school in an urban area to come to the school to counsel what he called emotionally disturbed children. In discussion with the principal the consultants indicated they were unwilling to do this sort of direct service. Instead they agreed to assist teachers by providing projects for them. The only stipulation imposed by the consultants was that projects must be initiated by the teachers themselves.
>
> Two or three members of the team were available at the school every day. They found they had to provide the teachers with considerable reassurance, emphasizing by their behavior and their comments that they were not spies for the principal but were in the school only to help teachers. Consultants avoided giving immediate advice when teachers raised problems focused on individual children; they reminded

teachers they would work actively with those who had a personal interest in some project.

During the fifth week the consultants sponsored a one-day workshop for teachers who wished to attend. There were small-group discussions and exercises designed to improve communication and problem-solving skills and to develop a sense of group commitment. At the end of the workshop teachers presented their ideas for projects, and different members of the consultation team were assigned to coordinate them. Projects included development of teacher skills in small-group work, videotaped recording and playback of teaching styles, behavior modification, psychodrama, motivational development in a special reading class, and discussion groups on interracial issues. Some projects were carried out in a three-month period; some were put off until the following quarter. The teachers' response was positive.

At the end of the six months, the principal who had invited the team into the school was appointed assistant school superintendent in another part of the city. The new principal did not support his predecessor's policies, however, and the consultants had to withdraw from the school. Some teachers kept in touch with the consultants and reported that staff and student morale had dropped under the new regime. Disruptions were frequent; there were sharp racial tensions. Many teachers did not return to the school the following year. Those who did described the situation as "worse than ever."

This case prompts us to recognize the need for an appropriate structure to support interventions, even those interventions in which structural change is not the immediate objective. Despite a favorable start with teachers, the consultants found their project terminated by an authority structure beyond the focus of their program. The interplay of structure and process has been apparent in a number of the examples we have presented: Communication in medical teams was impeded by the divisive structure of professional affiliation; the consultant to a daycare center concluded his intervention by accepting a seat on the board of directors, since only that body could do the restructuring necessary to make further improvements.

Often consultants who intervene in the processes of a system appear to consider structure only as an afterthought. Broskowski, in the last case, described the events that brought about the sudden termination of the project as a secondary matter presented only "for the sake of historical completeness and to demonstrate the importance of top-level commitment to any change program" (p. 56). But it can be argued that structural issues have such an impact on consultation that they deserve a central place when it comes to formulating consultation theory.

Graziano (1969), in his description of five frustrating years spent trying to introduce an innovative program for treating autistic children, has illustrated the need for a broader perspective in the mental health field. His attempts were blocked again and again by what Graziano called the mental health power structure. This consisted chiefly of mental health professionals who had the power to review new projects for funding but were wedded to old ways of doing things, no matter how inefficient. Abetting this power structure were funding sources—particularly a United Agency operated by conservative businessmen who seemed to be as threatened by change as were the professionals themselves. The troubles he encountered while trying to get official sanction for the autism program convinced Graziano that it is hard to make real changes without confronting the power structure. He noted that the sixties, when he was writing, produced many innovative ideas about mental health. But while the conception of those ideas depended on creative humanitarian and scientific forces, implementation depended on professional and political power structures. He concluded that those who would be innovators cannot afford to divorce themselves from the operation of authority structures.

In the next chapter we present a number of examples where structural change was the focus of intervention. In some of these cases, the consultants were attempting to bring about structural change; in others, they helped systems adapt to structural change imposed from without; and in still others consultants took the role of external critics of imposed change, helping people cope with the threat of changes that could disrupt their lives.

5

Initiating
and Facilitating
Structural Change

Settings have structures, and those structures may be implicated in the problems that invite consultation. In this chapter we look first at consultants as initiators or facilitators of structural change and then examine the consultant's role in helping people react to change when it is imposed on the community from external power sources.

Whether the consultant attempts to alter structure depends on more than his or her diagnosis of the problem. The consultant's status in the setting and mandate from the client also play a part in the choice of intervention. To engage with the basic structure of a setting usually requires a good measure of client trust and high consultant status. But there are substructural changes that can be accomplished without threatening the system as a whole. In the following pages we present examples of both sorts of change—those involving the main structure and those involving some substructure in a setting.

Reviewing a broad range of consultation cases, we might conclude that the consultant's theoretical orientation determines strategy. Behavioral interventions are most often employed to alter individual behavior, the human relations approach is usually applied to group process, and systems theory leads its adherents to focus on structure. But if these emphases are common, they are by no means necessary. An understanding of systems theory also helps the consultant appreciate the systemic forces impinging on group process and shaping individual behavior. A human relations background can generate ideas about the structure required for effective group functioning. The implications of behaviorism for structural change in society are apparent in B. F. Skinner's *Walden Two* (1962) and *Beyond Freedom and Dignity* (1971).

Our initial case narrative in this chapter provides evidence for the flexibility of conceptual models. At first glance it might seem that the cognitive approach would not lead the consultant readily to structural intervention. After all, this approach is grounded in laboratory experiments in social cognition—experiments that focus on the peculiarities of individual perception, judgment, and information processing. But, as usual, the first glance is misleading.

We have suggested that members' perspectives and beliefs are important elements of community group life. Just as individuals hold assumptions that guide their behavior, so groups have shared assumptions that act as prisms to refract incoming information and give meaning to ongoing experience. There are several broad categories of assumptions expected in all groups. The first category involves a shared view of issues and events, what might be called *issue assumptions.* Members can be expected to have a common point of view about the importance of a particular social issue and a common opinion about the issue's negative or positive aspect. Those who hunt seals think the seal hunt is important and good; those who belong to Greenpeace believe that hunt is important but bad.

The second category includes assumptions about the causes of events that are important to the group. Group members will often subscribe to similar *cause assumptions*; the extent to which some members deviate may be a significant source of friction. Members of a rape crisis center may be united in the view that rape is an extreme expression of the norm of male dominance over women in society; those favoring freedom of choice on the abortion issue may blame the Catholic church for antiabortion laws; an organization favoring nuclear energy may see antinuclear agitation as communist-inspired.

The third category comprises *action assumptions,* opinions about what the group's task should be. Often there is dissension in community groups about the preferred role of the group in relation to significant social issues. Those working in corrections may disagree about whether the prisons are to protect society or to rehabilitate offenders. A rape crisis group may be divided over whether its task is to teach self-defense or to work for changes in basic male–female relationships in society. An organization of parents of learning-disabled children may be torn between focusing on self-help strategies or entering the political arena and demanding more government funds for special programs.

Groups can be classified according to the category of assumptions that holds members together. It is possible to imagine pure types: common fronts that take a position on a certain issue but disagree on cause and group task; ideological groups that have a shared view of the underlying causes of social dynamics but quarrel over which issues are significant and what should be done about them; protest groups with a common enemy and action strategy but differing views of the main issues and varying causal theories.

A community group divided over issue, cause, or action assumptions will have to manage internal dissension and cope with threats to efficient functioning. It might be expected that disagreement about issue assumptions would be most problematic. If members do not have a common view of significant issues, what unites them? A woman who does not regard rape as a crucial problem is not likely to last long as a member of a rape crisis center. Someone who makes a living from the seal hunt would be ill advised to send dues to Greenpeace.

Nevertheless, there are community groups where different issue assumptions are built into the charter. These may be multiple-issue organizations where some members see one issue as significant whereas other members have other concerns. Members who are united in their stand on one issue may disagree about another. If such a group is to survive, it must find a structure that will permit it to function. That task was undertaken in consultation to the Women's Health Education Network in Nova Scotia, a group with a diverse and scattered membership embracing such concerns as well women's clinics, nutrition, mental health, and uranium mining. In a case description prepared for this book, Patrick O'Neill, Myriam Marrache, Patricia Reddy, and Emily Shimizu report on their use of action research to lay the groundwork for a structural intervention. The focus of consultation was on the issue assumptions of members and on the need to find a structure that would express these assumptions and respond to the diverse perspectives within the membership.

It was not until the mid-1970s that the province of Nova Scotia, on Canada's eastern shore, took any significant notice of the women's liberation movement. When it did, recognition of women's issues tended to be expressed in very practical ways, such as organization of well women's clinics. Many women in the province live in rural areas where human services are sparse. One essential service, salient even to women who have never heard of feminism, is health care. There were many problems with health delivery in the province: It was centralized in the few urban centers; families in small towns had little choice of doctor; health care information was not readily available. Most doctors were male, and some were blatant about their disinterest in the health needs of women. One rural doctor, the only physician in his small town, told two women researchers that he did not give Pap tests "because they're dirty."

Women in several towns around the province organized well women's clinics between 1975 and 1979. The clinics did routine tests and concentrated heavily on providing information—for example, about self-examination for cancer symptoms. The organizers usually managed to find at least one physician who was willing to cooperate, although many doctors felt that these clinics were either unnecessary or even harmful. The alleged harm lay in the possible disruption of the revered doctor–patient relationship.

These clinics had implications that went considerably beyond merely augmenting an antiquated health care system. They provided a way for women who were concerned with feminist issues to reach one another. They also put these active people in touch with other women who had been unaware of such issues. And, perhaps of most significance, they helped make women aware that what once seemed to be personal health problems had social implications. The family doctor who dealt with marital problems by giving the wife Valium might be just one example of professional neglect of women. So might be the physician who failed to give out information on cancer self-examination. The doctor who discouraged breast feeding might be expressing a personal attitude toward women, not just making an objective assessment of one patient's needs.

In 1979 enough interest had been generated through several years of clinics and conferences to bring women together to form a new provincewide organization. Individual women and representatives of women's groups realized there was a need for regular communication, mutual support, and education. The Women's Health Education Network (WHEN) was born. Its overriding philosophy was to promote consumerism in the health field. This orientation included an emphasis on the consumers' responsibility for their own health, a need for wide dissemination of health information so that consumers could make informed choices, and an emphasis on prevention rather than on merely dealing with health problems once they had occurred.

WHEN consisted of a board of directors, an executive, and a general membership of more than three hundred. Since some of the members were actually organizations rather than individuals, the membership base was even larger. A major development early in WHEN's history was its success in getting a substantial three-year grant from the Canadian government. This money permitted the group to establish an office in a centrally located town and to hire two full-time employees: a coordinator, and a fieldworker.

The coordinator's task was to keep the books, look after the finances, edit a monthly newsletter, represent the group to governments, and develop areas of research. The fieldworker maintained liaison with community groups, set up a resource information center, prepared and delivered health education presentations, and put together an extensive list of potential resources offered by groups and individuals around the province.

Two issues, both relating to the group's ability to attract and hold members and to be responsive to members' concerns, brought the consultation team into the picture during WHEN's second year of operation. The first problem was the reality that when the three-year government grant expired, the organization might well have to continue without paid staff members. Hence there was an urgent need to find an organizational structure that would be self-sustaining without the maintenance functions provided by the coordinator and the fieldworker. An important objective was to determine how WHEN should organize itself so that its network of diverse members would not fall apart.

The second issue, related to the first, was the need to build a structure that would satisfy a membership that had diverse assumptions about *which* health problems were significant. Under the general heading of health issues affecting women there were many different topics. One member might be interested in mental health; another might be concerned about the problems of proposed uranium mining. One might be concerned about nutrition while another was more interested in the topic of aging. The problem was even more complicated, in fact, since one could not presume that all WHEN's members would take the same side on the issues that did interest them. Because WHEN's constituency included all the women in the province, whether members or not, there was further opportunity for differences of opinion. Some women favored liberal abortion laws, for instance, but others opposed them. For one woman the health issue posed by uranium mining was pollution of the environment; but for another, whose unemployed husband might expect to get a job with the mining project, the issue would be one of nutrition—putting food on the family table. How was WHEN to maintain its members' commitment and increase its ties to its constituency in the face of such differences of opinion?

The major task of the consultation team was to employ an action research model to determine the distribution of members' assumptions about important issues. Earlier WHEN staff had made a survey with an open-ended question about WHEN's priorities. The staff was perplexed to find there were almost as many answers as respondents. The consultants were invited to make a more systematic survey.

The first step was to analyze responses from the earlier questionnaire so that apparently different answers could be grouped under a smaller number of headings. The consultants took about seventy answers and found that they were able to place them in thirteen broad categories ranging from environmental issues to nutrition. A questionnaire was made up containing the thirteen categories along with several examples for each. (Environmental issues, for instance, included the examples of uranium mining, nuclear energy, chemical sprays, and fluoridation.) The questionnaire was then sent to all the members, who were asked to respond twice to each category. They were asked to identify the issues they thought were actual priorities of WHEN and those that should be priorities of the organization.

More than one third of those who received the questionnaire provided data. The results gave the organization new insights into the concerns of members and the way that members perceived WHEN. The top priority for members was mental health followed by aging processes and physical and sexual abuse. Members perceived the organization to be most interested in maternal and infant health, followed by nutrition and gynecology.

Data provided by the consultants enabled those guiding WHEN to see where the organization was on or off track in the eyes of members. There was congruence on several topics. Members saw sex education as relatively important and thought WHEN was concerned with the issue. Members had little interest in intoxicants and thought their organization shared this lack of emphasis. But more important were those issues where members believed their own interests were not being shared by WHEN and vice versa. For instance, most members thought WHEN was relatively uninterested in mental health and aging processes, two priorities for the membership. In contrast, members expressed little concern over environmental issues, although they thought this topic took up much energy in the organization.

One advantage of the assessment technique developed by the consultants was that it permitted members to indicate issues that were priorities for them but should *not* be for WHEN. Most members did not give such responses, but a few members felt that the group as a whole had a different stand on an issue than they did themselves. Because it was a broad-based organization, WHEN included many people who agreed with the majority on some issues but disagreed on others. A women might join WHEN because she supported well women's clinics, but she might disagree on what she perceived as a prochoice stand on abortion. She might want information on nutrition but be opposed to sex education.

One matter of considerable interest was whether members would think WHEN was too broad-based. Perhaps the membership actually consisted of people who cared about only one or two issues, and WHEN got its multi-issue nature from its diverse membership and not because individual members were themselves diverse in their concerns. If that were the case, the organization could expect to become fragmented as different groups in the membership sought to capture WHEN for their own pet concern. This supposition was not borne out by the data. In fact, members checked many more items in describing their own priorities than they did when describing the perceived priorities of the organization. The consultants were surprised to find that 82 percent of the respondents listed more issues as their own priorities than they felt were active priorities of the organization. This suggested that WHEN's future lay in being even more diverse in its emphases or in communicating more effectively with members to convey the multi-issue nature of its work.

This finding had an important consequence for the group's structure. Acting on the earlier notion that individual members might have fewer concerns than did the organization, the staff had begun planning to develop single-issue committees throughout the membership. Those who were particularly interested in maternal and infant care would be attached to a committee devoted to that topic, people concerned about environmental issues could work on a committee with that focus, and so on. A preliminary step had been taken before the consultants began their work. At the annual conference, the staff had invited members to sign up for single-issue committees. They were surprised when only a handful did so. Various interpretations were advanced: Perhaps the members had no time for the involvement required of a committee; perhaps they felt they did not have the skills to take such an active role. The data provided by the consultants, however, suggested a different interpretation: Members were in fact fairly broad in their interests and probably resisted attempts to make them focus on only one concern. In pursuing the single-issue structure, WHEN had been flirting with the danger of fragmenting the group. The consultants suggested different organizational strategies, such as meetings organized geographically rather than in accord with any specific priority. This arrangement permitted local members to set their own agenda, but with flexibility to permit members to travel to different meetings if meeting topics suited their own priorities. Such a structure put a premium on developing a sense of community in the organization while allowing member involvement in a broad range of issues.

The consultants also sent the questionnaire to about seventy people who had failed to renew their memberships. As expected, the discrepancy between their own priorities and those of WHEN was greater than for renewing members.

Apart from its effect on the future structure of the organization, the research project had side effects on the immediate involvement of members. Usually communication flowed from directors and staff to members. For their membership fee, members received information of various sorts in various ways. But the members themselves had little opportunity to participate actively in WHEN's affairs. WHEN was always concerned to find possibilities for member involvement. When the group took a stand against extra billing by physicians, it gave its members practical advice on how to support this stand. In the province's program of socialized medicine, doctors are paid through a general insurance scheme financed by tax money. But physicians, unhappy with the amount they were paid for their services, adopted a general practice of charging patients an extra dollar or two for each office visit. WHEN advised members to refuse to pay the surcharge. This provided an avenue for members to express their commitment to the group's goals through their own action. But it was difficult for many members, because it meant a confrontation with their family doctor. Often women looked up to their doctor and found it hard to take the stand recommended by the organization. The survey gave them an opportunity to be active at little cost in terms of time and little expertise.

In any broad-based organization there is a danger that those who are prepared to give a good deal of time, and who have confidence in their own skills, will capture the group's direction from the less involved general membership. Members who thought this was happening in WHEN, perhaps in their assess-

ment of topics covered in the newsletter and at conferences, might have felt powerless to exert influence.
Their frustration would be expressed in continued inactivity, gradual disenchantment, and then in failure
to renew membership. The survey provided a means
for members to influence the policy and structure of
the organization. Their concerns, and their perception
of the group's direction, were taken seriously by
WHEN. The consultants, acting in concert with WHEN
staff, were able to communicate to members that
their input had influenced the direction of the group.

Community groups are founded on issue assumptions;
members share certain perceptions about which social issues
are important. Sometimes the fundamental assumption is very
broad and permits considerable variation in selection of group
priorities, as in the organization described by O'Neill, Marrache, Reddy, and Shimizu. Women united by an interest in
health issues might differ in their views of alcoholism, uranium
mining, nutrition, and aging.

There are both strengths and weaknesses in groups with
heterogeneous membership. Miller (1978) in his living systems
theory points out that the more complex the system, the better it can adjust to environmental stress. This ability may give
the group survival value if it can coordinate its internal processes. In Miller's view, a system with heterogeneous components tends toward segregation of functions and hence in-
creases the probability of conflict. Multiple objectives, with the
lack of a clear priority, also threaten the system with conflict.
Such organizations may have to use more and more of their
processes to resolve internal conflict rather than advancing the
group's goal.

Gamson (1975) defined a multiple-issue group as one
that gives programmatic attention to distinct subgoals in different institutional spheres. There are several reasons to think that
groups with a variety of goals should have an advantage. "First,
only a group that has survived for a little while can be expected
to begin the process of differentiating action programs in different areas" (p. 45). Thus the fact that a group has multiple con-

cerns ought to be a sign that it has some survival value. "Second, with many hooks in the water, it seems that one would be more likely to catch a fish or two" (p. 45). In the literature on community organizing there is a clear preference for groups having a variety of goals. Alinsky (1971) recommends that organizations be based on many issues. "A single issue is a fatal straitjacket that will stifle the life of an organization" (p. 120).

One of the major advantages of a multiple-issue group is the possibility of attracting a broad membership. In Alinsky's view, multiple issues draw in the many potential members essential to the building of a broad, mass-based organization. "Each person has a hierarchy of desires or values; he may be sympathetic to your single issue but not concerned enough about that particular one to work for it and fight for it. Many issues mean many members" (1971, p. 120). The broader and more diverse the membership, the more networks there will be connected to the focal group. In times of crisis, or when the group needs to mount a campaign with a show of general support, it can be essential to have links to a wide variety of other organizations. A diverse membership can provide these links.

A vivid example of this utility of diverse membership is provided by an event in the history of WHEN, the multiple-issue group described by O'Neill, Marrache, Reddy, and Shimizu. In late autumn of 1981, the Canadian government was racing toward the finish line in its efforts to have the Canadian constitution repatriated from Britain. A key issue dividing the federal government from the provincial governments was the federal government's insistence on the inclusion of a "charter of rights" in the constitution. In a dramatic breakthrough, a compromise was reached between the federal government and nine of the ten provincial governments.

When the package was made public, only days before it was to be sent to Britain for ratification, Canadian women's groups were shocked to find that one feature of the compromise was the watering down of equality of women in the rights charter. Through contacts in Ottawa, WHEN discovered that the two provinces insisting on this modification were Saskatchewan and Nova Scotia. In Saskatchewan, the left-leaning government was concerned that an equality clause would jeopardize its affirmative action programs, a concern that could be allayed. That left Nova Scotia, the home province of WHEN. The group had little time in which to work. The federal government had put its package before parliament, and there was to be only a short debate before the matter was sent to Britain.

The group mobilized in a single day. It learned that the premier of the province was out of the country but the cabinet had a meeting scheduled for that afternoon. All morning, WHEN contacted its members. Many of these belonged to other women's organizations, and they contacted these networks. Influence spread in ripples across the province. Each person was given the telephone number of the premier's office, which was located only a few feet from the room where the cabinet met. Calls streamed in from all around the province, representing opinion from a wide variety of organizations. The cabinet meeting apparently was interrupted several times. At last, in desperation, a long-distance telephone call went out to the premier from his colleagues. By the end of the day, he had authorized a telegram to the federal government indicating that Nova Scotia would not object to the inclusion of women's rights in the constitution. The package was changed, and equality between the sexes was included in its charter of rights.

This is a dramatic illustration of the power available to a group with a diverse membership. But it must be set against the difficulties such groups face precisely because of the need to coordinate a broad constituency. In a survey of American groups that challenged the status quo from 1800 to 1945, Gamson (1975) did not find that multiple-issue groups were particularly successful. But five of the nine groups he included in the multiple-issue category were minor political parties, which may have special problems in a country with a strong two-party tradition.

An aim of a multiple-issue group is to show a constituency that a variety of social problems really has a common thread. Health issues served that function for WHEN. One of the difficulties that must be overcome by a women's movement is the fact that women of different social classes and different ethnic backgrounds may seem to have more elements dividing them than uniting them. To bring women together in common cause, it is necessary to find issues that cut across distinctions created by economics and geography. Health is one unifying issue. Regardless of social stratum, women have health concerns that differ from those of men. Moreover, there is a tradition that the woman of the household is responsible for its health needs. She is the one who feels the forehead, takes the temperature, and makes the doctor's appointment. A "health education network" provided a peg on which to hang the fabric of women's organization.

The very breadth of such a group guarantees that there will be a variety of assumptions about which problems are most important. The challenge in working with the group is to find an appropriate structure that will use the distribution of assumptions within the group to maximum advantage. As the WHEN case suggests, a cognitive approach to group structure requires an assessment of how assumptions are distributed in the group. The assessment process may provide important information for the way the group shapes itself. In this illustration, the assessment suggested that assumptions about issues were distributed so that a structure based on single-issue committees would probably be counterproductive.

But as O'Neill and his colleagues indicate, the assessment process performed another function quite aside from giving information to WHEN leaders. It also offered an opportunity for members to exert influence over the organization's direction. Although WHEN was not a group marked by great discontent at the time of the intervention, the diversity of members, and their different priorities, posed a constant problem for internal coordination. Hirschman (1970) has analyzed situations in which discontented members will attempt to change the direction of an organization versus situations in which they will simply leave. He calls these the "voice" and "exit" options. Taking the voice option always involves an evaluation of the chances of getting the organization back on what the member considers to be the right track; and it also involves judging whether other options are more viable. A member may stick with a group, even though frustrated by it, if there are no comparable groups to join. Or the member may remain if he or she feels there is a reasonable chance that the group can be redirected.

The question for members may be: Are there avenues to exert influence in the organization? Hirschman points out that exit from a group requires nothing more than an either/or decision, but voicing one's discontent is an art that is constantly evolving in new directions. To make members' voices heard may require new channels of communication. The action research project described in the WHEN case probably had the side benefit of providing such a channel. In Hirschman's words, choice of the voice rather than exit option may depend on "the invention of such institutions and mechanisms as can communicate complaints cheaply and effectively" (p. 43).

Fragmentation of Services

Consultation in the preceding case was aimed at finding an organizational structure that would tolerate as much diversity of opinion as possible while sustaining group identification. This is a delicate balance; the danger of fragmentation is constant. Often the consultant's task is to work with systems that are in the process of fragmenting or have already fragmented. In the human service field, fragmentation can mean duplication of effort or failure to provide a coordinated approach. The result can be harmful to the clients on whose behalf the services were initiated.

McCann-Baker (1978) has described her consultation to a network of services for the intellectually handicapped, a network that had become seriously fragmented. Proposals for integration of various components into a functional service delivery system had foundered on the shoals of misunderstanding and acrimony. Rather than work at the level of "personality conflict," although this was the prevailing problem definition, the consultant decided to aim her intervention at the system itself. In this previously unpublished case, we recount her experiences in facilitating the development of a new structure for service delivery.

In a rural district, major vehicles for service to the intellectually handicapped consisted of two residences and three workshops. The residences were located in neighboring towns, and in theory they served somewhat different populations. The group home was intended as a residence for adults who functioned well enough to spend the full working day at the most effective and commercially viable of the three workshops. The developmental home served clients who were at a lower level of functioning. They needed care and supervision throughout the day, although some were able to attend their own small workshop for some periods.

Different and autonomous boards of directors operated each of the two residences and the largest workshop. While the Association for the Intellectually Handicapped had nominal authority to oversee service delivery, it was a weak organization that had little say over the way the different facilities operated.

There were many examples to indicate that the lack of cohesion in this system was impairing potential services that might be offered. Lip service was paid to the ideal of a natural progression of clients from the developmental home to the group home and then to full integration into the community. But the group home was uninterested in taking residents from the developmental home, even when the staff of the latter claimed that the functioning of its clients had significantly improved. The staff of the developmental home felt frustrated because a natural exit point for their residents was blocked, and they accused the group home of being unwilling to accept more difficult cases. On their side, officials of the group home believed the developmental home had made a number of errors in admitting particularly low-functioning individuals in order to keep the residence full and maintain the per-diem rate provided by government. Having made these supposed errors, the developmental home was believed to be trying to unload its problems by placing inappropriate cases in the other residence.

Another problem centered on the relationship between the largest workshop and the group home, a relationship that was strained even though both facilities served many of the same clients. The workshop provided training and some schooling for many higher-functioning handicapped people in the district, some of whom commuted from their parents' homes or foster parents' homes and some who came from the group home. Staff at the workshop felt that their facility was often treated as no more than a babysitting service by the group home; there was certainly little communication about treatment programs. Staff at the group home were suspicious of the treatment efforts made in the workshop, believing that the workshop should confine its activities to providing a daily work setting.

The consultant discovered that an ambitious plan for integration of all services in the district had been drawn up but never implemented. The plan would establish a community services board to oversee the residences and the workshops, providing a coordinated policy for all. It would work with district medical services, social agencies, and the school board on all issues affecting people with intellectual handicaps.

One problem with the integration plan was its source: It had been drawn up by the president of the developmental home. He was a dedicated man with a sincere desire to maximize services to the intellectually handicapped. He was also opinionated and expressed his views in a forceful way that alienated many officials and staff members in other facilities and made them suspect his motives.

The president of the developmental home proceeded in a fashion that suited his style. He failed to mend fences with other facilities. Instead he attempted to get the weak Association for the Intellectually Handicapped to take control, dissolve the various boards, and impose the integration program. Under pressure from all sides, the president of the Association for the Intellectually Handicapped shelved the issue. When the consultant talked with him he expressed doubts that the association actually had the legal power to impose integration.

Meetings were occasionally called to do something about the situation, but relationships were so strained that these attempts merely increased tensions. The consultant attended one such meeting held in the absence of the man who initiated the plan for a community services board. The embattled Association for the Intellectually Handicapped took tentative steps to establish a "residences board" that would coordinate policies between the group home and the developmental home. Not only was this proposal much more limited, on paper, than full integration, but the consultant realized from the tone of the discussion that this move was an attempt by the association to appear to be doing something while maintaining the status quo.

A good deal of groundwork with individual officials would be needed if the various autonomous boards were to agree to genuine integration. The consultant decided that she was in a position to do some of this work, since she was not identified as an advocate for any position or as a staff member at any of the facilities.

Her approach was to interview members of the various boards and, while gaining information about present and future services, to kindle interest in the integration notion. The consultant asked questions: Do you foresee changes in the kind of services that might be needed in the next few years? Is there a need for a broader range of services? How might these services come into being? What changes will be needed in the way things are presently organized? Whenever the respondent hit on some problem that an integration scheme might solve, he or she was encouraged to expand on it. The consultant did not encourage respondents to talk about the difficulty of integrating services; instead she showed enthusiasm when discus-

sion centered on the advantages of integration. She
also summed up points made by the officials in a way
that highlighted this identification with the need for
integrating services, although not with any particular
integration plan.

The interviews took several weeks. They led up
to a meeting at which the proposed community services board was to be discussed. When the meeting
took place, the consultant was pleased with the positive tone that was set at the outset; she perceived a
new willingness on the part of officials that she had
interviewed to consider some kind of amalgamation.
Those at the meeting tentatively adopted eventual integration, including the community services board.
The much more limited residences board was to be
referred to a committee to consider how it might be
worked into the broader plan.

But at that point the developmental home president intruded forcefully into the proceedings. He
failed to acknowledge that for the first time there was
general acceptance of his long-range plan. Instead he
appeared to shift ground, focused on the residence
board, and demanded that it be implemented immediately rather than considered by a committee. The
meeting ended in considerable confusion.

The consultant realized that she now had an
opportunity to see the developmental home president
as others saw him. He had excellent ideas, but his
abrasive style kept them from being implemented.
This was an area that the consultant had neglected,
with potentially serious consequences. Following the
meeting she met with the developmental home president and had a full discussion with him about what
had happened. He explained that despite the apparent
willingness of various board members to accept his
long-range integration plan, he was convinced that
some changes were needed immediately. For that reason he had seized on the residence board as a possible
vehicle; he was perturbed that even this limited improvement might be delayed by a slow-moving committee. The consultant made it clear that she under-

stood his position. But she was frank about her perception of his style and the effect it was having on those whose agreement he needed. She was successful in helping him to prepare for future meetings, at which real progress was made toward developing comprehensive services for intellectually handicapped citizens of the district.

The case reported by McCann-Baker indicates the balance between structure and process in consultation. Essential structural reforms had been delayed because of what those involved had defined as a personality clash. The consultant decided to promote the new structure rather than to emphasize personality issues. But in so doing she ran the danger of cutting her perceptions off from those of participants in the controversy. If they focused on personality problems, she had to deal with the reasons for their focus. Attempting to redefine the problem would be only partly successful as long as genuine clashes of style continued to disrupt relationships.

The ecological principle of interdependence suggests that it is important to understand how different aspects of a system relate to one another. The way in which roles, persons, and policies are matched can facilitate or block needed changes. In this case the person associated with an integration plan kept it from being implemented. Further, this link probably kept other integration plans from getting serious consideration. The notion of integration was associated with an abrasive individual who, despite his good intentions, reacted to others with such dominance that his motives were suspect.

This case again turns our attention to the need to understand a setting's traditions. How did things come to be the way they are? A consultant who neglects this long view is in danger of seeing problems as products of irrationality and proposing simplistic solutions. The consultant who created a climate of acceptance—even enthusiasm—for a new structure was dealing with only part of the problem. The reason why no integration had taken place was not because no one had thought of it and not because there was no enthusiasm for it. The problem was *who* had thought of it and *who* was enthusiastic. Only when she tackled this aspect of the problem was the consultant able to facilitate change.

In the two examples just discussed, the consultation task involved working with the overall structure of an organization. In the case of WHEN, the client group was seeking a new mode of organization; in the example given by McCann-Baker, the consultant promoted the integration of fragmented services. There are also situations in which the consultant undertakes a structural intervention to change some part of a general system. We turn now to a pair of cases that led consultants to develop new structures within public schools. The challenge in these circumstances may be to fit the new component into the existing system. Often a system will exert pressure to reject a new component, like a body rejecting a transplanted organ.

When Cherniss, Trickett, D'Antonio, and Tracy (1982) were consulting to a public high school in New England, they found that many problems were not being handled by existing departments. They decided to help students develop a new structure to take up a range of issues in the school.

> An assistant superintendent initiated the request for consultation in the high school, explaining that the guidance department was ill equipped to deal with the many problems displayed by students. He was concerned that students were apathetic and absentee rates were high. Psychological services at the school were almost nonexistent—the school had no social worker or psychologist on even a part-time basis. The learning difficulties and behavior problems of 1,100 students had to be dealt with, if at all, by five guidance counselors; only one of these had even minimal training.
>
> In their initial assessment of the school, the consultants found it to be a loose and confusing place. The noise level in the building was high, and students could often be seen roaming the halls during class time. There was considerable ambiguity over roles and procedures for dealing with such student behavior as lateness.

The majority of students could be broken down into four groups: first there were the athletes, cheerleaders, and club kids who were socially aware and involved in the formal offerings of the school; radicals and flower children constituted a second group; the black students who made up 10 percent of the school population were a third group; fourth were the quiet poor whites.

The consultants decided to act on a suggestion from the district superintendent that the school might profit from having a student committee modeled on the School Effectiveness Committee of the local teachers' union. This committee consisted of a small group of teachers who gathered concerns and suggestions from their colleagues about current policies and proposed changes in the schools. The consultants agreed that if students were given an organized voice in such troublesome areas as discipline, their commitment to the school might increase.

The school already had a student council that might have been expected to fill such a role. For some years, however, the council's large membership, thirty students, had been selected in class elections that were essentially popularity contests. Members of the council were unrepresentative of the general student population and certainly not the groups that were disaffected and apathetic. The council's time was taken up with elections and planning social functions. Its influence in the school was waning.

The consultation task was to develop a new Student School Effectiveness Committee in such a way that it would not threaten and be blocked by the student council. The principal, who was new to his job, indicated that he would support such a committee only if the student council agreed with the innovation. The consultants recognized the merit of this approach. The student council constituted the most extensive, stable student organization in the school. Its members were known to most of the student body, and its visibility and influence would be essential to gain legitimacy for the new group.

The principal called a meeting of the student

council at which the consultants would put their proposal. They knew that no matter how tactfully they proceeded, council members could not help but feel that the new group encroached on their turf. Many of the issues with which an Effectiveness Committee might deal were nominally the business of the student council, even if the council did nothing about them. The consultants hoped that eventually the new committee and the old council might be synthesized to create a strong student voice in school affairs.

The consultants approached their meeting with the student council as advocates of the idea of a smaller Effectiveness Committee, but with no specific prescriptions about composition or day-to-day functioning of the proposed group. Council members were told that the intent was to give students a greater voice in school policy and to rekindle student interest in the school.

A majority of the student council members were either uninterested or skeptical. Some questioned the need for a new group—why not work with the council to make it function better? The consultants said the group could succeed only if it was diverse with respect to grade, sex, race, academic track, and interests. The consultants were vague in response to questions about the precise functions of the group, explaining that its role would be developed gradually. The general mandate would be to solicit and consider student proposals to improve the education and quality of life in the school.

The issue was again considered at the next meeting of the student council. A new point was raised: Several council members said because they did not have any major problems with their own education in the school and they knew of no students with such problems, it was hard for them to see a need for an Effectiveness Committee. This confirmed that the council members were unrepresentative and somewhat out of touch with many students, but it was also an issue that had to be negotiated successfully to gain the backing of the council.

When the consultants pointed to student apathy, absenteeism, and discipline, the council decided to hold a general meeting of the student body to see if there was, indeed, concern about these matters. Only fifty students appeared at the general meeting, and half of those were on the student council. Some students agreed that there was a lack of school spirit and pointed to the low attendance at that very meeting as evidence of apathy.

At the next session of the student council, one of the consultants met with the group in the absence of any other school officials. There was a dramatic change in position by the students. Now they launched into an emotional cataloguing of complaints: criticism of specific school personnel, courses, injustices in discipline, and the unstimulating atmosphere of the school.

Mobilizing these expressions of concern, the consultant obtained the council's endorsement of the new committee. A few members now actively supported the idea. The majority took the position that since there did appear to be genuine problems in the school, the new group probably would not hurt and might even help.

It was decided that the Effectiveness Committee would be composed of twelve members: six who volunteered from the council itself and six who would be representative of various other groups in the student body. The six from the council were each assigned to find one other student whose membership would diversify the committee. But when the twelve members had their first meeting, the consultant noted that the composition was all white. Working through the informal networks available to them, the council members had failed to recruit a single black member. This became the first point for discussion for the committee, since it was clearly diagnostic of the social organization of the school. The group decided to add two more members, and two black students were recruited.

It had taken three months from the inception

of the idea to the first meeting of the Effectiveness Committee. But the long preparation period had been well spent. It was important to meet the student council at its convenience so that it would not feel pressured, and eventually the committee was able to emerge from its potential rival.

Over the space of two years, two different consultants worked with the Effectiveness Committee and helped it to deal with a variety of issues important in the functioning of the school. These issues included inadequate and incompetent teaching, a restrictive dress code, the need for more modern-language courses, the ethnocentric character of the history courses, lack of institutional rewards for sensitive and competent teachers, a double standard of treatment for black and white students, excessive drug use, student apathy, and lack of community support for educational programs. The efforts of the committee to bring about changes in school policies were sometimes successful, sometimes not. But the work of the committee, and the visibility it gave to student involvement with these issues, helped to mobilize student interest throughout the school.

In its work the committee was constantly reminded of the need for new structures to mesh with those already in place. Often the efforts of the new group were resented by those who thought their territory was being invaded. Black students were dissatisfied with the black history course offered by the school, a course that focused on African and Asian history and excluded black people in America. When the Student School Effectiveness Committee raised the matter with the history department, some history teachers became hostile. They felt the student group was intruding in departmental business.

The achievements of the committee were threatening to other groups. One success concerned the dress code, which was dropped after the Effectiveness Committee made representations first to school administrators and then to the district school board. The favorable reaction to this change reawakened the dormant rivalry between the new group and the existing student council. At the beginning of the second year, when the student council had to decide whether to reconstitute the Effectiveness Committee, there was considerable opposition once again. The consultant had to remake the case for the committee and offer to work with the council itself to make it more effective. Despite considerable resentment, the council agreed that the committee could continue its work.

At the end of the second year, the consultant and the committee reviewed the history of this innovation. There had been successes and failures. Although the committee had fulfilled its aim of increasing student interest in the life of the school, relationships with other groups remained problematic. It was decided to continue the committee's existence indefinitely; a faculty adviser would replace the consultant.

In their own review of this case, Cherniss and colleagues (1982) emphasized the importance of relating a new structure to a host system. Intricate relationships must be established to link a new component, such as the Student School Effectiveness Committee, with existing subsystems. Without skillful negotiation, the new enterprise may be sabotaged by groups that are threatened by encroachment on their territory—not only subsystems that might be in direct competition with the new group, such as the student council, but various other subsystems such as history department teachers.

The ecological approach encourages consultants to focus on the way a system manages its resources. In the case described by Cherniss and his colleagues, the overriding purpose of the new committee was to enable the school to make better use of resources. In the existing situation, with an unrepresentative student council, viewpoints of students in various subgroups had no impact on the school's policies. The major achievement of the Student School Effectiveness Committee was to unlock these resources, making divergent views known. This had effects on poor teaching, narrow subject matter, and rigid ways of handling student behavior.

In a case described by Weinstein (1982) a new structure

was created in a middle school to bring more resources to bear on particularly challenging problems. These problems were posed by thorny home/school interactions concerning children who were having major difficulties in school. Weinstein believed a new team approach might permit more flexible handling of these cases. In contrast to the situation faced by Cherniss and his colleagues, she found little opposition to launching the new structure. But once the new approach was established, the consultant had to take care that it did not threaten the traditional approach to problems in the school.

A new middle school was established in a school district to provide a transitional stage between elementary and high school. Specialist teaching was introduced to children for the first time. The twelve teachers in this school were excited by the experiment, and in this climate of innovation the consultants found it easy to introduce a new approach to handling problems posed by difficult children.

In the past, teachers had been expected to fend for themselves. When the problem passed beyond their ability to deal with it, they were expected to move the issue along the chain of command for disciplinary action—first to the school principal and then to the office of the superintendent.

The concept of a team effort to deal with these problems was introduced. The team consisted of two consultants, the principal, guidance counselor, school nurse, and four teachers. Weekly meetings were held, and teachers were free to consult the committee about difficulties with specific children.

As the committee began to formulate ways of handling different problems, the consultants were forcefully reminded that the team they had created with so little difficulty had to be seen in the context of a broader system with its own rules and procedures. Innovations by the team often ran afoul of established regulations.

Angelina, a thirteen-year-old who had recently moved into the district, was a source of exasperation for her teachers. With all but two teachers she broke the rules and challenged classroom authority. She was constantly being sent to the principal for discipline. Angelina was frequently absent from school; it seemed clear that suspensions were not productive since she preferred to be out of school in any event.

In their discussion of the case, team members made various suggestions that seemed to run counter to school district norms. Eventually the guidance counselor made three visits to try to improve the situation, even though such visits were not allowed except by a school social worker. This was the rule even though the school did not, in fact, *have* a social worker.

As a result of the illegitimate home visits, the team was able to gain enough information to put together a program for Angelina. This included a session each morning with the guidance counselor, attendance at school for just half of each day, having the girl go only to the two classes where she had some rapport with the teachers, and daily tutoring by the principal himself in the subjects she was missing. Under this program, real progress was evident. The principal enjoyed his "front line" involvement. Angelina was able to come to school more often and with fewer problems.

But just as the program began to show results, the team learned that the superintendent of schools, who had an office in the same building, was planning to call in Angelina's mother to announce the girl's dismissal from the school system. Dismissal would lead to her being placed in a residential facility. The principal went to the superintendent, reviewed the progress that was being made, and got him to cancel the dismissal meeting.

Repercussions were not long in coming. The superintendent was annoyed that his own decision-making powers and the proper line of authority were being circumvented by a group of school staff. Shortly after his meeting with the principal, the superintendent directed the principal to "tighten up" procedures in the school. Things were "too loose," he said. He demonstrated his opinion dramatically one day when he confronted Angelina, who had come to school in a miniskirt. The team was placing a high priority on her attendance, even at the expense of some formal rules in the school. Nevertheless, the superintendent ordered her to go home and change clothes.

It was apparent that the team would have to achieve better liaison with the superintendent. He was invited to a team meeting to hear another case discussed. It was hoped that when he had a look at the workings of the group, he would have more empathy for its methods. The team took up the matter of Fred, a twelve-year-old who had not returned to school after Christmas vacation. Fred's mother had reported that he was no longer interested in school; subsequent attempts to contact her had failed. The principal reported that he had gone to Fred's home, found the boy in his bedroom, and forcefully brought him to school. At this point the superintendent intervened, noting that the principal had broken the law by going to the boy's home. Standard procedure was to call the police, who served as truant officers in the town. With that, the superintendent announced that he had another meeting to attend and walked out. The team, which had hoped to gain his understanding, now felt intimidated.

Despite lack of support from the superintendent, the team continued its high-risk operation. In the case of Fred, rather than involving the police, the team contacted as many family members as possible and explained the seriousness of the situation. Finally one family member, a son-in-law, commited himself to going to Fred's home each morning and bringing the boy to school. After five very difficult mornings, Fred again attended school on a regular basis. Similar innovations were introduced in other cases.

To keep the team going into the next school year, attempts were made to recruit other teachers to serve on it. These teachers, however, even though they often came to the committee for help, were unwilling to put themselves in such a vulnerable position. The committee continued its work with the same membership. During the second year one of the teachers on the team was named principal of another school. This afforded an opportunity to broaden the team and change its procedures so that it spanned both schools. With two principals as members, the team had a more solid position in relation to the superintendent. The role of the consultant became less important; she was able to withdraw and leave the innovation in place.

As therapists are taught to tread cautiously when interfering in the lives of individuals, so consultants learn to respect the integrity of the systems in which they would intervene. Such systems have established roles, traditions, and habitual ways of getting things done. The fact that things might be done better does not mean there is no reason for the way things are done now. In the case described by Weinstein (1982) it was clear that a new approach would be helpful in handling children with serious school problems. Introduction of a team was facilitated by the fact that it was part of a school that was itself experimental. Nevertheless, there were still established ways of doing things in the school district. There were rules, in some cases even laws, that were challenged by innovative approaches. The superintendent, who acted out the role of guardian of the district's traditional operating modes, resisted attempts to bring him over to the new approach. Even without his sympathy, it was possible to keep the committee functioning, to keep it innovative, and to extend its team concept to another school.

The four cases presented so far in this chapter have several elements in common: All involved structural change, whether the whole system or just part of it was the focus of change; in all four, moreover, the consultants were working with an existing system. There is also a special set of cases in which community workers become involved in starting new organizations from scratch. Several cases in this book touch on this activity—the founding of a residential youth center described in Chapter Two, for instance, and the organization of parents of learning-disabled children to be discussed in Chapter Seven. Although we have not entirely neglected the consultant-as-creator, we recognize that this is a specialized function with its own special literature. We cannot hope to do justice, here, to the intricacies involved when the consultant takes major responsibility for founding a new setting. We refer interested readers to Seymour Sarason's *The Creation of Settings and the Future Societies* (1972) for a thorough discussion of the topic.

Coping with Imposed Change

We have considered consultants as ambassadors of change. But consultants may find themselves in different relationships to structural change imposed on a community from beyond its boundaries. Sometimes these changes have unintended consequences that must be worked out. At other times, the consultant's task may be to give local people a loud, clear voice in changes that will affect them. In still other situations, the consultant may find that he or she ought to lead opposition to imposed change.

We begin our look at these aspects of consultation with a situation where structural change has already created difficulties for some people in the setting. The challenge for the consultant is not how to bring change about but, in the wake of change, to help those who have been displaced to find a significant role in the new structure. Willis (1979) found himself in this situation when he consulted with a prison in Ontario. There were pressures on the prison system from those who wanted more treatment and rehabilitation and less emphasis on punishment and security. This changing philosophy was translated into new institutional arrangements that gave more power to the staff members who were involved in rehabilitation programs.

Although the consultant could readily agree with the philosophy that brought about these changes in prisons, he found that not enough had been done to integrate the system members whose position had been undercut. While correctional officers welcomed the changes, there was one important group, the supervisors, who found themselves psychologically stranded.

Although he was not brought to the prison specifically to deal with the role problems of the supervisors, Willis perceived this to be a significant issue in the prison. Moreover, he found the clients willing to have him define his intervention so that he could deal with this problem.

> The medium-security correctional facility had a population of a hundred adult male offenders who were not classified as serious security risks. Three years before the consultant arrived, a new "treatment" emphasis had been inaugurated with the appointment of an innovative superintendent, a man with a degree in sociology and many years of experience in the field.

> The supervisors, who defined their roles in military terms and placed a heavy emphasis on security, were adrift. In the past they had run the institution. From their office in the front of the building, they controlled entrance and exit, assigned staff, scheduled shifts, and handled all major problems. Having no new role, the supervisors tried to continue as they had in the past. But now their concern for security, which once had been valued, lacked support from above and below. Complaints about the supervisors from the correctional officers, who were carrying forward the treatment programs, resulted in a stream of memos from the administration that stripped the supervisors of much of their power. They became more resentful and isolated. They tended to use one another as models and to continue their reliance on the old methods.

> The consultant listened to the supervisors' own definition of the situation without attempting to impose a solution. He told the supervisors that they were experienced and capable staff who had worked their way up through the ranks. Their isolation not only created tension but deprived the facility of the benefit of their considerable experience.

> The consultant held a series of meetings over several months with the objective of assisting the supervisors to redefine their function in the institution.

The consultant guided the discussion so that the group was helped to stay within the limits likely to be accepted by the administration.

The result was a set of role guidelines that were produced by the supervisors themselves and accepted by the superintendent. These guidelines helped to integrate the supervisors, with their traditional responsibility for security, into the new institutional style that emphasized rehabilitation.

In this example the consultant saw that the supervisors were not merely obstacles to the new prison approach; they actually constituted a resource that was not being tapped. His ability to explain this to the supervisors provided them with a sense of self-worth that had been damaged when their position was undercut. Using a discussion format that permitted the supervisors to develop their own ideas, the consultant was able to help them adapt to change and create new, productive roles.

The consultant is not always the agent of change, nor will he or she always accept the premise that societal forces demand complete adaptation from those affected. Instead the consultant may define the task as one of helping communities withstand pressure to change—helping them, that is, to retain integrity, individuality, and a measure of autonomy in the face of powerful forces from outside. Ritchie (in press) outlined this consulting function in his model of a rural community psychology. He used the Canadian situation, with its multicultural tradition, as his reference point. We have suggested that the consultant should not merely tolerate but should value diversity in settings. Ritchie argues, similarly, that professionals working with communities should support the preservation of cultural and linguistic identities. Ritchie notes that social scientists are most likely to be invited to contribute their skills when communities are in transition. In times of change, minorities are vulnerable. Ritchie observes that strong pressures to change typically conflict with the community's desire to remain distinct and to maintain established patterns. This conflict is usually accompanied by stress that threatens the psychological well-being of the community.

The pressures that disrupt a community may be economic. Matthews (1976) has reported on the plight of small rural communities in Newfoundland, settlements threatened by the government's policy of relocating the province's population in urban centers. When Newfoundland joined the Canadian confederation in 1949 it had about 1,500 rural communities, most with fewer than 300 residents. Many of these were isolated, and the cost of providing services to them was high.

The Newfoundland government adopted a policy of urbanization in which entire communities would be moved. Since assistance was provided only if *every* community member agreed to move, group pressure and intimidation were pervasive. Nevertheless, many communities refused to move. In 1965, a similar program was reintroduced with sponsorship from both the Newfoundland and Canadian federal governments. The goal was the evacuation of 600 communities and the relocation of 70,000 people in selected growth centers. Matthews points out that these programs put the rural communities in a dilemma: "While life in urbanized areas offered some attractions, those affected knew that the land and the sea could at least provide them and their families with the necessities of food, shelter, and clothing" (p. 2). Moving to new and larger centers would mean that most adult breadwinners would find themselves in the welfare lines.

Under these pressures, many people chose to relocate and communities were broken up. But the government policy fell far short of its target. In the first program, sponsored by the Newfoundland government, 7,500 people were moved. In the second program, under joint sponsorship, about 16,000 chose to relocate. Matthews' book *"There's No Better Place Than Here"* is a perceptive and detailed study of representative communities that resisted strong pressure from outside. His research itself constitutes an intervention on the side of tolerance for diversity in communities.

In the Newfoundland case, pressure on local communities was a direct result of government policy. It was a policy undertaken with little regard for the traditions and psychological value of the life-style of the people who were affected. Not all outside threats to local community life are intentional. An ethnic minority may have its linguistic and cultural traditions threatened by the dominant majority—particularly as improved communication and transportation make contact between the dominant and minority groups pervasive. The challenge to a social scientist may be to help the minority acquire the skills that will enable it to compete with the dominant group while maintaining valued traditions and supporting the survival of the minority culture.

There are cases too in which the consultant's task is to seek a stronger voice for local people in the broad policies that affect them. In Ritchie's model, the consultant's task is to develop active and informed participation in decision making among community residents. He observes that application of this principle may invite the perception that progress is being resisted; nevertheless, consultants have an obligation to promote informed participation.

This discussion of pressures for change in a community, whether exerted intentionally or unintentionally, has brought us to the third area of focus for the consultant. In Part Three we explore the relationships among groups in the wider community and between a client group and its host environment. We shall see the issue of response to change raised again in the contexts of community conflict and power relationships in the community. In the next chapter, for instance, we consider a case in which an urban area was helped to make a positive adaptation to pressures for an integrated school system. And in Chapter Seven a case is presented in which the principal challenge was finding an effective voice for citizens in a sweeping plan being developed for their city.

Part Three

~~~~~~

Links Among Groups in the Wider Community

Community consultation goes beyond work *in* the community to embrace work that takes the community itself as its focus. Consultants are being drawn increasingly from a traditional work relationship with a particular client into the rough and rude world of community politics, social conflict, and disparity in wealth and influence among groups of citizens. Often consultants find themselves guided more by a combination of social ideals and the pragmatics of circumstances than by a formal contract with one client.

In the next two chapters our focus shifts from the internal processes of a specific organization to the links among groups in the community. Often consultants will be situated in a way that permits them to focus on these interrelationships directly. The client may then be conceived of as the whole community, and the objective may be to further what Iscoe (1974) calls the competent community. At other times consultants will find themselves working with groups whose central concern is with their links to the surrounding environment.

There are many ways of thinking about intergroup issues. We have chosen two broad topics around which to organize case material and analysis: intergroup conflict and the distribution of power among segments of the community.

6

Reducing Conflict Among Community Groups

Conflict among groups in the community often distracts organizations from broader goals and disrupts adaptive functioning. There are many potential sources of conflict. Some groups are sharply divided in their approach to important issues —for instance, those lobbying for and against liberal abortion laws or gun control. Some have similar goals but find themselves competing for scarce resources—for instance, two mental health organizations vying for funds to serve the same population. Some have a combination of similar and different goals—for instance, a union and management who both want the firm to be successful but argue over distribution of the fruits of success. There are also intergroup conflicts based on traditional animosities, even though the groups do not have different goals and are not competing for the same resources. This is sometimes the case in hostility among ethnic groups (O'Neill and Levings, 1979). With so many sources of tension it is not surprising that a good portion of the case literature is concerned with conflict resolution.

In this chapter we describe some cases in which consultants employed strategies to improve relations among community groups. In keeping with our emphasis on treating each case according to its peculiar circumstances, we shall also look at cases in which consultants found themselves sidestepping direct conflict resolution.

Our first narrative describes an intervention not in the resolution but rather in the prevention of conflict in the community. Prevention is an honored concept among social scientists who claim to have a community focus. But, as Emory Cowen has pointed out, it is a term that can be interpreted in unbelievably elastic ways. In an address given to the Community Psychology division of the American Psychological Association, Cowen noted that as primary prevention became popular, it became confusing. The term appears with increasing frequency in talks and articles, it now figures prominently in the deliberations of planners, and more and more people say they are doing it. He took issue with the breadth with which the term *prevention* is employed. Cowen specified two key aspects in the definition of primary prevention: It must have as its target large groups of people—often whole communities—and it must be employed before trouble occurs.

Short (1972) has outlined an example of anticipatory problem solving that admirably fits the notion of primary prevention in the community. The intervention in which she was involved created a demonstration project to help an urban school district move toward racial integration. It is an illustration of community planning that recognizes widespread evolutionary change in society and attempts to anticipate the effect on a local population. The preventive task is then to help smooth the path to new social arrangements without the conflict that might accompany a break with tradition.

There was an evolution toward racial integration of public schools in the United States. In metropolitan areas, as schools tended to draw their populations from their own neighborhoods, there emerged a racial imbalance with students reflecting patterns of neighborhood segregation. By 1970 the courts were becoming increasingly impatient with the rationalizations for such imbalances in school population. Pressure was building on cities to adopt plans to transport students into other neighborhoods for schooling. Apart from the potential for ethnic clashes over the shifting of students, busing also threatened district sovereignty. Suburbs and urban areas, administered by different school boards, were often racially homogeneous. Real integration of schools would require transportation of students across these boundary lines.

Although most observers recognized that change was coming whether local school officials welcomed it or not, still districts differed in the extent to which they prepared themselves. In this climate, programs that showed how transportation plans could be effected smoothly and to the benefit of students had a high potential for preventing future conflict in the community.

The setting was a metropolitan area in California with eleven autonomous school districts serving an urban area and adjacent suburbs. It was evident that racial integration of the schools would become a reality sooner or later and that, without some changes to permit interchange of students across district boundaries, educational officials would be unable to meet the challenge. While the urban district was 53 percent white, the suburban districts ranged from 88 to 99 percent white.

The eleven districts agreed to participate in an Urban Studies Project designed to develop a regional approach to school integration. Systems analysis indicated that there was little cooperation and no joint programming among the districts. The districts all had virtually identical organizational structures that defined the channels through which personnel and information must move. The districts tended to operate as though they were independent of one another economically, politically, and socially. There was an entrenched tradition of resistance to interdistrict or intercommunity collaboration; local autonomy was clearly held in high esteem.

Those involved in the Urban Studies Project knew that it could succeed only if officials in each district felt they were fully involved in planning and implementing any cooperative venture. Each step had to be taken carefully in order to prepare the way for the next step. First an advisory council was formed, including superintendents of all school districts, representatives of community agencies, and staff of the project. It took this group four months to draft a grant proposal acceptable to all the districts. The next committee was composed of supervisory staff and had the task of planning a curriculum. This committee had to draft guidelines acceptable to all superintendents before districts would commit teachers to the project. This task took another four months. When it was completed, teachers' in-service training sessions were instituted to develop the actual learning experience for children.

In the operational phase, a thousand children in fifth and sixth grade participated. Each child was involved in the project one day a week for nine weeks, working in small groups with an adult leader. At the beginning of the school day children were transported from their schools to a central staging area where they were divided into project classes composed of students from different ethnic groups, social classes, and school districts.

To pave the way for a successful educational experience, a careful sequential strategy had to be implemented involving teachers, parents, and the communities at large. The consultant was involved for three years implementing this strategy. She had to anticipate sources of difficulty or outright opposition in communities, school districts, or local agencies and develop avenues for constructive participation. Organized resistance to any sort of integration program already existed in the suburban communities.

The consultant worked through local news media and direct contact with community groups to provide accurate information about the project. This work tended to inoculate residents against the inevitable anti-integration campaigns. The value of such groundwork was demonstrated when parents, teachers, and even the students took it upon themselves to refute opposition campaigns and to defend the program and its goals.

It was important that the project be portrayed as providing a service rather than as taking over functions of local districts. In the construction of the various committees, representatives of each district had veto power and procedures were instituted so that no committee appeared to impose its will on another.

Another area of involvement for the consultant was in-service training of teachers. Those selected to participate were paid for their time out of project funds and were given the opportunity to receive college credit. The consultant also developed relationships with schools from which children would be drawn. Her task here was to find ways in which the teaching staffs of these schools could contribute to the project and would not feel suspicious that project teachers were receiving preferential treatment or that their own classroom autonomy was in jeopardy.

The consultant helped to develop parental participation. The Parents' Advisory Committee was the last group constituted. It was impossible to create this committee earlier because of the constraints under which the project operated. District officials had to approve the overall plan before teachers could be recruited, and curriculum and specific instructional plans had to be approved before the districts would agree to involvement of children and parents.

After the operational phase of the project, various evaluation techniques were employed to assess the value of the experience. The positive results were useful not just for what they showed about how such a program could be run but also because they provided data that dispelled fears and improved the climate for the structural changes that accompanied eventual school integration.

The ecological principle of succession emphasizes the need for a long time perspective in consultation. Settings are captives of their histories. Tomorrow's social change has its roots in yesterday's social tradition. The community's response to change can also be predicted from its previous ways of defining and dealing with problems. The demonstration program described by Short (1972) illustrates the need to be aware of the direction of social evolution and, moreover, its probable effect on the local community. Awareness of the inevitability of a demand for school integration led to an intervention intended to make it easier for the community to adapt to changing times.

Because those involved in the project had an understanding of traditions in their school districts, they were able to intervene with little disruption or conflict. The plan involved a step-by-step strategy that was attuned to local sensibilities and prerogatives. For instance, rather than involving parents in the program at the outset—a procedure that might look good on paper—the planners recognized that they could take this step only when approval had been granted from those in administrative positions, from the curriculum planners, and then from the teachers who were to be involved.

The intervention had a clear cognitive component: It was designed to change the way people thought about school arrangements. Any demonstration program has, as an important objective, the aim of showing that something can be done. In this case the program was intended to show not only that it could be done, but that it could be done smoothly and beneficially. Its success was not only in bridging institutional gulfs but conceptual gulfs as well.

Cognition and Conflict

A persistent theme in the conflict resolution literature concerns the central role of stereotyping in intergroup relationships. Consultants frequently find it necessary to understand and deal with distorted perceptions that each group has of others in its field of action. Of course there are many noncognitive causes of conflict in communities. But the view that cognitive aspects are mere by-products of sociological and economic forces (the view of Karl Marx, cited in Harding, 1969) had been undercut by findings from the psychological laboratory. The tendency to simplify and generalize, to deal with people in terms of stereotypes, is often a crucial component of troubled relationships among groups.

The process of understanding one's experience requires a constant fitting of new information to a previous framework of knowledge. As Miller (1978, p. 101) put it in his theory of living systems, "A decision about an information input is not made absolutely but with respect to some other information which constitutes a frame of reference." To point out the distortion that can occur, he used the analogy of a geometric figure drawn on a rubber sheet stretched in different directions.

As we perceive the world, we simplify by applying categories to people and events. We seek similarities within groups and differences between groups to reduce the complexity of crisscrossing human categorizations. This process produces stereotypes that are then used to predict the behavior of individuals from presumed characteristics of their group. Hamilton (1979) and Tajfel (1970) have argued that the basic difference between "them" and "us"—between the in-group and out-groups —is one of our most important principles of social order.

Many examples of stereotyping have been reported from the world of policy making (Janis, 1972; Etzioni, 1969). Relations among nations are complicated by the tendency to ignore positive information about the adversary and negative information about one's own country. Etzioni cited a study by Bronfenbrenner (1961) in which American schoolchildren were asked why Russians and Americans planted trees along the roadside. According to the children, Americans planted trees for shade whereas Russians planted trees to block vision and provide work for prisoners. Janis and Mann (1977) suggested that the stereotyping of rivals and enemies distorts the decision-making process. The more cohesive the group making decisions, the more likely such distortion is to occur. Opponents are seen as "too evil to warrant genuine attempts to negotiate, or as too weak or stupid to counter whatever risky attempts are made to defeat their purposes" (p. 130). Tversky and Kahneman (1973) have noted that people are biased toward believing that their own group's behavior is dictated by environmental pressures, including the pressures exerted by the initiatives of other groups, whereas the behavior of other groups is thought to be free from environmental pressure. People are more aware of their own moods and plans, and know less about those of others. A person "may tend to regard his opponent's strategy as relatively constant and independent of his own [behavior]" (p. 230). When the action of other groups is antagonistic, in-group members see it as intentional and willful because situational constraints are not apparent. We excuse ourselves but blame others for the same behavior.

Hamilton (1979; Hamilton and Rose, 1980) has examined the ways in which stereotypical beliefs about out-groups persist even in the face of contradictory information. One important mechanism seems to be the illusory correlation. Once a stereotype has been formed, people tend to overestimate the frequency of the events that fit the stereotype while underestimating those that contradict it. As Hamilton and Rose (p. 833) put it, "If one has previously acquired the belief that blacks are more likely than whites to be lazy, then the way one processes information would be biased in that direction, even in the absence of any actual difference between blacks and whites in the manifestation of laziness."

Stereotypical views of other groups in the community are a frequent underpinning of conflict or potential conflict. When consultants attempt to resolve conflict between groups, they often find themselves working directly with stereotypical notions. Blake, Mouton, and Sloma (1965) have described a case in which this consultative function is well illustrated. The consultation task was to help resolve long-standing hostility between management of a large industrial plant and an international union that represented a portion of the work force. There were many unresolved grievances; strike threats were commonplace.

Entry into the situation came as a result of organizational development workshops that the consultants had run for plant managers over a three-year period. Through their involvement with the firm, the consultants knew of the difficulties between union and management; they volunteered to become involved in the issue. Agreement was reached on a two-day workshop to involve union and company officials. One consultant worked with management personnel, another with those from the union, and both participated in joint sessions.

Each group was asked to develop a written "image" of itself and the other group. Management saw itself showing a balanced concern for production and people, but the union saw the company as having a single-minded concern with production. Managers saw themselves functioning autonomously in a decentralized decision-making system, but the union believed plant managers were part of a corporate hierarchy following dictates from headquarters. The union saw the company as opposed to all organized labor and determined to drive the international union from the plant. Management thought it was trying to improve relations with the international. The company saw itself as honest and aboveboard in labor relations; the union saw management as underhanded and lying.

The union saw itself as primarily concerned with people; this stance was viewed by management as a disregard for the company's financial health. The union believed it was governed by its members; the company thought the union was controlled by a scheming clique. Managers thought the union was inflexible in its interpretation of the contract; the union thought it was willing to resolve issues informally. Union officials maintained that they cared only about issues affecting their members; the company thought the union wanted a say in all decisions —the right to comanage.

Both sides shared the view that management preferred to deal with independent unions rather than with internationals; both agreed too that management had been inconsistent in its treatment of independent unions versus the international. Both sides concurred that union members were skillful and proud of their competence, and they agreed that one of the union's goals was to get more control over training its members.

A workshop like that described by Blake, Mouton, and Sloma (1965) can show antagonistic groups that they are operating on very different assumptions. Group members generally find it much easier to develop an image of the out-group than of themselves. One reason may be the tendency to form complex pictures of the in-group while holding a much simpler view of out-groups. As we noted in Chapter One, there is research evidence to support this hypothesis about in-group and out-group impressions (see, for example, Linville and Jones, 1980). Because there is less information to take into account in describing the out-group, it is an easier task. Thus Blake, Mouton, and Sloma reported that participants in their workshop found the task of developing an image of themselves much more difficult than producing a stereotype of the opponent.

The process of drawing out an image of one's own group and then comparing that image with the stereotype held by an opponent can be most instructive for a community group. But the educational process must go further if conflict is to be resolved. Each group must understand how its own mode of operating could have contributed to the views of antagonists. In the workshop described by Blake, Mouton, and Sloma, for instance, each group was asked to list all the events that could have led to the interpretation held by the other group.

Conflict resolution of this sort takes as one of its first objectives the narrowing of issues. What really divides the parties? In the process, groups may find that they have more areas of agreement than they realized. Of course, not all of their differences are products of mere misunderstanding. If they were, conflict resolution would be easy indeed. But although there are key issues about which the parties disagree, the act of focusing often removes minor irritants and gives each side a more objective understanding of the other's motivation. Whether the laboratory approach found in much of the organizational development literature is of merit depends, in part, on the balance between areas of common concerns and areas of real disagreement. As Blake, Mouton, and Sloma observe, if two parties are determined to continue conflict and to maintain a win/lose orientation, workshops will be of little value. In the case they described, the parties had some important common goals. The union wanted good conditions, wages, and benefits for its members, but these could only be achieved if the company prospered.

The use of superordinate goals—broad areas of common interest that override smaller points of conflict—has long been recognized as a basis for conflict resolution. In a set of classic studies, Sherif and his colleagues (1961) showed that competitive groups can be brought together if they are aware of a serious problem that can only be solved if they work together. There is also a cognitive component in this form of conflict resolution. It is not enough that superordinate goals exist or that they exist in the mind of an observer to the conflict such as a community consultant. They must also be salient to the contending parties.

An important consultation task may be to make such common problems salient at a time of conflict. This was the approach taken by consultants during a teacher's strike in New York City. The strike was the result of a dispute involving the Board of Education, the United Federation of Teachers, and an experimental school district in the Ocean Hill-Brownsville section of Brooklyn. When the new district attempted to transfer some teachers to another district, it incurred the anger of the union, which opposed semiautonomous school districts. The union's intervention brought charges of racism from the predominantly black Ocean Hill-Brownsville community.

The strike began in September, coinciding with the start of a school year, and ended in November. During the strike, parents were outraged and the educational system of the city was in chaos. It was in this atmosphere, at the height of the strike, that a community mental health center ran a forum on school-community relations that was designed to help some of those involved to find common ground. Levin and Stein (1970) have reported on the way in which this forum attempted to make superordinate goals salient in order to reduce hostility in the community.

The district in which the forum was run served 180,000 residents. It was undergoing a transition from white to minority populations and also a downward shift from blue-collar to lower socioeconomic status. The mental health center found itself in a squeeze during the strike. Principals asked that school consultation services be continued, even though teachers were on strike. Some parents wanted the center to offer classes outside the school while others wanted the existing schools kept open.

Although a resolution of the strike itself would require successful citywide negotiations, the center believed it could play a useful role in reducing conflict among those in its immediate community. Two forums on the conflict were scheduled to help people with strong feelings examine issues objectively, to reduce stereotypes, to encourage members of different groups to find ways to work together, and to provide a model that might resolve future conflicts.

> The mental health center drew from various community groups to plan the forums. In this process it became clear that the planners confronted one another with sharply drawn stereotypes: Parents believed all teachers supported the strike, which was untrue; charges of antiblack prejudice and anti-Semitism were tossed about freely whenever opinions differed.
>
> The forums involved parents, teachers, students, merchants, clergy, and school board officials. As people arrived they were divided into five groups; the organizers took care to keep cliques dispersed. Each group's task was to formulate an educational program for the city and then nominate one of its members to run for mayor in a mock election. The group's educational program was to be his or her platform.
>
> Those nominated included members of various groups; there was no clear bias in nominations. Each candidate made a campaign speech outlining the group's agreed educational objectives. A variety of goals was voiced, but a persistent theme was the need to have contending groups work together for the good of the city's schools.
>
> While ballots were being counted, members of the five groups shared with everyone their experience in working on the task. Although the exchange of views had sometimes been heated, it was common for participants to express surprise at being able to see others as individuals rather than as stereotypical foes. After the intervention, professionals from the mental health center concluded that although differences re-

mained, the emotional tenor of the conflict had improved and stereotypes had been weakened.

Often consultants are situated in a role that prevents them from intervening at the heart of a conflict. In the case of the teachers' strike, the community mental center was in no position to affect the citywide dispute. But, as Levin and Stein (1970) indicate, this does not render consultants impotent. Broad conflicts have important effects on people at a local level. The general dispute is often played out in microcosm in each school district and neighborhood. Any intervention that helps people to develop a better working relationship can have significant benefits for the health of the community.

The task used in the forum described by Levin and Stein required a cooperative problem-solving approach. At least for the evening people found themselves confronted by a task in which they had to work together. The superordinate goal of achieving a better educational system for the city, an objective in which all could share, was made salient. Consultants used a technique that cut across existing group lines and created, however temporarily, a new group identification. The success of this maneuver was apparent in the tendency of artificial groups to support their own candidate for mayor, resisting the pull to vote for a member of one's own professional group.

The previous two cases illustrate circumstances in which the consultant can be successful in bringing contending groups together in a workshop atmosphere and applying conflict resolution techniques. Many variations on the strategies used in these workshops can be found in the specialized literature on this intervention style (see Blake and Mouton, 1976). But rather than give further examples of such techniques, we return to our theme that the consultant must be aware of the context in deciding when conflict resolution techniques are likely to be successful.

When Conflict Resolution Fails

Conflict resolution is less likely to work when parties to the dispute have stronger reasons for competition than for cooperation. In such a setting, focusing on central issues in the battle may simply sharpen hostility. Workshops may not only fail; they may be perverted by the parties to gain an advantage in the struggle.

The consultant's task is to make an early diagnosis of the issues—as well as the motives of those involved in the dispute—to decide whether there is really much common ground to be found. Sebring and Duffee (1977) have reported an intervention in which a problem-solving approach was impossible. The case involved a dispute over a vocational rehabilitation program in a women's prison. The conflict began as a disagreement between the black education director and a white home economics teacher who had recently been hired as part of a new commitment by the state to improving facilities for rehabilitation. The educational director accused the teacher of using an old-fashioned approach to make black inmates into good domestics. The teacher felt the director did not recognize her focus on consumer-oriented home economics.

What seemed at first to be a clash between two individuals actually ran much deeper. It divided personnel on issues of race and educational philosophy. By the time consultation was requested the conflict had been recycled on many levels. Ultimately it was expressed as a dispute between the commission of corrections and those who guided the state's educational program.

Each side had its stereotypes of the other. Each had its own version of the facts. Motives were suspect. Cadres had support from significant groups beyond the prison walls. Some prisoners used the tension to play one group against the other; others became discouraged and stopped going to class. At one point the teachers were working with less than 10 percent of the prison population.

> In the women's prison, consultants had to determine the best level and mode of intervention. Should they work at the state or the local level? Should they press for staff changes or try to promote mutual problem solving? Did participants really want

to work together? Or were they merely committed to defeating their opponents?

After an initial meeting with parties to the dispute, the consultants decided there might be some room for negotiation in the prison. But this strategy proved impossible to carry out. Meetings of participants were strained, then sabotaged. There were many attempts to draw the consultants into the prevailing organizational paranoia. Consultants found themselves responding in kind, keeping careful records, being cautious about anything they said to one group or the other, and finally sending copies of their report to all parties at the same time by registered mail.

When it was clear that conflict resolution involving the parties was destined to fail, the consultants decided to use their report itself as an instrument of change. They recommended to top officials in both corrections and education that all funds for vocational education be withheld from the prison until staff problems were resolved. The consultants included various options for solving these problems.

Unfortunately, high-level officials were able to use the one clear recommendation as an excuse to cut funds while picking, choosing, and interpreting the options in line with their own prejudices. In fact, they used the report as a rationale for cutting funds throughout the correctional system. The main parties to the dispute remained in place, but the prison superintendent was removed a month after the report was presented.

This case is another testament to the difficulty consultants have in predicting unintended consequences of their interventions. Not only did their initial problem-solving strategy fail, but the report they filed as an alternative intervention had effects they neither expected nor predicted. Sebring and Duffee (1977) recommend that when consultants must rely on a final report to exert pressure, they should throw all their weight behind one solution. When a conflict has become acute and disruptive, the consultants may need to recommend sweeping changes—such as removing a whole group—rather than giving options for halfway measures. The virtue of an unequivocal final report is that it can be used by top administrators as an objective rationale for decisive action.

Earlier we discussed cases bearing on the question of who the consultant should consider the real client to be. The example recounted by Sebring and Duffee raises this point again. Conflict frequently puts the consultant in a dilemma of accountability. Sebring and Duffee are among those who argue that when the consultant is working in public institutions, he or she owes final allegiance to those receiving and paying for the institution's services—in this case the inmates and taxpayers. It is they who lose most in a win/lose conflict that disrupts institutional functioning.

The ecological perspective encourages the consultant to look beyond an immediate conflict to discover the sources of external pressure that are contributing to the problem. If a local problem is merely an expression of contending forces in the broader environment, the chances of resolving it locally are not very good. In the case reported by Sebring and Duffee, many factors contributed to the dispute in the women's prison: racial tension, difficulty in meshing organizational arrangements between two powerful state bureaucracies, and external political ties of those within the institution. The parties to the conflict were able to maintain their position and keep the fight going largely because of the support they had beyond the prison walls.

In our discussion of the ecological approach, we have emphasized the need to take a long view of current problems to see where they are influenced by evolutionary change in the community. In time institutions are pressured by public sentiment to change their emphases. Strain among groups in an institution may be a reflection of the difficulty involved in meeting new objectives. In the women's prison, pressure on the institution came from a shifting of public concern from punishment to rehabilitation. One result was an injection of educational funds—and with the funds came the intrusion of a different state bureaucracy into the prison system. In this case the consultants were not placed at a level where they could exert influence on the real wellsprings of conflict.

McRee and colleagues (1974) have reported a case that illustrates the need to take account of the surrounding environment to understand conflict situations. They discovered that the evolution of a community's educational system had unanticipated consequences for the functioning of a neighborhood school. The school, which served first through twelfth grades, had been all black for much of its existence. It served as the primary center for social activities in the community. Pressures toward integration had resulted in a population shift in the student body, a name change for the school, a new organizational structure that included only junior high school grades, and the merging of the school's parent–teacher association with another school's PTA. A new administrative plan was imposed on the school: There was a black principal (who did not live in the community) and a white vice-principal; black and white counselors were hired; racial quotas were established for student government. In this state of flux, most social functions at the school were canceled to avoid racial problems.

> The problem presented to the consultants was a recent outbreak of theft and vandalism in the school. Suddenly the school found itself with the highest vandalism rate ever reported in a school in that county. As many as 583 window panes were broken in a matter of weeks. Everything not nailed down was stolen. Local police had given up on the problem. Typing teachers began taking typewriters home at night as a last resort against repeated theft.
>
> The consultants learned that since general social pressures had been translated into changes in the school's structure and function, there had been considerable resentment from members of the community. Prior to integration, the school had served as a major resource to the surrounding black community. It was a community center and major recreational facility. The onset of vandalism coincided with the de-

nial of these services. There was no legitimate arena
in which grievances could be aired.

To resolve the issue, the consultation team concentrated on the ecological question of the school's
relationship to the wider community. A separate PTA
was reinstituted for the school and facilities were
again made available for recreational and social activities and on weekends. There was a sharp drop in vandalism and theft. The consultants also recommended
that school facilities be used for a medical screening
clinic, adult education courses, and various other community activities. The State Department of Social Services was asked to assign a worker on school grounds
at specific evening hours to assist community members and provide information regarding social service
programs. Vandalism and theft dropped dramatically
once the school's use was again broadened.

In the case reported by McRee and her coworkers
(1974) the wave of vandalism and theft in the school indicated
that a conflict existed, but the parties to the conflict were not
immediately apparent. With a narrow approach—treating the
problem simply as an outbreak of lawlessness—conflict resolution would have been most difficult to achieve. Only by taking
a wider reconnaissance of the situation, and understanding the
community pressures, were the consultants able to repatriate
the school to its neighborhood.

There are many situations in which direct conflict-resolu-
tion techniques may be inappropriate. Sometimes an attempt to
bring rival groups together will disclose that they are actually
further apart than they realize. If conflict often arises because
groups mistakenly think they have no common ground, it is
also true that community organizations can function parallel to
one another without realizing how divergent they are in philosophy and goals. The consultant who approaches such groups
with a textbook model, failing to survey the situation carefully,
may simply make things worse. Chappell-Ivey (1980) became
involved in a case where, at first glance, it appeared the obvious
task was to bring two groups together. The organizations served

overlapping populations, and they seemed to have stereotyped conceptions of one another that might limit the degree to which they could work together. But she soon discovered that what had seemed to be mere misunderstanding, based on lack of contact, was really an expression of deeply divergent philosophies.

The Shelter was founded in a Canadian city to provide service for women and their children who were in need of temporary housing as a result of domestic physical (and sometimes emotional) abuse. The funding came from private donations and from per diem support provided by municipalities in which clients normally resided. The house was open and staffed around the clock each day of the year. Shelter, meals, safety from physical danger, comfort, and emotional support were provided. Specific services offered by the staff included education in basic life skills and self-care for the woman (and for her children, if present). The thrust of this self-help program was to prepare clients for independence.

Staff also provided individual counseling designed to help the client assess her situation and make her own decisions regarding the future. The explicit orientation of the staff was to support the woman's decision whatever it might be. If she elected to return home to the abusive husband, staff urged that it be under new conditions including such possibilities as marriage counseling, involvement of children's services, and other community resources. If the woman decided to reestablish herself and her children in the community independently, referrals were made to such resources as legal aid, family court, daycare, employment counseling, and housing services.

The founders of The Shelter discovered they were going against the prevailing orientation of existing agencies—particularly against traditional ideas about the sanctity of the family and the need to keep families from breaking up. It took four years of dedicated, patient work to find the funding needed to establish the facility. The first few years of its operations involved constant struggle to win acceptance

from police, family court, and municipal agencies
that had to provide per diem money.

At the time of the consultant's involvement
The Shelter had survived its embryonic difficulties,
but it still faced suspicion or outright hostility from
certain community groups. This hostility was principally related to the supposed feminist orientation of
the founders and staff. While this perception was generally accurate, the staff disputed the accompanying
view that they were dedicated to breaking up families.

The consultant focused on one representative
disagreement between The Shelter and another community group, the Relatives Association (RA). This
was an organization of spouses and other relatives of
alcoholics. Members held weekly meetings to share
their experience in living with an alcoholic. The Relatives Association regarded alcoholism as an illness
that could be arrested: Alcoholism frequently involves
difficulties in a family, just as any other serious illness
might disrupt family life. In the view of RA, family
and friends are important sources of emotional support in the treatment of alcoholism. Changes in family attitudes toward alcoholism were thought to be
crucial to the recovery of those suffering from this illness. If the spouse abandoned the alcoholic, treatment would be retarded.

There was a significant overlap in the families
of concern to RA and The Shelter. These organizations first came into contact when RA received a
grant to open its own crisis center for battered wives
in another city. To gather information that would
help them start their house, which was to be a one-
year demonstration project, RA arranged a meeting
with staff of The Shelter. The meeting ended acri-
moniously because of differences in the philosophy
stated by the groups. At the time of consultation,
moreover, there were rumors that an RA meeting had
been devoted to an attack on The Shelter, which was
characterized as promoting "the disintegration of the
family."

The consultant decided to analyze difficulties
between the groups and see if rapprochement was

possible. Since her work had been initiated by The
Shelter, it seemed likely that its staff was prepared to
improve relations. On first contact with RA, the consultant was pleasantly surprised to learn that the difficulties did not seem significant. Her preliminary
view of the situation suggested that each group had
been viewing the other stereotypically but both shared
a good deal of common ground. It was not true, for
example, that The Shelter habitually advocated the
breakup of marriages; nor was it true that RA always
counseled women to remain with alcoholic husbands,
even in the face of physical abuse. In fact, RA had
made several referrals to The Shelter.

The picture that emerged was one of two community groups with slightly different emphases both
providing service to women who were abused by alcoholic husbands. Depending on the case, both
groups found there were times when clients should be
supported to return to their spouse and times when
they should be helped to make an independent life.
With this much agreement it might be expected that
the consultant would lead representatives of the two
groups to a new understanding.

Further analysis of the groups indicated that
there were deep divisions in philosophy dividing them,
however. Although each group could point to cases
where it supported women to take the course of action implied in the other group's guiding orientation,
these were exceptional cases. The Shelter encouraged
women to return to their abusive spouses, alcoholic
or not, only when it was the strong wish of the woman herself. Seldom did the staff, with its feminist orientation, actually believe that this was the best course
of action for the client. And the cases in which RA
believed that wives of alcoholics, battered or not,
should abandon their spouses ran counter to the
group's orientation. Although RA was prepared to admit that such circumstances did exist, these cases
were highly exceptional and involved physical abuse.
The norm for each organization, then, was the rare
exception for the other.

No doubt these fundamental differences would

have surfaced again had the consultant attempted to
bring the two groups together. Such a meeting would
have highlighted differences in philosophy, and animosity would have been renewed. The consultant
concluded that her best course of action was to leave
the two community organizations with the minimal,
though functioning, relationship that already existed.

Chappell-Ivey (1980) found herself in a situation where
an uneasy truce might be the best interaction possible for two
community groups with divergent views of a social problem.
The best intervention was to leave things as they were. In other
situations, however, circumstances may require that the consultant take action even though there is little hope of dealing with
deep-seated prejudices and stereotypes. The community may
face a crisis requiring that stereotypes be handled by professionals. Shellow (1965) described a case in which the consultant had
to make sure that the personal views of police officers did not
interfere with their ability to handle a civil rights demonstration.

The consultation took place in a suburban Maryland
county shortly before the huge civil rights march on Washington, D.C., in the summer of 1963. When the march was announced, law enforcement officials worried that an overflow of
protesters into the counties surrounding Washington might result in clashes. A community field station of the National Institute of Mental Health was invited to help with an intensive one-
week program given to the civil disturbance unit of the county's
police force. The consultants had to work in a tight time frame.
They had only six hours in which to help the police prepare
themselves psychologically for what might be an extremely
stressful situation.

Group discussions brought out the private attitudes of the police. Officers who felt that blacks had
legitimate grievances were in the minority. Most held
stereotypical, prejudiced views on race. Most extreme
was a small group of arch-segregationists who sat
through most discussions in silence. One was heard to

remark during a coffee break, "That's just fine, let them come. I'm gonna bust me a nigger's head or two."

The consultants avoided trying to change the men's minds or confront their attitudes. Instead they attempted to provide clear models of police behavior in various crowd situations. The role of the police was made salient. It was pointed out that the lack of structure gives police officers an opportunity to set the stage for nonviolent resolution of issues because they are a visible authority.

The officers were encouraged to identify with their group, particularly because it was a closed unit designed for special assignments. This group identification allowed the consultants to capitalize on pressures for conformity. Withdrawal from the unit or poor performance at the scene of an incident was virtually unacceptable for each officer. Therefore the conflict between group norms and private attitudes —even though those private attitudes were shared by a majority of officers in the unit—were resolved in favor of behavior befitting their role.

There were no incidents during the rights march. The first real test of the unit came that fall, when two housing projects were picketed by the Congress of Racial Equality (CORE). The unit acquitted itself well, maintaining a high standard of police work, and an official of CORE was so impressed with the unit that she wrote a letter of appreciation to the police department.

In this case the consultants were concerned with encouraging role-appropriate behavior rather than changing private attitudes. Of course it is possible that, since behavior ran counter to attitude, attitudes might subsequently be modified to reduce dissonance. But role demands, made salient by the training effort, would probably provide sufficient justification for professional behavior at variance with private opinions.

The case reported by Shellow (1965) is a good example of the instances in which intervention must aim at behavior rather than delve into deep-rooted attitudes. Although it might be laudable to press for change in the way groups view one another, in a crisis the consultant may not have the luxury or the authority to take on such a project. The immediate task may be to help role occupants act according to their own professional standards, even in situations that might make their personal prejudices salient.

There are many times when professionals must resolve discrepancies between private attitudes and role demands. For instance, Baluk and O'Neill (1980) found that health professionals working with abortion patients are often in this dilemma. They studied attitudes toward abortion patients held by doctors, nurses, and social workers. The research focused on professional stereotypes about the psychological consequences of abortion for patients; these stereotypes were then compared with actual test scores of abortion patients. The researchers discovered that all three professional groups vastly overrated the extent of anxiety, depression, and guilt that accompanied abortion. Working with patients did not change this stereotype. Each professional category was divided into students and professionals who had had experience with such patients, but there was no improvement in the stereotype as a result of experience. Drawing on the notion of the illusory correlation, it appears that professionals saw what they expected to see—despite evidence that might have moderated their impressions. Private feelings about abortion almost certainly influenced the professional perspective of these doctors, nurses, and social workers. As Shellow indicated in the case of the civil rights demonstration, a consultative function in these circumstances might be to reinforce professional identification and hence reduce the effect of private attitudes.

Stereotypes and Group Solidarity

It is natural that the cases we have reviewed all focus on the *negative* aspects of stereotypes. But, like most issues in consultation, this one has two sides. Stereotypes serve a function in community groups, and the consultant who does not recognize the functional value of a particular stereotype will be limited in designing a useful intervention. It can even be argued that for some groups, stereotyping other groups can be adaptive. This fact, if it holds true in a specific case, must be weighed against the consultant's natural desire to help a group see the world with unprejudiced eyes.

Sozonchuk (1980) confronted this problem in her work with a women's health organization. This group, which was described in the preceding chapter in connection with another intervention, had an antagonistic relationship with a significant portion of the medical profession in its environment.

The consultant became involved with the Women's Health Education Network when it was still in its formative stage. Her work in the group focused on building membership and creating an identity that was sufficiently strong to attract funds from granting agencies. The problem of gaining members was complicated by geography: The group was scattered across a whole Canadian province, and general meetings involved considerable travel.

It soon became apparent that to overcome the challenge of geography members would need a strong sense of mission. The consultant found that this sense of mission was fueled by the members' view of the medical establishment. Members were genuinely indignant about the state of health care in many areas of the province. And, although there was strong opposition from some doctors, group members tended to cherish a stereotype of the male-dominated medical profession that exaggerated the amount of antagonism actually present.

Male physicians were assumed to support the status quo and hence were expected to resist change. It was a surprise for members of the organization when they were (occasionally) faced with a male physician willing to donate time to help a well women's clinic or encountered female doctors who were uninterested or unsupportive. For their part, the majority of doctors also had a stereotypically negative view of the women's organization. They were frequently threatened by well women's clinics, assuming that the service would be unprofessional, or would infringe on the traditional doctor–patient relationship, or both. They failed to take into account the fact that clinics might provide useful information that the doctors had neither the time nor the resources to dispense routinely to their patients. Stereotypes held by group members and doctors were mutually reinforcing.

The consultant found that the tendency to exaggerate the amount of opposition they would encounter, and to stereotype existing health services, provided the women with a valuable sense of purpose. Their zeal encouraged them to devote time, energy, and effort to the enterprise, overcoming distance and internal personality clashes that might otherwise have stalled the group early in its life.

Even when conflict seems functional at a certain stage, no doubt there comes a point where differences should be resolved. In the case described above, tension between the women's organization and the existing medical services would surely have an unproductive side. Doctors might actively interfere with operation of well women's clinics, they might pressure colleagues not to participate, they might block sources of funding. The women's group might overlook potential allies in the medical community and fail to incorporate potential resources into their services. Keeping these cautions in mind, the point remains that consultants need to examine each situation to determine what functions are served by intergroup conflict.

In this chapter we have presented a spectrum of cases that deal with conflict in various ways. We saw a consultant at work on a demonstration project designed to reduce the dissension expected to accompany racial integration of a city's schools. In two cases, consultants used conflict resolution techniques to improve intergroup relations; in a third case, similar techniques proved inappropriate. Some conflicts could be handled only by recognizing the community pressures beyond the immediate situation. We have reviewed cases in which the consultant had to avoid deeper issues and concentrate on role demands as well as cases in which a focus on stereotypes might have done more harm than good.

These examples have raised many issues that face consultants in conflict situations. What functions does the conflict serve, and for whom is it functional? When should stereotypes be confronted, and when should they be left alone? Do contending groups share common ground, and is this ground firm enough to support their real differences in perspective or objectives? If groups are indeed locked in a win/lose struggle, can the consultant serve a useful purpose—and useful to whom? Is the conflict confined to the area in which it is expressed, or does it draw its energy from forces in the broader environment? If a conflict recycles itself at various levels, where should the consultant intervene for maximum effect? Answers to these questions in the particular cases presented here may not be translatable to other circumstances, but we hope that consultants can draw on these dilemmas to inform their approaches to community conflict.

An underlying theme of conflict resolution strategies is that conflict is dysfunctional—something to be resolved. This suggests the corollary that the way things would be in the absence of conflict is acceptable. If the consultant focuses on a conflict that disrupts the system, there is an assumption that the system should be preserved from disruption. There are many cases where this stance is reasonable, but there are other cases in which an unresponsive system, one filled with inequities, requires some degree of intergroup confrontation if it is to change and grow. In such cases the consultant may have to choose between becoming an advocate for a party to the conflict rather than being an agent of system maintenance.

Gamson (1968) has summarized these different perspectives on conflict with his contrast between social control and social influence. In a social control orientation the concern is with helping a system deal with threats to its stability. The social influence orientation puts the consultant on the side of a particular community group that seeks to enhance its position relative to others in the environment. It is this perspective that will predominate in the next chapter, as we focus on power relationships in the community.

Organizing Disadvantaged Groups

Who gets what? That may be the quintessential question in community life, rivaled only by a related question: Who *decides* who gets what? The ecological perspective turns the consultant's attention to the way in which resources are cycled through a system. It sensitizes the consultant to the need for mobilizing resources in community development and to resource distribution as a central theme in relations among segments of the community. Iscoe (1974), in his emphasis on the concept of the competent community, links competence to the provision and use of resources. We would expect to find that consultants concerned with enhancing community competence would become involved in the cycling of resources.

One measure of a community's competence is the way decisions are made and the degree to which various groups of citizens share in decision making. Do people have any real power over the events that affect their lives? In particular, can citizens make their voices heard in issues of resource allocation, questions about who gets what in the community? Iscoe comments: "One of the criteria of a competent community is the change in which power is transmitted to once powerless citizenry" (p. 612). He notes that shifts in power challenge the status quo. This makes it unlikely that a consultant who is responsible to established authority will have freedom to facilitate any significant transfer of power. Consultants whose efforts are centered on this aspect of community competence are likely to find themselves allied with groups mobilizing to increase their share of power and resources.

In the contrast between the social control and social influence perspectives outlined by Gamson (1968), the consultant's choice is between helping a system maintain itself or helping disadvantaged groups change the system. This choice does not rest entirely on the consultant's own values, of course, but is affected by the port of entry and mandate. In our discussion of the distribution of power and resources, we shall see consultants organizing disadvantaged groups so they can compete more effectively for influence. Sometimes disadvantage means poverty. But in some cases members of the middle class find themselves shut out of important decisions made by a powerful establishment.

Two views of conflict sharpen the contrast between the control and influence perspectives. According to Gamson (1968) the social control perspective sees conflict as a disruption that must be managed and reduced so that the system can continue functioning. The control emphasis is on resolution of conflict. But for the disadvantaged group, a conflict situation can be an opportunity to make gains. From the social influence perspective, conflict provides a state of flux in which useful changes can occur. Adopting the influence perspective, the consultant becomes less concerned with techniques of conflict resolution and more interested in developing tactics to help disadvantaged groups come through the upheaval in an improved position.

Any evaluation of the power structure in a community will conclude that power distribution is a function of social conditions rather than individual psychological variables. But consultants who become involved in organizing the disadvantaged will soon be struck by the importance of beliefs and attitudes in maintaining the status quo. The cognitive orientation turns the consultant's attention to the importance of citizens' perceptions of their powerlessness. Overcoming defeatism and introducing new hope about the possibility of fighting city hall is one of the fundamental problems for the organizer. In Iscoe's view: "Characteristic of disadvantaged communities today is not only the economic condition of the members but their psychological disadvantages, as exemplified by feelings of hopelessness and powerlessness" (1974, p. 609). Saul Alinsky, in a manual for training organizers, talks about citizens who are "numb, bewildered, and scared into silence. They don't know what, if anything, they can do" (1971, p. 194). Si Kahn, in another manual, tells potential organizers that "one of the most destructive legacies of paternalism which exists in almost every poor community is the destruction of poor people's faith in themselves and their own abilities" (1970, p. 51). We have no intention of blaming the victim; we are not suggesting that people are disadvantaged by their own attitudes rather than by the power structure. But in that context we shall focus on the psychology of powerlessness that must be overcome to facilitate successful action.

The psychology of powerlessness can be summed up in several comments. Each represents a pervasive belief:

> "Things are as they should be."
> "Things can't be changed."
> "*I* can't do anything to change things."

The consultant must deal with these three opinions to mobilize citizens for social action.

An important component of the belief that "things are as they should be" has been characterized in the social psychological literature as the Just World hypothesis. O'Neill (1981) has argued that this hypothesis has considerable relevance for community psychologists working with disadvantaged groups. The Just World view provides a way for people to understand and rationalize social conditions, even conditions that victimize them. The Just World view probably has its roots in childhood. The notion that our parents ultimately were acting for our own good provided some comfort at a time of disturbing powerlessness. The belief in benevolent authority persists into adulthood, where it influences our beliefs about the way rewards and punishments are distributed. People get what they deserve, and deserve what they get.

The Just World hypothesis becomes a source of distortion in our thinking when it persists in the face of contradictory information—and as we gain experience with life it is hard to avoid contradictory information. Many people seem to get what they do not deserve. The hypothesis may serve to fill gaps in information so that events seem consistent with the Just World view. A person now works backward from effect to presumed cause: If a bad end befalls a man, he must have been a bad man. This cognitive bias lends itself to blaming the victim.

The Just World hypothesis has been studied extensively in social psychological laboratories, where it has been shown that it influences the attributions we make about others. People tend to blame victims for their own misfortunes (Jones and Aronson, 1973; Lerner and Simmons, 1966), and they assume that even arbitrary rewards must have been deserved in some way (Lerner, 1965). The Just World hypothesis can also be used by people to rationalize their own disadvantaged social position, and it is here that it poses the most direct problem for the organizer. People may apply the hypothesis to themselves in two ways: They deserve what they get either because of their behavior or because of the kind of people they are. Jones and Aronson (1973) asked mock jurors to decide whether a rape victim was responsible for what happened to her. All the subjects received the same set of facts, but different groups were told that the victim was a divorcee, married, or a virgin. The divorcee was blamed least, but the rapist was given the lightest sentence in her case. Jones and Aronson interpreted their results as supporting the Just World hypothesis. The divorcee, stigmatized as a Bad Woman by society, got what she deserved. A bad event befell a bad person. But rape of the married woman and the virgin, stereotyped as Good Women, violated the Just World view. They must have *done* something to bring misfortune on themselves. Although there is little research on the way people apply the Just World hypothesis to themselves, we might speculate on how these results would translate: People can justify their own social disadvantage, and that of their group, by adopting the stigmas applied to them by more favored groups. Or their disadvantage can be rationalized by assuming that they did something wrong, or failed to do something right, and hence deserve their fate.

Research on the Just World hypothesis usually implies that it is pernicious, and indeed it represents a distortion in the way people perceive and interpret events. But some version of the Just World view may be necessary to supply the thrust for building an organization. Although the Just World hypothesis can be destructive when people use it to rationalize their own disadvantage, it can also provide notions of justice that specify how people ought to be treated in society. It can engender a sense of injustice that prompts social action. It encourages the disadvantaged to make comparisons between their lot and that of others. Disappointed expectations can be transformed into a healthy sense of outrage at inequity. To be upset by the injustice meted out to a group implies that a norm of justice, based on the Just World hypothesis, is being assumed. The organizer's obstacle is not the Just World notion per se but that version of the notion which is used to rationalize inequality and injustice. The general view that the world is and ought to be just provides a valuable framework to use in pointing out the unfairness of certain social arrangements.

Can Social Conditions Be Changed?

The belief that things cannot be changed is conceptually distinct from the Just World view. A person may believe that his or her group is being treated unfairly and yet feel powerless to do anything about it. According to French social analyst Roland Barthes (1977) a belief in the permanent and necessary nature of social arrangements is a powerful instrument for maintaining the status quo. He cites the tendency to turn culture into nature—the belief that man-made conditions are a function of natural law or human nature. Barthes argues that social change requires that the disadvantaged realize that social arrangements have been made and they can be remade.

A person may believe that the world is not as it should be and that it can be changed, but one may also believe that one has no power to change social conditions. This feeling of personal impotence has been studied by social psychologists conducting research into internal versus external locus of control. When this research has focused on involvement in social action, the usual finding is that those least likely to take action tend to believe that they lack control over events in their lives (Rotter, 1966). Unfortunately, work in this area is limited because the most widely used instrument, the Internal-External (I-E) Scale, confounds the belief in personal control with the belief in a Just World and the belief that social conditions are immutable. Orientations that are conceptually distinct are blurred on the scale. One item—"In the long run, people get the respect they deserve in this world"—suggests that things are as they should be. Another item—"The world is run by the few people in power and there is not much the little guy can do about it"—suggests that conditions cannot be changed. Both items, however, are designated on the scale as measures of a belief in the individual's personal efficacy. For a thorough analysis of these problems with the I-E Scale see Collins (1974). The point to be made here is that citizens may believe that they do *not* get the respect they deserve, and they may believe that this condition is produced by the present power structure. The question is this: What can they do about it? The consultant's task may be to develop a strategy that gives disadvantaged groups new confidence in their ability to work for social change.

The willingness of people to join a nascent organization dedicated to some specific social action may depend on what they see as the source and target of the conditions to be confronted. In his theory of social alienation, Stokols (1975) proposed that disadvantaged groups often feel that their legitimate aspirations have been thwarted. But there will be important consequences for action depending on whether they perceive it as "neutral" or "personal" thwarting.

In personal thwarting, some institution or group is regarded as the direct cause of a frustrating circumstance that is seen as being aimed directly and intentionally at the individual and similar people. For instance, an oil company may be accused of deliberately withholding supplies of heating oil from ghetto residents in an effort to drive up prices. In contrast, neutral thwarting exists when the institution is not thought to be actually responsible for the frustrating circumstance, the condition is not aimed at a particular group, and unfortunate consequences are regarded as unintentional. A worldwide shortage of energy may result in depleted supplies and a lack of heating oil for homes, despite the apparent best efforts of oil companies to allocate supplies fairly.

Stokols suggests that to predict behavioral response to oppressive social conditions one must know whether the frustration is seen as personal or neutral thwarting; and one must know whether the individual sees himself or herself as having any optional course of action. People who think they have no options make passive adaptations. This passive response will take the form of subjugation if the individual perceives personal thwarting; it will lead to isolation if neutral thwarting is perceived. Drawing on the comparison-level theory of Thibaut and Kelley (1959), Stokols argues that the lack of options leads people to lower their expectations—to accept cultural stigmas applied to their group, for example, and assume that group members get less because they deserve less.

The response is more likely to be active when a person sees the possibility of options. In the case of personal thwarting, people may experience the outrage that leads to rebellion. If they experience neutral thwarting, people are more likely to engage in problem solving. But if repeated attempts at problem solving fail to change the situation, people run out of perceived options and become isolated.

Although Stokols does not mention it, there is another possibility for people who engage in problem solving until they run out of options. Rather than becoming isolated, they may redefine the problem. They may change perspectives and conclude that the cause of thwarting is not neutral but personal—with a defined source, with the individual's own group as the target, and with some degree of intent in the thwarting circumstances. Often the consciousness raising in which organizers engage is intended to accomplish this change in perspective.

From Stokol's model we can take the important point

that an organizer must show those in disadvantaged groups that there are options available for action: If this cannot be demonstrated, the organizing effort founders on the Scylla of subjugation or the Charybdis of alienation. But it seems that the value-laden distinction between rebellion and problem solving may be somewhat simplistic. Organizers may achieve problem solving if they can introduce strategy and tactics, and if the group correctly targets the source of the problem. Choosing the correct level to engage a problem is important, particularly when confrontation tactics are employed. When the issue is defined as too general and the source too far removed from the reach of the disadvantaged group, members may believe the problem is just too big. It may simply reflect "the system" or "human nature." But operating at a level too low, too local, may also be counterproductive. Kahn (1970, p. 16) notes that "confrontation tactics are basically aimed at the redistribution of wealth and other resources; and it is not always true that within a given community there is enough wealth to redistribute."

In the case literature we would expect to see consultants dealing with the psychology of powerlessness—including beliefs that victims deserve what they get, or conditions cannot be changed, or individuals lack the skill and power to confront the status quo. While helping citizens to gain a sense of their own efficacy, the consultant must also identify the right target for change efforts and develop a strategy for action. We begin this chapter with several cases that show the community worker functioning as an organizer; we conclude with a discussion of the difficult position of the organizer who is imported by those who hold power in a community.

When the consultant has information about the community and the social circumstances that provide the context for intervention, the first task is to bring people into contact with one another to build an organization. The archetypical image is that of an organizer striding unannounced into a poor neighborhood, talking on street corners, turning apathy into action. Alinsky (1971, p. 103) outlines such a conversation:

Organizer: Do you live in that slummy building?
Answer: Yeah. What about it?

Organizer:	What the hell do you live there for?
Answer:	What do you mean what do I live there for? Where else am I going to live? I'm on welfare.
Organizer:	Oh, you mean you pay rent in that place?
Answer:	Come on, is this a put-on? Very funny! You know where you can live for free?
Organizer:	Hmm. That place looks like it's crawling with rats and bugs.
Answer:	It sure is.
Organizer:	Did you ever try to get the landlord to do anything about it?

And so on. Often this mode of entry, imported from the early days of the labor movement, is unnecessary. Local people may already be organized into a group and then talk to a consultant about developing a plan of action. This was increasingly true with Alinsky himself as he gained a national reputation for his ability to champion the poor and challenge the powerful.

The model of street corner organizing makes several assumptions. The first is that people in a geographical area will identify with one another and turn their attention to a common problem; the second is that a geographical area ("the poor district") is the natural unit of organizing. The next two cases depart from these assumptions: Local people may be sharply divided, however much they are disadvantaged in society; and the target issue may cross geographical boundaries and require a network approach to organizing.

Traditional hostilities among segments of a disadvantaged group constitute a major barrier to community organizing. In London, West Indian immigrants and the white working class have stronger feelings about one another than they have about the establishment. The organizer faces the same problem trying to unite Portuguese and Pakistanis in Toronto or Anglophones and Francophones in Montreal. In an earlier chapter we noted the dilemma faced by organizers in the American South trying to build an organization to address problems that affect poor whites as well as poor blacks.

The first task of the organizer, then, may be to help people recognize that factions have superordinate goals which deserve more energy than the old arguments that divide them. An example of this approach can be found in the work of British community worker Mike Lucas, described by Bender (1976). Lucas was organizing in the Beckton area of East Ham, a poverty-stricken district in which the government maintained second-class accommodation for six hundred families who could get no other homes. The turnover was high; anyone who *could* leave did. Those who remained were the less able, especially unsupported mothers and young children.

> The community worker's objectives were to get more efficient provision of existing services; to press for introduction of new services; to involve tenants in the provision and management of services; to encourage residents to take advantage of their rights. These aims required the development of a cohesive organization in the community, but a major obstacle was long-standing hostility between two factions making up the Beckton district.
>
> At one time Beckton had been considered the best part of West Ham. Many residents who had spent their whole lives in the community remembered this tradition and resented the changing fortunes of the area. They particularly resented the influx of people who had come into Beckton as part of the Housing Department's policies. Community workers were told that it would be impossible to build an organization that included old-time residents as well as the newcomers in the housing project. These groups were said to be utterly antagonistic.
>
> To circumvent intergroup hostility the community worker joined the staff of a legal aid service and they developed a tape-and-slide show that would convince residents that they had many common grievances. The show included many color slides taken in the community and tape-recorded interviews with local people. Word spread that neighbors had been interviewed for the program, and when the organizers

distributed leaflets in Beckton to announce their show a large crowd came to the auditorium to see it.

The novelty of seeing their neighborhood portrayed in a show and hearing themselves and their neighbors was a big incentive in getting people to attend. But once in the auditorium, they were exposed to the more important message of the production: There was a community of interest among those in Beckton; there were common problems; all experienced some degree of neglect from those who had the power and resources to make the community a better place. That evening a tenants' association was formed, including old-time residents and tenants of the housing project.

Lucas and the legal aid workers found an innovative solution to the intergroup tension that divided those they wanted to organize. We offer the case for two reasons: to point out that consultants must take intergroup hostility into account and to give an example of one novel method used to bridge the gap among factions. But we know that most long-standing hostilities, often based on ethnic prejudice, will not be resolved by a one-night slide show. Even in the Beckton case, although the technique brought different groups into the same hall and led to the founding of an organization, we can only guess at the problems faced by factions as they worked to develop a common definition of the problem and a united approach to action.

Consultants must be resourceful indeed to bring together groups who habitually think of one another in stereotypical terms, and feel more threatened by the out-group than by social arrangements that lead to their mutual disadvantage. It is this problem that has made it so difficult to give practical application to Sherif's important finding that superordinate goals can be used to resolve intergroup conflict (Sherif and others, 1961). It takes a considerable shift in perspective for groups with traditional animosity to recognize that a social condition affecting both is more significant than their mutual hostility.

In some cases, prospective organizers will have to solve the problem posed by intergroup hostility before they can build a cohesive organization. The many factors involved in stereotyping and prejudice outlined in the last chapter will be relevant to this task. But in other cases the consultant will decide that too much time and too many resources would be required to build a rapprochement; energy must be invested in social action rather than in conflict resolution. The consultant will work with one cohesive population, hoping in time to build bridges to other groups who might come to see that they have common cause. The approach will depend, as usual, on a good reading of the environment. The consultant must understand the prejudices that exist, determine how deep tensions run, and discover whether stereotypes are shared by significant portions of the target groups.

Organizing the Middle Class

The prototype of street corner organizing neglects issues that cross geographical and social class boundaries. Shortly before his death, Alinsky (1971), who had spent his life working with the poor, predicted that the next great task would be to organize the middle class. He did not have time to articulate this position fully or to explain how such efforts would differ from organizing poor communities. Recent work, however, gives us some insight into these differences.

Organizing across social class lines generally involves a single issue. People from different backgrounds, living on different sides of the tracks, may find they have a common concern: improving facilities for the handicapped, fighting a proposed nuclear power plant, or trying to stop a school board from banning books. Alinsky (1971) argued against single-issue organizations in poor communities on the assumption that a disadvantaged group would have a number of mutual concerns. But in organizing across class lines and geographical boundaries, a single salient issue may be all the consultant has to work with.

Another difference between organizing the poor and the middle class is a shift in the psychology of powerlessness. Earlier we noted that the psychology of powerlessness has three components: The world is as it should be; the world cannot be

changed; *I* cannot change it. A belief in personal powerlessness
may be the most significant obstacle to organizing poor people.
They have had a lifetime to discover that their actions do not
lead to power and prosperity. But in the middle class personal
efficacy is less likely to be a problem. The consultant will find
that these people have experienced success and are more likely
than the poor to expect that their actions will be effective. But
more than the poor, they may have accepted cultural myths
about the inherent justice in society. The consciousness raising
necessary to build an organization that is predominantly middle
class will focus on contradictions in the Just World view.

A third difference in building a single-issue group that
crosses geographical lines is the pragmatic problem of *finding*
those affected by the issue. In the classic Alinsky model of
organizing, a drive through town is sufficient to pinpoint the
poor neighborhood. But how does one find those who care
about nuclear power, those who oppose strip mining, those who
support equal rights for women, those who have handicapped
children? The following case, in which a predominantly middle-
class organization was developed by O'Neill and Loomes
(1982), deals with these aspects of organizing. The single issue
was a need for improved educational facilities for children with
learning disabilities. The consultants had to find people affected by the problem, mostly parents, and had to demonstrate
that much more could be done for their children than local
school officials admitted.

> In Canada's Atlantic provinces a combination
> of economic underdevelopment and traditional, con-
> servative politics has hampered the introduction of so-
> cial programs taken for granted in most other parts
> of North America. In the province that was the set-
> ting for this intervention, the needs of learning-dis-
> abled children were neglected by the education sys-
> tem. Despite the fact that such children were typically
> of at least average intelligence, the tendency was to
> deal with their specific problem in the area of reading
> or writing by relegating them to "special classes" de-
> signed for the intellectually handicapped or to leave

them in regular classes of thirty to forty children with no supportive services.

In the absence of any effective learning disabilities program with which their efforts could be compared, school officials were able to give parents the impression that nothing more could be done. But in one school district the situation changed when a private school for learning-disabled children was opened, providing a standard of comparison. The private school was dramatically successful. Most parents could not afford the high tuition, but when news of the school's accomplishments became known many parents were indignant about the lack of services in public schools.

The consultants decided to assist parents to found an organization aimed at helping children with learning disabilities. The organization could include a number of activities: running workshops for parents to help them tutor their children, demanding more services from local schools, putting pressure on the provincial government for additional funds.

The first task was to locate parents of children with learning disabilities. This proved to be a major problem. Because the schools avoided facing problems presented by these children, no files were kept on them. Even if such files existed, even if the schools would have permitted the organizers to see them, they would have omitted many children because of inadequate diagnostic procedures. Often parents themselves knew about their child's disability only because they had had the child assessed by neuropsychologists in a nearby city.

Through informal contacts the consultant managed to get a handful of names of parents. This, at least, was a starting point. As each parent was called, he or she was asked about other parents who might have children with similar difficulties. Usually parents were able to add one or two names to the list. Despite the lack of an organization, parents seemed to be aware of a few others in the same circumstances. It seemed that the emotion attached to the problem sensitized parents so that when they heard bits of information about other people they tended to remember whether the person had a child with learning problems. In fact, parents often provided names of people they had never met but who did have a child with a learning disability.

The consultants knew that the initial conversation with parents would be crucial to recruitment. They hoped to create an organization in which the members, not the consultants, would be in control. But it was unlikely that parents would commit their time to even one meeting if they had no idea at all of the sort of group they were joining. The consultants also wanted to be honest about their own opinion on the general direction of the organization. They had to mention the possibility of confronting government.

When parents were contacted, they were told that an organizational meeting would be held and at that point parents would decide what the new group would do. As expected, parents always asked what the group *might* do. The answer was that at some point pressure would have to be put on the government to get resources committed for introduction of learning disabilities programs in the schools. The parents were primarily midde class, presumably not a militant group, yet the suggestion of social action did not deter any of those called. It seemed that this was an issue of such emotional significance for parents, and one that had caused them such frustration, that they were prepared to demand that politicians do something.

The first call was carefully structured. Rather than asking the parents for even the commitment to attend a meeting, the consultant simply said "I'll telephone you again when the first meeting is set up. In the meantime I'd like you to think about what you would want from a group like this." Parents did not have to decide whether to attend the meeting until the second call was made. Between calls they were asked merely to think about the matter. This was a request that was hard to refuse, yet it had the effect of preparing parents psychologically to join the new group. When they were called again, every parent agreed to come to the meeting.

In the second round of phone calls, one parent announced grandly that she was the local representative of a provincewide organization called the Association for Exceptional Children (AEC). She seemed to feel that the present organizing attempt was treading on her turf. The consultants decided they should learn more about AEC before the first meeting. They found that AEC was almost dormant. Its activities appeared to be limited to appointing local representatives in various school districts. A group of parents in a nearby school district had organized, become affiliated with AEC, and had never been heard from again. This was not a good omen; nor was the comment from the local representative just before she hung up the phone: "If this is just going to be another meeting where parents whine about their problems, I'm going to walk out."

At the initial meeting the group was reminded that there had been a general consensus to press for more resources to help children with learning disabilities. One of the consultants felt obliged to act as chairperson for the first meeting, since he had called it. One woman reluctantly responded to his request for a secretary, "but only for this meeting." A questionnaire was handed out asking parents to indicate their interest in the group and whether they would be willing to serve on the executive. It turned out that this step was premature; those responding were noncommittal or negative. The consultant collected the forms and asked the group to come up with ideas for an agenda. He was met by silence. The meeting had started disastrously; everything was going wrong. But at that point the AEC representative, quite unwittingly, came to the rescue.

To break the awkward silence that followed his call for agenda items, the consultant said one option the new group would have involved joining AEC. He recounted the story of the group that had affiliated with AEC and then apparently vanished. Until now, he had not known whether the woman from AEC was present or not. In fact she was sitting in the back row. (Later the consultants found that on her question- naire she had written "You're asking for trouble.") When the consultant expressed doubts about her group, the woman exploded. She denounced the con- sultant bitterly for what he had said about AEC and stated that everything necessary in the field of learn- ing disabilities was already being done by AEC. Final- ly she was scornful about the prospect of a group of parents such as this having any impact whatever.

When she finally paused for breath, one man remarked "I don't think we should join AEC right now." There were nods of agreement. This was the first time a parent had offered an opinion, and it was an opinion that presumed the existence of the group. Within moments there was a clear division in the au- dience. A small group at the back turned to listen to the angry whispers of the AEC representative, but most ignored this faction and began an animated ex- change of stories detailing the difficulties they had encountered in the school system. By the end of the meeting parents from this faction were volunteering to take on various tasks.

The consultants decided the second meeting would be a good time for a solid stump speech. They brought in a guest speaker, a dynamic woman who was active in pushing for learning disabilities programs in the province's capital city. Her enthusiastic talk was followed by a discussion in which parents showed real optimism that their efforts could be successful.

The third meeting was the last in the formative stage of the organization. Parents were now ready to elect an executive and divide tasks among commit- tees. These tasks included funding the organization, developing strategy for approaching government, edu- cating the public about learning disabilities, and pro- viding direct service to children. The committee deal- ing with the last task was first off the mark. It began planning a workshop to teach parents techniques to use with their children. Another self-help strategy was to have parents tutor each others' children—tutoring that was often successful because it defused the emotion involved when parents tried to help their own children.

The consultants recognized that there was a certain danger in these self-help strategies. They could be implemented quickly and would bear fruit much sooner than the long-term task of negotiating with government for more resources. There might be a tendency to focus entirely on this area and neglect the political strategy, but these self-help strategies could not solve the underlying problem. The consultants attempted to keep the group's activities in balance by giving particular attention to the political committee.

A year after its formation the group was still in existence, all its committees active. Government had been approached, with some results. Under pressure, the province agreed to pay tuition for children diagnosed as needing the services of the private program. The government considered this to be a major concession. But since the private school was quite small it could never hope to enroll more than a fraction of the learning-disabled children in the province. While the government was admitting it had a financial responsibility for helping such children, it was refusing to admit that public schools were the right settings to provide the help. Nevertheless, the government's concession helped several parents significantly and it had symbolic importance. It signified official recognition of the fact that there were children with educational needs not being met by the existing education system. It also validated the intensive and costly approach used by the private program, a fact that could be used later by the parents' group. Finally it gave the new group a taste of success and encouraged members to press on.

In the example provided by O'Neill and Loomes (1982) most of the parents that were recruited for the organization were drawn from the middle class. There were several reasons for this. Wealthy people, who were not numerous in the district where the consultation took place, have the resources to find private solutions to problems such as having a child with exceptional needs. Among the poor, diagnostic services that would detect a learning disability are almost unknown. Finally, it will be remembered that the network was created by asking each person who was called to provide other names. This procedure made it highly likely that having started in one social class, more names from that class would be generated. Middle-class people are more likely to live in the same neighborhoods, work in the same professions and trades, and meet in the same social circles.

Whatever the reasons, it was clear in this organizing effort that those drawn from the middle class can be organized and prepared for social action. What is needed to accomplish this is a clear-cut issue that carries strong emotional significance for the families being recruited. Given these circumstances, the middle class may actually be easier to organize than people in poor communities. Because of their history of personal efficacy they are ready to believe that an unjust social condition can be changed and that they themselves have the power to do something about it.

It is their tendency to believe in a Just World, based on their own experience and that of their families and neighbors, that stands between the middle class and social action. In the case described by O'Neill and Loomes, this belief disposed parents to trust school officials when they argued that they were doing everything possible for learning-disabled children. But this explanation was inconsistent with the evidence provided by a new private school that achieved dramatic results with learning-disabled children. We have noted that the belief in a Just World, rather than a belief in immutable social conditions or personal impotence, is usually the chief psychological barrier to middle-class organizing. Once parents became aware of the contradiction between the assurances of school officials and the demonstrated effectiveness of the private school, it was not difficult to convince them that they could take effective action.

This project also illustrates the ecological assertion that

consultants should try to identify indigenous resources. Parents represented such resources, and often their skills could be best used in a program of tutoring each other's children. Parents who become extremely frustrated with their own child, primarily because of the intense personal significance of the child's disability, may be able to work effectively and objectively with someone else's child. It was this psychological factor that was employed in the self-help strategy of the organization. But at the same time, the consultants were constantly aware of the seductive power of self-help. We have frequently noted that the fundamental aim of consultation is systemic change. No amount of self-help would change a system in which children with special needs were shortchanged by the schools.

Strategies of Social Action

The cases presented so far in this chapter have focused on the initial organizing process. Once a group is organized, the consultant's challenge is to develop tactics that will help citizens to influence social policy, alter the distribution of resources, or both. No doubt there are as many strategies as there are situations. Our argument against a textbook approach to consultation discourages us from reciting rules and cataloguing tactics. Nevertheless, we have chosen a classic case from the community organization literature to give a flavor of the way organizations operate and how events can offer both opportunities and obstacles. The case is drawn from Alinsky's *Reveille for Radicals* (1946), written while the author was in jail as a result of his organizing activity. (Alinsky recommended jail with its solitude and enforced inactivity for anyone who wants to find time to write a book.) Although the case is a prototype of old-time organizing, with a clear division of Good Guys versus Bad Guys, it provides a useful touchstone with which to study not only the ways in which organizing has changed in light of modern conditions but also the ways in which the process remains the same.

In a poverty-stricken community of 120,000, business was dominated by one major department

store. The firm had its headquarters on the other side
of the tracks from the squalid community where its
money was made. The size and commercial connections of this store ensured that it would be able to sell
goods more cheaply than the corner stores that eked
out a living in the same community.

The public relations of this store were abysmal.
Over the years it was unresponsive to requests for
help on every conceivable issue. It failed to contribute to local churches or other organizations. The best
it could offer was a meager contribution to the annual fund organized by people in the community to
provide Christmas baskets for needy families. The
usual contribution to the fund from the big store was
$3.50 worth of hard candy, which probably cost the
firm forty cents wholesale. Residents of the town
well knew the tight-fisted attitude of the store; it was
a standing joke for residents to remark bitterly as
Christmas approached that maybe this year the firm
would increase its contribution . . . from forty cents
to fifty cents.

Local people, led by priests and ministers, peri-
odically tried to boycott the store to make it more responsive to the needs of the town. But the power of
the firm was such that economic tactics always failed.
The store's ability to keep prices low, and to cut
prices even further when it had to, undermined boycotts. Poor people could not afford to take their business elsewhere.

A poor people's organization was formed in the
community. Its leaders, many of whom were church-
men, knew that with the right issue they could mobilize local people. They also knew that the large store
was most likely to offer the issue. But the years of
failed boycotts had left their mark; people thought
the store was invincible. It would take an emotionally
charged issue, a major campaign, and some new tactics if the organization was to be successful.

In mid-November, 250 of the store's employees
joined a labor union and went on strike. The dispute
occurred at a time when the community began to

think about the store's miserly response to the Christmas fund. The strikers were local; people knew them by name—often by first name. They had been baptized and some had been married in the neighborhood churches. They were members of various local organizations, including sports teams. The sympathies of the community were with them.

The store now made its only clever move in the entire dispute. Representatives of another labor organization suddenly appeared; it was a large union with reputed racketeering connections and no support among the striking employees or in the town. This outside union said it was trying to sign up the employees. The store, which had covertly brought the outside union into the picture, painted the matter as a jurisdictional dispute with itself as victim. The company's position had the kind of technical merit that might stand up in court.

The poor people's organization was in a difficult position. If it mobilized on behalf of the strikers, it could appear to be backing one union against another rather than rallying the community against the store's owners. The leaders of the organization worked to keep tempers cool while they planned a strategy that would outmaneuver the store. Keeping a firm hold on those it represented was a tough job for the organization. Members of the community were outraged by the store's behavior. Every rumor became magnified. If someone said a threat was made against a local priest, the next person heard "Father Smith's been slugged" and then someone would claim he was in hospital. It was a climate in which people might well act on their own, perhaps with vandalism and violence. Such random actions would discredit a communitywide campaign before it was under way. To keep residents in check the organizers spread the word that a grand strategy was being prepared that would deal the store a real blow. But members of the group could only be mollified for so long. The time was approaching when the leaders would have to make good. And when they took action, they would have to be careful to observe the technicalities of the supposed jurisdictional dispute between the unions.

The organization announced that it planned to hold a people's court to hear arguments on all sides and then render a verdict. A representative telephoned the office of the store president to invite him to the court, but the secretary said he was in conference. The leaders of the organization drafted a telegram. Speaking in the name of all the churches, social, fraternal, and ethnic organizations in the town, they said, "We have been requested by our people to inquire into the merits of the case of the present strike going on at your store." Identifying the community group with all local organizations and churches meant that any rejection by the store could be seen by residents as a rejection of the clubs and churches with which they identified strongly. The telegram went on to invite store management to attend the people's court. It concluded, "It has always been and will be the policy of this organization to give a fair hearing to both sides before taking action."

Store officials indignantly refused to attend. Instead they tried to smear the organization, charging that people's courts were appropriate in Russia, not America. "We believe in American law, not in people's courts." When the court was held, only the local union representing the strikers attended and presented a case. The packed community hall listened attentively and then solemnly passed judgment in favor of the striking union. The organization's leaders immediately issued a statement asking the store management whether they saw any reason, in light of the verdict, why the organization should not "take action" on behalf of the strikers. No specific action was mentioned.

Within an hour of this statement being made public, the store's lawyer telephoned to insist that the leaders of the community group come to his office. The person taking the call glanced out the window and saw a driving snowstorm. He agreed. It would make a good public impression for community leaders to gather from all parts of town and make the difficult trek through the snow to visit the fancy suite of the store's lawyer.

Five priests, three ministers, four owners of small businesses, and three union men made it through the snow to the lawyer's office. These representatives of a disadvantaged community found themselves in luxurious surroundings furnished at a cost of thousands of dollars. When the group entered the conference room there were not enough chairs. The lawyer grandly told one of the priests to go out to the hall and get one. The impression was that of a wealthy store and its opulent legal firm behaving like an arrogant aristocracy.

The lawyer had to admit that the vast majority of the store's employees were members of the striking union; but he continued to insist that this was really a jurisdictional battle between two labor groups. When representatives from the community accused the store of bringing in a union known for its racketeering connections, the lawyer angrily demanded to know whether they were challenging the integrity of his clients. When a spokesman said they certainly were, the lawyer got out his pen and legal pad and asked for their names.

"What for?"

"For the record."

"What record?"

"The record . . . you know . . . the record!"

The flustered lawyer asked if they were afraid to give their names. One after another they gave their names, and the lawyer carefully noted them. The meeting was over. The priests, ministers, union men, and small businessmen trudged back through the snowstorm.

Beginning the next morning and over the next several days, every person who had attended the meeting was confronted by thugs who professed to be from the outside union. The community people were given warnings that were all variations on one theme: "If you want to stay healthy, get out of this fight." Word quickly spread in the community that threats

were being made against local representatives, including ministers and priests. Leaders of the poor people's organization called the lawyer. He admitted that
he had turned the names over to the outside union
but disclaimed responsibility for any action it might
take. He began to sound nervous when the community leaders made it clear that they would hold him
responsible.

That night the organization decided the time
was right for action. The blustering of the outside
union and the mistake made by the store's lawyer put
store management in an extremely vulnerable position. They were acting out of desperation, and the
failure of these desperate acts must be making them
even more nervous.

A strategy session was held. The leaders of the
community group made sure that a store stool
pigeon was present so that store management would
have advance warning; it was hoped they would ca-
pitulate without a fight. The key move was to be a
legal one: The poor people's organization would go
into court in two days and seek an injunction re-
straining the store from murdering those who had
been threatened, in particular the Protestant ministers
and Catholic priests. Privately the leaders knew that
this injunction was unlikely to be granted. But the
bad publicity would bring a public outcry. It might
well produce sufficient indignation to make a boycott
work no matter how much the store lowered its
prices. When the threat of this court action was
leaked to the store, it brought immediate action. The
night before the scheduled appearance in court the
president of the company personally telephoned and
surrendered unconditionally.

The case of the big store versus the poor community is
drawn with simple brush strokes. The consultant four decades
later would rarely find matters so neatly defined or succeed so
dramatically in turning around oppressive conditions of long
standing. Nor is it quite so easy in most situations to tell who
is on the side of the angels. But precisely because of its sim-

plicity the case is useful as a starting point for some general observations about psychological aspects of organizing, the importance of strategy, and a consideration of tactics.

A distinction has been made between those who view social movements as essentially *reactive* or *proactive* (Gamson and McEvoy, cited in Grady, 1978). In the reactive framework, people become organized and politically active only when they suffer acute social strain or personal anxiety (or both). Such people, connected only loosely to society, can be easily manipulated. Strong leaders, often branded as outside agitators, take this discontent or personal maladjustment and put it to work in the service of some cause. This view is contrasted with the proactive framework in which citizens are seen as goal-directed actors pursuing social change through collective action. The more embedded people are in social groups, the more likely they are to be attracted to causes that advance group interests. Leaders and activists are less likely to be outsiders manipulating local people; they are more likely to be insiders who embody the group's norms and values and with whom group members can identify.

The big store/poor community case, as presented by Alinsky, expresses the proactive orientation. People came together in an organization because of a common group interest, not to act out a personal neurosis. Those already identified with local organizations such as sports clubs and churches were most likely to be actively involved. Social action was not a matter of stirring up and manipulating residents but a question of keeping their tempers in check and giving them a constructive focus for their discontent. Although such an organization is often built with the help of an outside consultant, local leadership provides the real dynamic. The fact that residents identified with the organization's representatives, including their own priests and ministers, produced outrage when those representatives were threatened. It was this sense of outrage that made dramatic action possible.

The case illustrates the importance of strategy over tactics. More than anything, strategy involves doing something when the time is right whereas tactics involves how that something is done. An effort to bring about social change may be successful with good strategy and poor tactics, but rarely the reverse. In the big store/poor community case, previous boycotts had failed in the absence of other circumstances that would put pressure on the business firm. Unionization of employees and a strike by these local people provided the climate in which mere threat of legal action and a possible boycott were highly effective.

Ecological principles, because they emphasize a long time span and a broad environmental context of action, are particularly relevant to strategic aspects of organizing. In this case, the way resources were cycled through the local community system was important both in defining the problem and in attempting to solve it. The store's predominance as a source of material goods at low prices, as well as its unwillingness to use any of its profits for the community's welfare, provided the basis for conflict. The nature of interdependence between the store and its customers put residents at a disadvantage. Only when the store was denied a resource it needed—the labor pool provided by the community—was the battle won.

The failed boycotts that preceded the strike contributed to a psychology of powerlessness. By focusing the community's attention on the store's policies, leaders highlighted the injustice of the store's actions. Residents knew things were not as they should be and, more important, they saw the store as the agent of injustice. The failure of earlier boycotts, however, reinforced the notion that things could not be changed.

The community was in the situation we have called personal thwarting (Stokols, 1975). Residents saw the store as the source of the conditions that frustrated them. They believed its policies were intentional and were aimed at members of their own community—their Christmas fund, their boys on strike, and finally their priests and ministers. When people who perceive personal thwarting also believe that they have no options, they are likely to be subjugated by power holders. In this case, subjugation was to a powerful business enterprise. When people did see some options, their actions tended to be violent and sporadic. The poor people's organization had to hold these impulsive gestures in check and to convince residents that it made more sense to work together in concerted action against the store.

When the time is right for action, the matter of tactics becomes crucial. Some of the tactics used in the big store/poor community case remain viable. It is still true that what the opponent *thinks* you can do is more important than what you can do. The history of pressure campaigns with grass-roots membership is a history of battles won by convincing those in power that the organization has the numbers and the daring necessary to do whatever must be done. The technique of making sure that an informer was present when militant plans were made is a trademark of the Alinsky-style organization.

In the 1960s, the civil rights movement gained great publicity with such tactics as marches, sit-ins, demonstrations, and information picket lines. These were effective when they produced widespread public pressure on the target of the campaign and pushed the opponent into taking repressive measures. Repression then provoked public sympathy for the mistreated and anger toward the mistreaters. But those in positions of power also learned from the success of the civil rights tactics. Kahn (1970, pp. 80-81) points out, "Most power structures know by now that the Alabama State patrol did more to help the civil rights movement than to hurt it and will go out of their way to avoid being responsible for similar situations." Kahn argues that marches and picket lines no longer scare the opposition unless they are symbols for other sorts of power. The tactics that were popular in those civil rights campaigns are being abandoned in favor of political and economic pressure.

Because its major weapons were economic (boycott, strike), the community organization described by Alinsky was particularly modern in its approach. But the case also illustrates the obstacles encountered in using such economic tactics successfully. In a poor town, a boycott that will really hurt the opposition may put the local residents through unbearable economic hardship. A different sort of economic tactic was attempted by Alinsky in a campaign in Rochester, New York. Alinsky was consulting with a community coalition called FIGHT, which had as its opponent the powerful Eastman Ko-

dak company. The dispute was finally settled, with a good deal
of compromise on both sides, after three years of conflict. On
the way to a settlement, Alinsky and FIGHT leaders invented
the stock-proxy tactic. They noted that large blocks of Kodak
stock were held by foundations, universities, and churches—institutions with liberal sympathies that had publicly supported
Alinsky's efforts in poor communities. The tactic involved trying to persuade these institutions to allow the community organization to have the voting proxies associated with their stock
holdings. If it had worked, it would have given the community
group a powerful voice in Kodak stockholders meetings. Alinsky had high hopes for the use of stock proxies as a tactic in
future campaigns with large corporations (Saunders and Alinsky, 1970). But—at least in the Kodak case—the tactic failed.
Those institutions that paid lip service to social action were unwilling to open their books and let a citizens' group see how
much stock they actually held.

The lessons learned by power structures as a result of civil
rights demonstrations in the 1960s include the importance of
refusing to be goaded into using repressive action. It was repression in the form of physical threats against local priests and
ministers that defeated the big store in the case outlined above.
It is more usual now to find that power structures will try to
co-opt members of a community organization—even the organizers themselves.

Today's organizer may find that his or her project is
funded by business or government leaders, those who seem to
have little to gain from significant transfers to power and resources. Lyndon Johnson's War on Poverty in the United States
put many community workers in this position, and the post
mortems on that social experiment often deal critically with
this very feature (Hersch, 1972; Iscoe, 1974; Sarason, 1978).
Opinions differ about establishment motives for initiating social
change—ranging from the optimistic view that enlightened leaders know that a competent community benefits everyone to the
cynical notion that such sponsored efforts deflect attention
from real issues. But whatever motives are at work, when the
powerful employ consultants to engage in social action, both
sides often get something different from what they expected.

There is no more striking example than the case of consultants who were hired by a business organization to undertake motivation workshops among the people of Curaçao, an island near Venezuela (Berlew and LeClere, 1974). After a brief survey of conditions on the island, the consultants decided that social change of a more profound nature was needed. They also decided that the chamber of commerce, which brought them to Curaçao, was not a fit client to support the ambitious project they had in mind. They created their own client: a foundation with representatives from all important segments of island society. Despite its apparent independence, the foundation was to be bankrolled primarily by the same businessmen whose direct sponsorship was considered unfit by the consultants.

The results of this daring enterprise are chastening for those who decide to create their own context for action, ignoring the traditions of the host setting. Government officials paid lip service to the project but failed to give it crucial support. Businessmen financed the project only during the phases that seemed related to the original mandate they had given the consultants. After the consultants departed, leaving behind an optimistic blueprint for far-reaching social change, funding stopped and the foundation died. The client created by the consultants for their purposes lacked the roots and the institutional support to sustain itself.

An ecological perspective encourages the consultants to fit interventions to host settings, to see how change efforts will interact with community traditions, and to gauge possible side effects that can distort intended effects. This perspective was lacking in the Curaçao case. To give just one example, the consultants assumed that if they gave achievement motivation training to island residents, they would turn a happy-go-lucky people into entrepreneurs who would willingly train others in similar techniques. But it turned out that the image of Curaçao people as carefree and rather lethargic was largely a stereotype developed by tourists. In fact, this was a society dominated by the psychology of power. The voodoo tradition remained strong. The consultants were seen as offering something—achievement motivation—that carried implications of hidden personal power. Those lucky enough to gain this power were not about to share its secrets with others, any more than voodoo charms and spells would be freely given away. The rippling effect of trainees training other islanders failed to occur for reasons that could have been predicted on the basis of a thorough analysis of the host setting and its people. Berlew and LeClere have been generous in sharing insights drawn from these mistakes so that others can benefit. Consultants tempted by ambitious social change projects are referred to Berlew and LeClere's original article (1974) for all the excruciating details.

In the Curaçao example, the initial consultation was sponsored by a business organization. In many cases, governments are hiring consultants with the ostensible task of organizing local people. Grady (1978) says that such government-sponsored efforts often leave established power politics unchanged, and in fact they may be used to protect the status quo. What may seem to be an activity in the social influence context may actually be undertaken to maintain social control. Grady has described a governmental attempt to create a citizens organization that would authenticate—but not alter—an ambitious redevelopment scheme. But the maneuver was undercut when a group of citizens spontaneously formed a genuine influence organization and demanded a real say in planning.

> The provincial government in one of Canada's Atlantic provinces established what were to be systematic planning procedures for the capital city and the area around it. The need for a comprehensive development plan was recognized by the provincial cabinet; planning was done primarily by a group called the Planning Secretariat, a group of professional planners who advised the cabinet.
>
> The official goal was "development of social and material well-being under conditions of rapid technological and social change." The first step was establishment of the Metropolitan Planning Committee. This Metro Committee included elected officials from various levels of government and professional planners and technical experts.
>
> From early in the planning process, the Plan-

ning Secretariat was committed to its own version of citizen participation. It arranged a week-long Encounter on Urban Development, in which a dozen specialists of international reputation would study the region, question citizens, and recommend the general direction in social and economic development. There was nothing in the terms of reference of this seminar to suggest that citizens would actually participate in the planning. The public's role was to provide information for the specialists to digest.

Government planners did not wait for the seminar to decide what ought to be done. In the months between the idea and the reality of the seminar, the Planning Secretariat and the Metro Committee developed a preliminary plan for the region. This draft provided for involvement of the public, but with clearly defined limits on how citizens would participate. First, the Metro Committee would try to reach the population with information about the proposed plan. Second, there would be a series of public information meetings at which elected officials and paid planners would make formal presentations and listen to comments. Third, comprehensive summary meetings would be held in which planners would justify the final plan to members of the public. The whole thrust of this approach to citizen involvement was to have experts do the planning and the public authenticate it.

The seminar was held with appropriate fanfare and media coverage. Visiting experts asked questions and made suggestions. Following the seminar, the Metro Committee created a program for public involvement stipulating that it should be well organized; this meant that it should be closely supervised by the Metro Committee. The plan also restricted citizens' contributions to the sort of regional development already envisioned by the government planners, avoiding local issues and neighborhood meetings.

This controlled, top-down model of public involvement was tried out in a series of public meetings over a two-month period—meetings sponsored by the

Metro Committee and highly structured. Slide shows
and diagrams were presented, and further meetings
were designed to inform the public about economic
development, public services, physical environment,
and government organization. Citizens were cast in
the role of consumers of policy recommendations rather than partners in the planning process.

But at this point the structured model of participation began to fall apart under pressure from
citizens themselves. At the first meeting, members of
the audience asked penetrating questions. More than
half of these questions either criticized the plan or demanded concrete and continuous participation by
members of the public. Toward the end of the meeting the mayor of the capital city clashed with a member of the audience who pressed for an end to "the
con game" and "let's pretend" planning.

The formal meeting ended, but some twenty
members of the audience stayed behind to talk. They
expressed dissatisfaction with the tight control of the
meeting and discussed how future meetings could be
opened. A series of informal meetings took place in
private homes. People began to work out a strategy
they could use in the public meetings.

Government staff members quickly became involved in the nascent citizen's group and influenced
its direction. An ad hoc committee on citizen involvement was formed; its demand for a special open
forum with the Metro Committee was granted. Government staff members helped to prepare the ad hoc
committee for the confrontation. They pressed the
group to make a specific demand: that government
sponsor a workshop on citizen involvement. Rather
than focusing on the current issue—a plan that was
proceeding without real public involvement—the citizen's group digressed into working out minute budget
details of the proposed workshop. At the open forum
the Metro Committee was very agreeable to the workshop proposal, and the provincial government agreed
to finance it.

The workshop involved representatives of thirty-one organizations in discussions about the right and wrong way for citizens to become involved in government planning. Government staff members did much of the coordination. With their guidance, the workshop participants concluded that the best structure for public participation was a board of directors that would channel all public concerns and the best mode of action would be cautious negotiation with government bodies. At the conclusion of the workshop, seven individuals were elected to the new board of directors.

Rather than turn its attention to the immediate problem—the major redevelopment plan that was proceeding with little public input—a majority of the board had a different priority. Accepting suggestions from government staff members, they decided to work for establishment of a long-term training center that would teach people how to participate in public policy.

When the training center idea was unveiled at a public meeting, there was a great deal of heated discussion about whether this was really the grass-roots organization it was made out to be. The model of citizen participation being proposed avoided any challenge to the authority of government agencies engaged in planning. Planning was something to be done by elected representatives and their paid experts. Conflict between citizens and government planners over the goals in a regional development plan was to be discouraged. This orientation was typified by the training proposal. Over three years, experts would set up a center where professionals would teach citizens how to participate. Lack of participation by citizens was supposed to reflect lack of competence in the citizens themselves. The professional-citizen relationship in the structure of the training center would duplicate the relationship between government planners and the public. At the meeting, a vocal minority pointed out that planning was already under way. A spontaneous citizens' movement had arisen out of a need to have some impact on what was being done.

By deflecting that immediate concern to a long-term training project, the training center proposal was clearly missing an opportunity to influence current planning.

Once the citizens' organization was firmly committed to the training center, it was encouraged to present a budget to the provincial government for funding. After some delay the government rejected the proposal and government staff members ended their involvement with the group. With all its energy directed into a grand scheme that had now met a dead end, the group seemed finished. Government planners could now anticipate returning to the old, comfortable model of public involvement: highly structured public meetings that were essentially exercises in public relations.

But with the rejection of the training center, control of the group had now passed out of government control. Although members committed to the training center dropped out, the minority who cared about active participation in the current plan was able to regroup. A new board of directors was elected, serving as an umbrella organization for specific interest groups that wanted to take social action and influence government planning. The group returned to its original objective with great vigor.

It matters little whether government officials consciously planned the strategy that undercut citizen participation in the case reported by Grady (1978). Perhaps they did not. The social control orientation is so pervasive among the powerful that they may naturally expect citizen participation to fall into place. If citizens are to be heard from, it must be in a way that does not interfere with the orderly conduct of business. However conscious the strategy, the practical implication of government involvement was to make the efforts of citizens as irrelevant as possible to the current redevelopment plan. The perspective on social action was reactive rather than proactive. If citizens were to participate, they must be taught to do so in workshops and training centers. This model of public involvement ignored the fact that citizens were clearly ready to make their voices heard

—without training and without the help of professionals. The spontaneous organization of a group set to campaign for involvement in planning was testimony to the fact that citizens were ready for involvement. It was the policy makers and planners who were unready and unwilling.

It may seem that the government made a serious mistake in its handling of the participation planning case. If it had funded the training center, it might have kept vocal citizens firmly deflected from considering the immediate planning process. The rejection of the training center concept succeeded in discouraging a number of people who were concerned with citizen participation, but it also allowed a hard core to recapture the organization and turn its attention back to current planning. The government may have thought that the training center proposal, even though it had the benefit of drawing attention away from the redevelopment plan, posed long-term dangers. If an astute consultant had been advising the government from a social control perspective, he or she might have made the Machiavellian suggestion that government keep the ad hoc group working on the training center without ever making a firm commitment. Those involved in the proposal could have been asked to rework their plans over and over again until the redevelopment plan had become history. It will be recalled that this strategy was used against a parents organization in a case reported by Graziano (1969) and discussed in Chapter Four.

The participation planning case, the last to be presented in the book, illustrates the utility of the ecological and cognitive perspectives in understanding community consultation. From an ecological viewpoint we have emphasized the importance of context. Consider the contexts of the participation planning case described by Grady and the Curaçao experience mentioned earlier. There were similarities. Organizing efforts were sponsored or influenced by those who held power in society. There was an attempt to disengage these efforts from the status quo—to adopt an influence rather than a control orientation. In both cases, organizations created to deal with the powerful were undercut by those who benefited from maintaining the status quo.

There were also differences between the settings, and these

were probably crucial to the different outcomes. Take the Curaçao case: Once the consultants had departed, the foundation
they created to sponsor their project soon died. But in the participation planning case, when the government withdrew its support the ad hoc organization was able to change direction and
provide a vehicle for direct and immediate citizen participation.
Why were the outcomes different? On Curaçao the foundation
was created by the consultants as an expression of their own
vision about what the island society needed. In the participation planning case the organization arose spontaneously as an
expression of the need of active citizens to have a voice in major planning that would affect their community. The ecological
perspective encourages us to take a long time perspective, to
understand how a community is evolving, and to assess accurately the local resources for change.

A cognitive orientation focuses on the relationship between belief and action. At the beginning of this chapter we
outlined concepts from Stokols's (1975) model of alienation. In
that model, the perception of personal thwarting was expected
to have important implications for the action that citizens
would take or fail to take. Those who regard themselves as victims of personal thwarting will be subjugated if they believe
they have no choices; they may rebel when they think they
have the strength to succeed. This is a highly unstable situation
for those in power. A subjugated group may be moved to rebel
if circumstances indicate they have more options than they
thought. In a situation of personal thwarting, there is an ever-
present threat that the powerless will take action and demand
fundamental change. One way of reducing this threat is to turn
personal thwarting into neutral thwarting. When neutral thwarting is perceived, the disadvantaged engage in problem solving
when they have options and are alienated when they have none.
Often the problem solving is directed at surface features of the
system rather than at social arrangements themselves (for instance, helping victims rather than changing the circumstances
that victimize them). Alienation keeps people isolated, identi-
fies the problem with the victim, and undercuts the possibility
of collective action.

This analysis suggests a motive for power holders to become involved in sponsoring what seem to be efforts at social change. Both the fact of their involvement and their strategy itself may be aimed at convincing disadvantaged groups that frustrating social conditions represent neutral rather than personal thwarting. The message is this: "We are not responsible for the problem—we have compassion for those of you who suffer from it." If this perspective shift is successful, problem solving can be directed at symptoms rather than at underlying causes of social distress. The analysis also suggests some directions for consultants. They will find it useful to focus on the perception of social problems by those who are victimized. Communication skills and knowledge of belief-change techniques are definite assets for the consultant. Consciousness raising can be aimed at identifying the real sources of social problems and then helping people to recognize their options in confronting them.

8

Conclusion: Successful Approaches to Community Consultation

Marvin Minsky, a computer scientist at MIT, says the primary purpose of problem solving is to get a better grasp of the problem space and to find representations within which problems are easier to solve: "The purpose of search is to get information for this reformulation, not—as is usually assumed— to find solutions; once the space is adequately understood, solutions to problems will more easily be found" (1975, p. 259). That sums up both the theme and the objective of this book. We have implied in various ways that the principal consultation task is not to impose solutions to problems but to help groups redefine the problem space so that solutions can be found. And in this book we have avoided precise prescriptions, hoping instead to help consultants look at old problems in new ways—to get a better grasp of their own field's problem space.

We have seen consultants using many skills in a wide variety of settings, yet we have not classified consultation by skill nor defined it by setting. Instead we have focused on the generic

254

themes that cut across settings. The impact of consultant characteristics was as important in an alternative high school as in the U.S. State Department. The psychology of powerlessness was as important in creating a network of middle-class parents as in organizing the poor of Muddy Flats. The traditions of a setting had as much of an impact on an American police department as on a Liberian school district. The assumptions that divide people posed as much of a problem in a rape relief organization as in an industry–union dispute.

If consultants need to get a good reading of settings, as we have argued, what stands in their way? Sometimes it is the threat of an outsider causing those in a setting to withhold trust and information. Sometimes it is an initial contract that restricts time and opportunity for thorough assessment. Consultants must deal with xenophobia and be skillful in negotiating their mandates. These barriers to understanding lie more in the setting than in the consultant. But we have suggested that significant barriers may lie in consultants themselves—tendencies to approach different settings with a fixed perspective.

Two factors that contribute to a rigid approach by consultants are overreliance on past experience and overreliance on specific models of consultation. These factors produce cognitive biases that have been referred to as availability and representativeness heuristics (Kahneman and Tversky, 1972; Tversky and Kahneman, 1973). Experience is a useful guide, but it can distort intervention when the consultant fails to recognize important differences between the current situation and those of the past. Models of consultation can help the consultant develop plans of action, but they also distort intervention when they focus the consultant's attention on features of the model rather than features of the setting.

In our review of the case literature, we have seen many examples in which problems could be attributed to an excessively technological approach. Sometimes the technology was drawn from a formal model of consultation. Often it consisted of informal notions about how consultants should behave and what should happen as a result. The idea that consultants should avoid being directive led one team of consultants to neglect a leadership vacuum in a new setting. The idea that intervention should be addressed to broad social problems led another team to ignore the lack of institutional support for such an intervention. The idea that consultants should generate choices for clients led a third team to produce a report from which contending factions pulled out options that supported their political position. Although none of these ideas is wrong, in the three examples they were employed without an adequate recognition of the needs of the setting.

But the cognitive-ecological approach also provides a way of organizing information about reality, and it might be argued that this model too has the power to distract the consultant from focusing on the needs of a setting. We could respond that the *sine qua non* of a cognitive-ecological approach is its emphasis on setting. We recognize the paradox, however, in suggesting that a model which warns about models does not warn about itself. It seems appropriate to examine the ecological analogy and the cognitive orientation to see what dangers they present for the consultant.

Ecology and Action

The ecological analogy draws its power from the theory of biological evolution, including the doctrine of natural selection. One of the traps that evolutionary theorists must avoid is the tendency to assume that anything that has evolved is necessarily good. This way of thinking tends to honor the status quo and to discourage social action.

In an assault on the naturalistic fallacy, Flew (1967) has quoted from a variety of sources to show how easy it is to deify evolution. For instance: "From the war of nature, from famine and death, the most exalted object which we are capable of conceiving, namely the production of higher animals, directly follows." And this: "The growth of a large business is merely the survival of the fittest . . . the working out of a law of nature and a law of God." And finally this: "If we did not respect the law of nature, imposing our will by the right of the stronger, a day would come when the wild animals would devour us—then the insects would eat the wild animals, and finally nothing would exist on earth except the microbes." With these quotes from Charles Darwin, John D. Rockefeller, and Adolph Hitler, Flew illustrates the tendency to treat the law of natural selection as though it were a commandment. He points out that the premises of the evolutionary argument are descriptive, but the shift is made to a conclusion that is prescriptive. Anything that *is,* since it is a product of natural selection, *ought* to be.

This theoretical shift can be used by those in power to justify anything they care to do. But it also has a more insidious effect: It can be taken as a justification for inaction by those who want a better world but are seduced by the view that all present social conditions are a product of the inexorable workings of natural evolution. Flew (1967), writing about evolutionary ethics, points to the logical nonsense involved in this notion. For if any and all present conditions are products of evolution, so are the actions we make to change and improve those conditions. The rebel, no less than the emperor, can appeal to natural law. Only time will indicate who has the winning hand in any particular case.

In this book we have presented many cases where ecological thinking was used to inform action, not to obstruct it. The principles of interdependence, adaptation, cycling of resources, and succession have all been employed in the service of positive change.

The principle of *interdependence* focuses on the links among components of an ecosystem. In the field of consultation, it suggests that an intervention can ripple through a setting having many indirect effects. The consultant can use this notion to watch for unintended consequences of action. Nevertheless, not all consequences can be known perfectly in advance of action, and the possibility of unknown side effects should not paralyze the consultant. In fact, the rippling effect is often used by consultants as a way of maximizing the impact of their intervention in a system. We have seen several cases in which consultants worked with schoolteachers in the expectation that the intervention would have positive indirect effects on students. In another use of the interdependence principle, we saw an insider-outsider team working to bring change to a county jail. The outsider provided technical skills; the insider provided knowledge of the system and also credibility. Neither could have accomplished much alone, but by linking their strengths they had a beneficial impact on a previously closed institution.

If an organism is to survive it must be able to adapt to changes in the environment. The principle of *adaptation* emphasizes the impact of settings on the behavior of organisms. The consultant gains an appreciation of the reasons for behavior once he or she learns to look at the way behavior is tied to the norms of the setting. This understanding can shape intervention. We have seen consultants employ adaptation information in various contexts. For instance, one team was faced with the task of preparing a Maryland police department for an imminent civil rights march. There was neither the time nor the mandate to change deep-seated racial attitudes. The consultants focused on the role identification of police officers and the constraints on their behavior provided by occupational norms. The team correctly calculated that these norms, if made salient, would exert more control over behavior than would personal prejudices.

The fate of organisms in an ecosystem is bound up with the availability of resources, and relationships among groups are tied to resource distribution. The *cycling of resources* principle turns attention to the way in which resources are defined and developed. We have seen many cases where the consultant's task was to identify potential resources. For example, a new residential youth center was structured so that staff members with diverse backgrounds could bring their own talents to bear on cases regardless of their professional credentials. Life experience—whether as a ballplayer, a police officer, or a mechanic—was seen as a resource to be valued and nurtured.

Perhaps it is the principle of *succession* that could most easily be distorted into a rationale for inaction. This principle asserts that ecosystems are products of their histories. It encourages the consultant to take a long view, to understand present problems in light of past traditions, and to appreciate the direction in which settings are moving. But if this sounds like a wait-

and-see attitude, the emphasis is on the *see* rather than the wait. Consultants are always working with evolving settings, and information about where they have come from and where they are going can be an invaluable guide to action. A lack of such information can make consultation, however technically adept, of little use in the long run. In Chapter Five we reported a case in which a consultant helped prison supervisors find a new role in a changing correctional system in Canada. But the evolving political context proved the intervention, although immediately successful, to be of little use. In preparing cases for this book we talked with the consultant involved and he told us how the story ended: An increasingly conservative government closed the facility; it explicitly took the Southern road gang as a model, killed rehabilitation programs, and put all the prisoners to doing road work. The principle of succession can be used positively by consultants. In one case, we saw the creation of a demonstration project to ease the evolutionary path toward busing in a metropolitan school system.

Although the ecological analogy may be vulnerable to a bias in favor of the status quo, we have presented ample evidence throughout this book that it can also be a guide to thoughtful intervention. The naturalistic fallacy is a danger but hardly a necessary outcome of the evolutionary perspective. Another criticism of the ecological analogy lies in the fact that, like systems theory, it provides analytical tools that permit generalization across various species. In so doing, it may have a tendency to shortchange what is uniquely human about human affairs. One remedy is to infuse the ecological metaphor with information from the study of social cognition, an approach taken in this book. Now we shall consider ways in which this cognitive perspective may bias consultation.

The Function of Beliefs

We can quickly dispose of one possible criticism of the cognitive approach—that it emphasizes the individual over the system. Because findings in social cognition were drawn principally from laboratory experiments with individual subjects, it might be assumed that cognitive and systems thinking are anti-thetical. On the contrary, we have presented many examples in which social systems, group assumptions, and personal beliefs were all interdependent. We cite a few here from the many possible illustrations. In one case, theory about shared assumptions in groups was employed to help an organization develop a structure that would permit both cohesion and diversity of opinion. In our discussion of conflict resolution among groups we pointed to the central role of stereotypical thinking. When reviewing cases concerned with community organizing and social influence, we noted the ways in which consultants can deal with the psychology of powerlessness. If there is any residual doubt about the systems relevance of cognitive concepts, we can point to our conjunction of these concepts with the ecological analogy, which has impeccable system credentials.

A second objection is that social processes rather than personal beliefs are the wellsprings of action. There is no doubt that every social condition has its rationalization and that some of these rationalizations are employed consciously and cynically to suit the convenience of those who profit by existing arrangements. Nevertheless, there is a great deal of evidence that cognitive biases predispose people to actions that are not optimal for them or for the organizations and communities to which they belong. To cite two examples: We know that the illusory correlation is an important component of the stereotypes that underlie race prejudice; moreover, we have good reason to believe that biases such as the Just World hypothesis are strong impediments to collective social action.

A much more serious objection to the cognitive approach is that it may imply that the consultant's primary function is truth-telling. If group members are victims of cognitive bias, why not just straighten them out? We can put aside the question of how often consultants *know* the truth, and indeed how often they know that they know it. Even when consultants are certain that their viewpoint captures more of the truth than the beliefs of a client group, the consulting role seldom consists of pontificating. Before deciding on how to deal with the shared assumptions in a community group, the consultant must understand how these assumptions developed and what function they serve.

Group assumptions have specific functions depending on the time and setting in which they arose. Furthermore, there may be some general functions that are served by all such shared assumptions. French social analyst Roland Barthes (1977) argues that cultural beliefs, which he calls myths, help to preserve the status quo. They make historical conditions seem natural and immutable. This process helps organized society to rationalize the way things are; it reassures individuals and integrates them into their social system.

Barthes concluded that revolutionary movements would have no need of myths. But an earlier French political theorist, George Sorel, notes that groups working for social change were also guided by strong myths: "Men who are participating in great social movements always picture their coming action as a battle in which their cause is sure to triumph. . . . The syndicalist general strike and Marx's catastrophic revolution are such myths" (cited in Burnham, 1970, pp. 135-136). Although Barthes and Sorel are in disagreement, we can distill common themes from their work about the general function of shared assumptions: They reassure members about the group's purpose, integrate members into the group, and give members confidence about the eventual success of the group's project. Assumptions integrate group members by providing them with a common code to use in deciphering events and determining their significance. Because codes only work for those who share certain information, values, and past experiences, they strengthen bonds among group members and give them a sense of community.

We have seen many situations in which consultants had to recognize the functional value of shared assumptions in a group. The cohesiveness provided by a common viewpoint, whether or not that viewpoint contains some distortion, may be essential to keeping a group from fragmenting. In one case a rape crisis center broke up when views clashed about the cause of rape. In another case, a major consultation task was to help a group maintain a measure of cohesion even though members differed in their assumptions about the goals and priorities of the group. A shared assumption may give members a strong sense of mission. We discussed a case in which the members of a new group had a common belief that the community establishment was against them. This belief, whatever its objective truth, encouraged members to devote their energies to group tasks.

There are also drawbacks to shared assumptions, especially as they simplify reality and rob events of unique aspects. A rape crisis group in which members all have a strong bias concerning the cause of rape in society may enjoy cohesiveness at the expense of its ability to give sensitive counseling to a variety of rape victims. An organization that gains a sense of purpose from the common view that other groups are hostile may miss opportunities for productive interaction with those other groups. These are among the features of particular cases that consultants must weigh when planning interventions.

A focus on the function of beliefs provides an answer to another criticism of the cognitive approach—namely that biases and false beliefs should be self-correcting in time. The application of evolutionary theory to the realm of ideas suggests to some that false beliefs will be selected out eventually. Neisser (1976, p. 194) takes this position: "The outcome of any single encounter between cognition and reality is unpredictable, but in the long run such encounters must move us closer to the truth." There are many who have a less optimistic view, however. Biologist Jacques Monod argues that ideas have the power to confer cohesiveness, ambition, and confidence on the groups that hold them; as the group's influence grows, the idea is promoted. "Its capacity to 'take,' the extent to which it can be 'put over,' has little to do with the amount of objective truth the idea may confer" (1971, p. 166). Skinner (1966) has demonstrated learning procedures that result in the maintenance of false beliefs, even when they are nonadaptive. Campbell (1965) suggests that there is a selection and retention system in the evolution of ideas that is biased toward rigid retention of present beliefs whether they are true or not. Thus consultants cannot ignore shared assumptions in the hope that they will become more realistic in time; nor can they adopt a simple truth-telling approach that neglects the function of assumptions in the client group.

The assertion that beliefs evolve, and that we must understand the functions they serve for a group, provides a useful melding of the ecological and cognitive approaches. Ideas are interdependent, and any intervention that changes them should take side effects into account. Ideas have their adaptive value, and in each case the consultant must consider how this value meshes with their truth value. Ideas can be resources in a community setting; indeed, the ideas of the consultant are one of the principal resources that he or she can offer to a client group. Ideas have their traditions, for which the consultant must have a healthy respect. Sometimes the consultant will decide to work within these traditions; sometimes it will be essential to make a clear break with them. We saw the case of an innovative facility for the mentally retarded that refused to accept building funds or to house beds. A new approach required a challenge to traditional assumptions about institutions. In another case, a pioneering way of working with troubled adolescents dispensed with the usual vertical authority structure. A new approach required a challenge to traditional assumptions about professional responsibility for service delivery. The decisive actions in these cases symbolized the determination to change fundamental and previously unquestioned assumptions.

In this book we have focused on the links between the consultant and the client, within a community group, and among groups in the community. Our emphasis has been on generic themes that provide the context for consultation across settings and on the need to respond to the unique aspects of each setting. We have seen the consultant as a resource to the groups with which he or she works. We hope, in turn, that this book will provide a resource for the consultants who read it. If we have not solved specific problems, we hope to have outlined the problem space and introduced ways of thinking about issues that make the problems easier to solve.

References

Abelson, R. P. "Script Processing in Attitude Formation and Decision Making." In J. S. Carroll and J. W. Payne (Eds.), *Cognition and Social Behavior.* Hillsdale, N.J.: Lawrence Erlbaum Associates, 1976.

Abelson, R. P. "Psychological Status of the Script Concept." *American Psychologist,* 1981, *36,* 715-729.

Alinsky, S. D. *Reveille for Radicals.* New York: Random House, 1946.

Alinsky, S. D. *Rules for Radicals.* New York: Random House, 1971.

Allen, V. L., and Wilder, D. A. "Impact of Group Consensus and Social Support on Stimulus Meaning: Mediation of Conformity by Cognitive Restructuring." *Journal of Personality and Social Psychology,* 1980, *39,* 1116-1124.

Alpert, J. L., and Associates. *Psychological Consultation in Educational Settings.* San Francisco: Jossey-Bass, 1982.

Anderson, C. A., Lepper, M. R., and Ross, L. "Perseverance of

Social Theories: The Role of Explanation in the Persistence of Discredited Information." *Journal of Personality and Social Psychology,* 1980, *39,* 1037-1049.

Andolfi, M., Stein, D. D., and Skinner, J. "A Systems Approach to the Child, School, Family, and Community in an Urban Area." *American Journal of Community Psychology,* 1977, *5,* 33-43.

Argyris, C. *Intervention Theory and Method: A Behavioral Science View.* Reading, Mass.: Addison-Wesley, 1970.

Argyris, C. "Dangers in Applying Results from Experimental Social Psychology." *American Psychologist,* 1975, *30,* 469-485.

Asch, S. E. "The Doctrine of Suggestion, Prestige, and Imitation in Social Psychology." *Psychological Review,* 1948, *55,* 250-276.

Baluk, U., and O'Neill, P. "Health Professionals' Perceptions of the Psychological Consequences of Abortion." *American Journal of Community Psychology,* 1980, *8,* 67-76.

Barthes, R. *Image-Music-Text.* (S. Heath, Trans.) New York: Hill and Wang, 1977.

Bender, M. P. *Community Psychology.* London: Methuen, 1976.

Bennis, W. G. "Bureaucracy and Social Change: An Anatomy of a Training Failure." In P. H. Mirvis and D. N. Berg (Eds.), *Failures in Organization Development and Change.* New York: Wiley, 1977.

Berg, D. N. "Failure at Entry." In P. H. Mirvis and D. N. Berg (Eds.), *Failures in Organization Development and Change.* New York: Wiley, 1977.

Berlew, D. E., and LeClere, W. E. "Social Intervention in Curaçao: A Case Study." *Journal of Applied Behavioral Science,* 1974, *10,* 29-52.

Berlin, I. N. "Learning Mental Health Consultation: History and Problems." *Mental Hygiene,* 1964, *48,* 257-266.

Berlin, I. N. (Ed.). *Advocacy for Child Mental Health.* New York: Brunner/Mazel, 1975.

Birnbaum, M. H., and Stegner, S. E. "Source Credibility in Social Judgments: Bias, Expertise, and the Judge's Point of View." *Journal of Personality and Social Psychology,* 1979, *37,* 48-74.

Blake, R., and Mouton, J. *Consultation.* Reading, Mass.: Addison-Wesley, 1976.

Blake, R., Mouton, J., and Sloma, R. L. "The Union-Management Intergroup Laboratory: Strategy for Resolving Intergroup Conflict." *Journal of Applied Behavioral Science,* 1965, *1* (1), 25-27.

Briggs, C. H. "Transition in School Psychological Services: A Case Study." *Journal of School Psychology,* 1973, *11,* 88-91.

Brockbank, R. "Aspects of Mental Health Consultation." *Archives of General Psychiatry,* 1968, *18,* 267-275.

Bronfenbrenner, U. "The Mirror Image in Soviet-American Relations: A Social Psychologist's Report." *Journal of Social Issues,* 1961, *17,* 45-56.

Broskowski, A. "Concepts of Teacher-Centered Consultation." *Professional Psychology,* 1973, *4,* 50-58.

Burnham, J. *The Machiavellians.* Chicago: Henry Regnery Co., 1970.

Campbell, D. T. "Variation and Selective Retention in Socio-Cultural Evolution." In H. R. Barringer, G. I. Blanksten, and R. Mack (Eds.), *Social Change in Developing Areas.* Cambridge, Mass.: Schenkman, 1965.

Caplan, G. *Principles of Preventive Psychiatry.* New York: Basic Books, 1964.

Caplan, G. *The Theory and Practice of Mental Health Consultation.* New York: Basic Books, 1970.

Chapman, L. J. "Illusory Correlation in Observational Report." *Journal of Verbal Learning and Verbal Behavior,* 1967, *6,* 151-155.

Chappell-Ivey, W. "Consultation Report." Unpublished manuscript, Acadia University, 1980.

Cherniss, C. "Creating New Consultation Programs in Community Mental Health Centers." *Community Mental Health Journal,* 1977, *13,* 133-141.

Cherniss, C., Trickett, E. J., D'Antonio, M., and Tracy, K. "Involving Students in Organizational Change in a High School." In J. L. Alpert and Associates, *Psychological Consultation in Educational Settings.* San Francisco: Jossey-Bass, 1982.

Clark, R. D. III. "Group-Induced Shift Toward Risk: A Critical Appraisal." *Psychological Bulletin,* 1971, *76,* 251-270.

Coiner, M. C. "The Port of Entry in School Consultation: One Stormy Passage." Unpublished manuscript, Yale University, 1977.

Collins, B. E. "Four Components of the Rotter Internal-External Scale: Belief in a Difficult World, a Just World, a Predictable World, and a Politically Responsive World." *Journal of Personality and Social Psychology,* 1974, *29,* 381-391.

Cowen, E. L. "The Wooing of Primary Prevention." Address to Division 27 at the Annual Convention of the American Psychological Association, New York, 1979.

Cowen, E. L., Lorion, R. P., and Dorr, D. "Research in the Community Cauldron: A Case History." *Canadian Psychologist,* 1974, *15,* 313-325.

Crockett, W. J. "Introducting Change to a Government Agency." In P. H. Mirvis and D. N. Berg (Eds.), *Failures in Organization Development and Change.* New York: Wiley, 1977.

Drotar, D. "Death in the Pediatric Hospital: Psychological Consultation with Medical and Nursing Staff." *Journal of Clinical Child Psychology,* 1975, *4,* 33-35.

Eagly, A. H., and Himmelfarb, S. "Attitudes and Opinions." In M. R. Rosensweig and L. W. Porter (Eds.), *Annual Review of Psychology.* Vol. 29. Palo Alto: Annual Reviews, 1978.

Edney, J. J. "The Commons Problem." *American Psychologist,* 1980, *35,* 131-150.

Edney, J. J. "Paradoxes on the Commons: Scarcity and the Problem of Equality." *Journal of Community Psychology,* 1981, *9,* 3-34.

Etzioni, A. "Social-Psychological Aspects of International Relations." In G. Lindzay and A. Aronson (Eds.), *The Handbook of Social Psychology.* (2nd ed.) Reading, Mass.: Addison-Wesley, 1969.

Fischoff, B. "Hindsight/Foresight: The Effect of Outcome Knowledge on Judgment Under Certainty." *Journal of Experimental Psychology, Human Perception and Performance,* 1975, *104,* 288-299.

Flew, A. "Evolutionary Ethics." In W. Hudson (Ed.), *New Studies in Ethics.* New York: Macmillan, 1967.

Frederick, V., Fretta, N., and Levin-Frank, S. "Women Mental

Health Consultants—'Cutie Pies or Libbers'?" *Psychiatric Opinion,* 1976, *13,* 26-32.

Freud, S. *The Future of an Illusion.* New York: Liveright, 1955. (Originally published 1928.)

Fuehrer, A. E., and Keys, C. B. "Law Enforcement in the Court: Role Identity and Interpersonal Relations Training of Deputy Sheriffs." Paper presented at the Academy of Criminal Justice Sciences Annual Meeting, New Orleans, March 1978.

Gamson, W. A. *Power and Discontent.* Homewood, Ill.: Dorsey Press, 1968.

Gamson, W. A. *The Strategy of Social Protest.* Homewood, Ill.: Dorsey Press, 1975.

Gamson, W. A., and McEvoy, J. "Police Violence and the Mobilization of Public Support." *Annals of the American Academy of Political and Social Science,* 1970, *391,* 97-110.

Glidewell, J. C. "The Entry Problem in Consultation." *Journal of Social Issues,* 1959, *15,* 51-59.

Gluckstern, N. B., and Packard, R. W. "The Internal-External Change-Agent Team: Bringing Change to a 'Closed Institution.'" *Journal of Applied Behavioral Science,* 1977, *13,* 41-52.

Goldenberg, I. I. *Build Me a Mountain.* Cambridge, Mass.: M.I.T. Press, 1971.

Gooden, W. "Racial Issues and Consultation; Schools: A Case Example." Unpublished paper, Yale University, 1977.

Goodstein, L. D. *Consulting with Human Service Systems.* Reading, Mass.: Addison-Wesley, 1978.

Gordon, J. S. "Consultation with Alternative Services for Young People." In F. V. Mannino, B. W. MacLennan, and M. F. Shore (Eds.), *The Practice of Mental Health Consultation.* New York: Wiley, 1975.

Grady, D. J. "Community Organization as Political Praxis: A Nova Scotia Experience in 'Citizens' Participation.'" *Social Science Monograph Series,* 1978, *11,* 105-128.

Grady, M. A., Gibson, M. H. S., and Trickett, E. J. *Mental Health Consultation: Theory, Practice, and Research 1973-1978.* Washington: National Institute of Mental Health, 1981.

Graziano, A. M. "Clinical Innovation and the Mental Health

Power Structure: A Social Case History." *American Psychologist*, 1969, *24*, 10-18.

Hamil, R., Wilson, T. D., and Nisbett, R. E. "Insensitivity to Sample Bias: Generalizing from Atypical Cases." *Journal of Personality and Social Psychology*, 1980, *39*, 578-589.

Hamilton, D. L. "A Cognitive-Attributional Analysis of Stereotyping." *Advances in Experimental Social Psychology*, 1979, *12*, 53-83.

Hamilton, D. L. (Ed.). *Cognitive Processes in Stereotyping and Intergroup Behavior*. Hillsdale, N.J.: Lawrence Erlbaum, 1981.

Hamilton, D. L., and Rose, T. L. "Illusory Correlation and the Maintenance of Stereotypic Beliefs." *Journal of Personality and Social Psychology*, 1980, *39*, 832-845.

Hansen, R. D. "Commonsense Attribution." *Journal of Personality and Social Psychology*, 1980, *39*, 996-1009.

Hardin, G. "The Tragedy of the Commons." *Science*, 1968, *162*, 1243-1248.

Harding, J., and others. "Prejudice and Ethnic Relations." In G. Lindzay and E. Aronson (Eds.), *The Handbook of Social Psychology*. Vol. 5. (2nd ed.) Reading, Mass.: Addison-Wesley, 1969.

Hersch, C. "Social History, Mental Health, and Community Control." *American Psychologist*, 1972, *27*, 749-754.

Hilliard, A. G. "A Helping Experience in African Education: Implications for Cross-Cultural Work." *Journal of Non-White Concerns in Personnel and Guidance*, 1974, *2*, 133-144.

Hirschman, A. O. *Exit, Voice and Loyalty*. Cambridge, Mass.: Harvard University Press, 1970.

Hovland, C. E., and Weiss, W. "The Influence of Source Credibility on Communication Effectiveness." *Public Opinion Quarterly*, 1951, *15*, 635-650.

Huang, L. N. "The Role of Ecological Factors and Consultant Characteristics in the Entry Phase of School Consultation." Unpublished manuscript, Yale University, 1976.

Iscoe, I. "Community Psychology and the Competent Community." *American Psychologist*, 1974, *29*, 607-613.

Janis, I. L. *Victims of Groupthink*. Boston: Houghton Mifflin, 1972.

Janis, I. L., and Mann, L. *Decision Making: Psychological Analysis of Conflict, Choice, and Commitment.* New York: Free Press, 1977.

Jenkins, H. M., and Ward, W. C. "Judgment of Contingency Between Responses and Outcomes." *Psychological Monographs,* 1965, *79* (1, whole no. 594).

Jervis, R. *Perception and Misperception in International Politics.* Princeton, N.J.: Princeton University Press, 1976.

Jones, C., and Aronson, E. "Attribution of Fault to a Rape Victim as a Function of Respectability of the Victim." *Journal of Personality and Social Psychology,* 1973, *26,* 415-419.

Jones, E. E., and Nisbett, R. E. *The Actor and the Observer: Divergent Perceptions of the Causes of Behavior.* Morristown, N.J.: General Learning Press, 1971.

Kahn, S. *How People Get Power: Organizing Oppressed Communities for Action.* New York: McGraw-Hill, 1970.

Kahneman, D., and Tversky, A. "Subjective Probability: A Judgment of Representativeness." *Cognitive Psychology,* 1972, *3,* 430-454.

Kahneman, D., and Tversky, A. "On the Psychology of Prediction." *Psychological Review,* 1973, *80,* 237-251.

Kahneman, D., and Tversky, A. "Prospect Theory: An Analysis of Decision Under Risk." *Econometrica,* 1979, *14,* 263-292.

Kelley, H. H. "Attribution Theory in Social Psychology." In D. Levine (Ed.), *Nebraska Symposium on Motivation.* Vol. 15. Lincoln: University of Nebraska Press, 1967.

Kelley, H. H. "Causal Schemata and the Attribution Process." In E. E. Jones (Ed.), *Attribution: Perceiving the Causes of Behavior.* Morristown, N.J.: General Learning Press, 1972.

Kelly, J. G. "Ecological Constraints on Mental Health Services." *American Psychologist,* 1966, *21,* 535-539.

Kelly, J. G. "A Quest for Valid Interventions." In C. Spielberger (Ed.), *Current Topics in Clinical and Community Psychology.* New York: Academic Press, 1970.

Kelly, J. G. "Qualities for the Community Psychologist." *American Psychologist,* 1971, *26,* 897-903.

Kelly, J. G. " 'Tain't What You Do, It's the Way You Do It.' " *American Journal of Community Psychology,* 1979, *7,* 244-261.

Kelly, J. G. "Ecological Theorems and Citizen Participation: Methods and Process of Research." Paper presented at the Annual Convention of the American Psychological Association, 1980.

King, L. W., Cotler, S. B., and Patterson, K. "Behavior Modification Consultation in a Mexican-American School." *American Journal of Community Psychology*, 1975, *3*, 229-235.

Korten, D. C. "Beyond Accustomed Territory." *Journal of Applied Behavioral Science*, 1974, *10*, 53-60.

Kukla, N. A. "Foundations of an Attributional Theory of Performance." *Psychological Review*, 1972, *79*, 454-470.

Lerner, M. J. "Evaluation of Performance as a Function of Performer's Reward and Attractiveness." *Journal of Personality and Social Psychology*, 1965, *1*, 355-360.

Lerner, M. J., and Simmons, C. H. "Observer's Reaction to the 'Innocent Victim': Compassion or Rejection?" *Journal of Personality and Social Psychology*, 1966, *4*, 203-210.

Levin, G., and Stein, D. D. "System Intervention in a School-Community Conflict." *Journal of Applied Behavioral Science*, 1970, *6*, 337-352.

Levy-Warren, M. H. "The Delicate Balance: Consultation in an Alternative Inner-City High School." Unpublished manuscript, Yale University, 1976.

Lewicki, R. H., and Alderfer, C. P. "The Tensions Between Research and Intervention in Intergroup Conflict." *Journal of Applied Behavioral Science*, 1973, *9*, 423-468.

Lindzay, G., and Aronson, A. (Eds.). *The Handbook of Social Psychology*. (2nd ed.) Reading, Mass.: Addison-Wesley, 1969.

Linville, P. W., and Jones, E. E. "Polarized Appraisals of Out-Group Members." *Journal of Personality and Social Psychology*, 1980, *38*, 689-703.

Locksley, A., Ortiz, V., and Hepburn, C. "Social Categorization and Discriminatory Behavior: Extinguishing the Minimal Intergroup Discrimination Effect." *Journal of Personality and Social Psychology*, 1980, *39*, 773-783.

McCann-Baker, M. E. "A Community Consultation Project with the Canadian Association for the Mentally Retarded." Unpublished manuscript, Acadia University, 1978.

MacFarlane, P. "Consultation with Halifax Rape Relief." Unpublished manuscript, Acadia University, 1978.

MacGillivray, R. G. "The Robin Hill Child Care Centre: An Ecological Analysis." Unpublished manuscript, Acadia University, 1980.

McGregor, D. "The Major Determinants of the Prediction of Social Events." *Journal of Abnormal and Social Psychology,* 1938, *33,* 179-204.

McGuire, W. J. "A Syllogistic Analysis of Cognitive Relationships." In M. J. Rosenberg and others (Eds.), *Attitude Organization and Change.* New Haven: Yale University Press, 1960.

McIntyre, D. "Two Schools, One Psychologist." In F. Kaplan and S. B. Sarason (Eds.), *The Psycho-Educational Clinic: Papers and Research Studies.* Boston: Massachusetts Department of Mental Health, 1969.

McRee, C., and others. "Utilizing Psychiatric Intervention Techniques as a Model for Consultation in School-Community Crises: A Case History." *The Psychiatric Forum,* 1974, *4,* 6-10.

Mannino, F. V., MacLennan, B. W., and Shore, M. F. (Eds.). *The Practice of Mental Health Consultation.* New York: Wiley, 1975.

Matthews, R. *"There's No Better Place Than Here."* Toronto: Peter Martin Associates, 1976.

Milburn, M. A. "Sources of Bias in the Prediction of Future Events." *Organizational Behavior and Human Performance,* 1978, *21,* 17-26.

Mill, C. R. "Short-Term Consultation in Organization Development for Mental Health Agencies." *Hospital and Community Psychiatry,* 1974, *25,* 83-88.

Miller, J. G. *Living Systems.* New York: McGraw-Hill, 1978.

Minsky, M. "A Framework for Representing Knowledge." In P. H. Winston (Ed.), *The Psychology of Computer Vision.* New York: McGraw-Hill, 1975.

Mirvis, P. H., and Berg, D. N. (Eds.). *Failures in Organization Development and Change.* New York: Wiley, 1977.

Monahan, J. *Community Mental Health and the Criminal Justice System.* New York: Pergamon, 1976.

Monod, J. *Chance and Necessity.* (A. Wainhouse, Trans.) New York: Vintage Books, 1971.

Mullin, M. L., Blakeney, R. N., and Bell, E. C. "Training Paraprofessionals as Community Mental Health Counselors Through Consultation." *Journal of Community Psychology,* 1974, *2,* 251-253.

Neisser, U. *Cognition and Reality.* San Francisco: W. H. Freeman, 1976.

Nisbett, R. E., and Borgida, E. "Attribution and the Psychology of Prediction." *Journal of Personality and Social Psychology,* 1975, *32,* 932-943.

Nisbett, R. E., and Wilson, T. D. "Telling More Than We Know: Verbal Reports on Mental Processes." *Psychological Review,* 1977, *84,* 231-258.

Nixon, G. "Systems Approach to Pediatric Consultation." *Journal of Clinical Child Psychology,* 1975, *4,* 33-35.

O'Neill, P. "Cognitive Community Psychology." *American Psychologist,* 1981, *36,* 457-469.

O'Neill, P., and Levings, D. E. "Inducing Biased Scanning in a Group Setting to Change Attitudes Toward Bilingualism and Capital Punishment." *Journal of Personality and Social Psychology,* 1979, *37,* 1432-1438.

O'Neill, P., and Loomes, P. R. "Building a Community Group to Improve Local Schools." In J. L. Alpert and Associates, *Psychological Consultation in Educational Settings.* San Francisco: Jossey-Bass, 1982.

Orvis, B. R., Cunningham, J. D., and Kelley, H. H. "A Closer Examination of Causal Inference: The Roles of Consensus, Distinctiveness, and Consistency Information." *Journal of Personality and Social Psychology,* 1975, *32,* 605, 616.

Platt, J., and Wicks, R. *The Psychological Consultant.* New York: Grune & Stratton, 1979.

Quattrone, G. A., and Jones, E. E. "The Perception of Variability Within In-Groups and Out-Groups: Implications for the Law of Small Numbers." *Journal of Personality and Social Psychology,* 1980, *38,* 141-152.

Reddin, W. J. "Confessions of an Organizational Change Agent." *Group and Organizational Studies,* 1977, *2,* 33-41.

Reddy, W. B., and Lansky, L. M. "Nothing But the Facts—And

Some Observations on Norms and Values: The History of a Consultation with a Metropolitan Police Division." *Journal of Social Issues,* 1975, *31,* 123-138.

Reppucci, N. D., and others. "We Bombed in Mountville: Lessons Learned in Consultation to a Correctional Facility for Adolescent Offenders." In I. I. Goldenberg (Ed.), *The Helping Professions in the World of Action.* Lexington, Mass.: Heath, 1973.

Ritchie, P. L.-J. "Issues in Rural Community Psychology: Implications for Practice and the Development of a Model." *Canadian Journal of Community Mental Health,* in press, *1.*

Rogeness, G. A., and others. "School Intervention Program to Increase Behaviors and Attitudes That Promote Learning." *Journal of Community Psychology,* 1977, *5,* 246-256.

Rotter, J. B. "Generalized Tendencies for Internal Versus External Control of Reinforcement." *Psychological Monographs,* 1966, *80* (1), entire issue.

Russell, B. *Power: A New Social Analysis.* London: Allen & Unwin, 1938.

Sarason, S. B. *The Culture of the School and the Problem of Change.* Boston: Allyn & Bacon, 1971.

Sarason, S. B. *The Creation of Settings and the Future Societies.* San Francisco: Jossey-Bass, 1972.

Sarason, S. B. "Community Psychology, Networks, and Mr. Everyman." *American Psychologist,* 1976, *31,* 317-328.

Sarason, S. B. "An Unsuccessful War on Poverty?" *American Psychologist,* 1978, *33,* 831-839.

Sarason, S. B., Zitnay, G., and Grossman, F. K. *The Creation of a Community Setting.* Syracuse: Syracuse University Division of Special Education and Rehabilitation and the Center on Human Policy, 1971.

Sarason, S. B., and others. *Psychology in Community Settings: Clinical, Educational, Vocational, Social Aspects.* New York: Wiley, 1966.

Saunders, M. K., and Alinsky, S. D. *The Professional Radical.* New York: Harper & Row, 1970.

Schelling, T. C. *Micromotives and Macrobehavior.* New York: Norton, 1978.

Schmuck, R. A. "Helping Teachers Improve Classroom Group

Processes." *Journal of Applied Behavioral Science,* 1968, *4,* 401-435.

Schmuck, R. A., and Miles, M. (Eds.). *Organizational Development in Schools.* Palo Alto: National Press Books, 1971.

Sebring, R. H., and Duffee, D. "Who Are the Real Prisoners? A Case of Win-Lose Conflict in a State Correctional Institution." *Journal of Applied Behavioral Science,* 1977, *13,* 23-40.

Shannon, C. E. "A Mathematical Theory of Communication." *Bell Systems Technical Journal,* 1948, *27,* 379-423, 623-656.

Shellow, R. "Reinforcing Police Neutrality in Civil Rights Confrontations." *Journal of Applied Behavioral Science,* 1965, *1* (3), 243-254.

Shellow, R., and Newbrough, J. R. "Working with the Juvenile Police—A Possible Role for the Psychologist in Community Mental Health." In F. V. Mannino, B. W. MacLennan, and M. F. Shore (Eds.), *The Practice of Mental Health Consultation.* New York: Wiley, 1975.

Sherif, M., and others. *Intergroup Conflict and Co-operation: The Robber's Cave Experiment.* Norman: University of Oklahoma Book Exchange, 1961.

Sherwin, S., and Renner, K. E. "Respect for Persons in a Study of the Use of Force by Police Officers." *Clinical Research,* 1979, *27,* 19-22.

Short, B. L. "Community Psychology and School Integration: Programs for Training and Community Change." Proceedings of the 180th Convention of the American Psychological Association, 1972.

Skinner, B. F. *Walden Two.* New York: Macmillan, 1962.

Skinner, B. F. "The Phylogeny and Ontogeny of Behavior." *Science,* 1966, *153,* 1205-1213.

Skinner, B. F. *Beyond Freedom and Dignity.* New York: Knopf, 1971.

Smith, B. L., Lasswell, H. D., and Casey, R. D. *Propaganda, Communication, and Public Opinion.* Princeton: Princeton University Press, 1946.

Smith, E. R., and Miller, F. D. "Salience and the Cognitive Mediation of Attribution." *Journal of Personality and Social Psychology,* 1979, *37,* 2240-2252.

Sozonchuk, K. "Community Consultation Report." Unpublished manuscript, Acadia University, 1980.

Stokols, D. "Toward a Psychological Theory of Alienation." *Psychological Review,* 1975, *82,* 26-44.

Tajfel, H. "Cognitive Aspects of Prejudice." *Journal of Social Issues,* 1969, *25,* 79-98.

Tajfel, H. "Experiments in Intergroup Discrimination." *Scientific American,* 1970, *223,* 96-102.

Taylor, S. E., and Fiske, S. T. "Salience, Attention, and Attribution." In L. Berkowitz (Ed.), *Advances in Experimental Social Psychology.* Vol. 11. New York: Academic Press, 1978.

Tefft, B. M., Hamilton, G. K., and Theroux, C. "Community Psychology in Canada: Toward Developing a National Network." Paper presented at the meeting of the Canadian Psychological Association, Quebec, June 1979.

Thibaut, J., and Kelley, H. H. *The Social Psychology of Groups.* New York: Wiley, 1959.

Toland, A. "Political Participation as a Function of Time, Desirability, and Probability of a Future Event." Unpublished master's thesis, Department of Psychology, University of Illinois at Chicago, 1981.

Trickett, E. J., Kelly, J. G., and Todd, D. M. "The Social Environment of the High School: Guidelines for Individual Change and Organizational Redevelopment." In S. Golann and C. Eisdorfer (Eds.), *Handbook of Community Mental Health.* New York: Appleton-Century-Crofts, 1972.

Trickett, E. J., Kelly, J. G., and Vincent, T. "Explorations in Ecological Inquiry: Topics, Methods and Processes of Community Psychology." In E. Susskind and D. C. Klein (Eds.), *Knowledge Building in Community Psychology.* New York: Praeger, in press.

Tversky, A. "Elimination by Aspects: A Theory of Choice." *Psychological Review,* 1972, *79,* 281-299.

Tversky, A., and Kahneman, D. "Availability: A Heuristic for Judging Frequency and Probability." *Cognitive Psychology,* 1973, *5,* 207-232.

Tversky, A., and Kahneman, D. "Judgment Under Uncertainty: Heuristics and Biases." *Science,* 1974, *185,* 1124-1131.

Walton, R. E. "Interpersonal Confrontation and Basic Third Party Functions." *Journal of Applied Behavioral Science,* 1968, *4,* 327-344.

Wedge, B. "A Psychiatric Model for Intercession in Intergroup Conflict." *Journal of Applied Behavioral Science,* 1971, *7,* 733-761.

Weick, K. E. *The Social Psychology of Organizing.* Reading, Mass.: Addison-Wesley, 1969.

Weinstein, N. D. "Unrealistic Optimism About Future Life Events." *Journal of Personality and Social Psychology,* 1980, *39,* 806-820.

Weinstein, R. "Establishing a Mental Health Team in a Middle School." In J. L. Alpert and Associates. *Psychological Consultation in Educational Settings.* San Francisco: Jossey-Bass, 1982.

Westermeyer, J., and Hausman, W. "Cross Cultural Consultation for Mental Health Planning." *International Journal of Social Psychiatry,* 1974a, *20,* 34-38.

Westermeyer, J., and Hausman, W. "Mental Health Consultation with Government Agencies: A Comparison of Two Cases." *Social Psychiatry,* 1974b, *9,* 137-141.

Wilder, D. A., and Thompson, J. E. "Intergroup Contact with Independent Manipulations of In-Group and Out-Group Interaction." *Journal of Personality and Social Psychology,* 1980, *38,* 589-603.

Willis, J. "Behavioral Approaches to Changing Institutions: A Case Study in a Correctional Center." *Corrective and Social Psychiatry,* 1979, *25,* 39-46.

Index